KU-269-254

No Gods and Precious Few Heroes

The New History of Scotland
Series Editor: Jenny Wormald

Original titles in the New History of Scotland series were published in the 1980s and re-issued in the 1990s. This popular and enduring series is now being updated with the following published and forthcoming titles:

Vol. 1 *Conceiving a Nation: Scotland to* AD *900* by Gilbert Markus (new edition to replace *Warlords and Holy Men* by Alfred Smyth)

Vol. 2 *The Beginning of Scotland 900–1304* by Dauvit Broun (new edition to replace *Kingship and Unity* by G. W. S. Barrow)

Vol. 3 *Power and Propaganda: Scotland 1306–1488* by Katie Stevenson (new edition to replace *Independence and Nationhood* by Alexander Grant)

Vol. 4 *Court, Kirk and Community: Scotland 1470–1625* by Jenny Wormald (reissued second edition with new foreword)

Vol. 5 *Union, Revolution and War: Scotland 1625–1745* by Laura Stewart (new edition to replace *Lordship to Patronage* by Rosalind Mitchison)

Vol. 6 *Enlightenment and Change: Scotland 1746–1832* by Bruce P. Lenman (second revised and updated edition of *Integration and Enlightenment*)

Vol. 7 *Ourselves and Others: Scotland 1832–1914* by Graeme Morton (new edition to replace *Industry and Ethos* by Olive and Sydney Checkland)

Vol. 8 *No Gods and Precious Few Heroes: Scotland 1900–2015* by Christopher Harvie (fourth revised and updated edition)

www.edinburghuniversitypress.com

No Gods and Precious Few Heroes

Scotland 1900–2015

Fourth Edition

Christopher Harvie

EDINBURGH
University Press

In memory of
Virginia Harvie, 1944–2005,
John Brown, 1937–2012 and
Jenny Wormald, 1942–2015

And for Geraldine Brown and
Sandra and Ian MacDougall

Edinburgh University Press is one of the leading university presses in the UK.
We publish academic books and journals in our selected subject areas across the
humanities and social sciences, combining cutting-edge scholarship with high
editorial and production values to produce academic works of lasting importance.
For more information visit our website: www.edinburghuniversitypress.com

© Christopher Harvie, 1981, 1993, 1998, 2016
First edition published 1981 in the *New History of Scotland* series by Edward
Arnold (Publishers) Ltd, reprinted with corrections and additions 1987
Second edition published 1993 by Edinburgh University Press
Third edition published 1998 by Edinburgh University Press,
reprinted with corrections and additions 2000

Edinburgh University Press Ltd
The Tun – Holyrood Road
12 (2f) Jackson's Entry
Edinburgh EH8 8PJ

Typeset in 10.5/13 Sabon by
Servis Filmsetting Ltd, Stockport, Cheshire,
and printed and bound in Great Britain by
CPI Group (UK) Ltd, Croydon CR0 4YY

A CIP record for this book is available from the British Library

ISBN 978 0 7486 8236 2 (hardback)
ISBN 978 0 7486 8256 0 (paperback)
ISBN 978 0 7486 8257 7 (webready PDF)
ISBN 978 0 7486 8258 4 (epub)

The right of Christopher Harvie to be identified as author of this work has been
asserted in accordance with the Copyright, Designs and Patents Act 1988 and the
Copyright and Related Rights Regulations 2003 (SI No. 2498).

In 2015 Professor Harvie was made a Global Vision Lecturer by the National
Geographical Association. EUP would like to acknowledge the generous grant assistance from the author towards the publication of this work.

WITHDRAWN

UNIVERSITY
OF
GLASGOW
LIBRARY

Contents

Tables

Foreword

Who hold Zam-Zammah hold the Punjab!

On 29 January 2015 a Scots politician gave up governing a hundred million people after eighteen months. Mohammad Sarwar's palace was in Lahore, where Rudyard Kipling in *Kim* (1900) started his hero from the great gun Zam-Zammah. In a Pakistan seized by the world's disorder, the Labour MP for Govan (1997–2010) tried to administer a population three times larger than it was when he left in 1972. His wife mourned the distance from her Glasgow friends. In 2011 one of his predecessors had been shot dead.

Nearby, western intervention in Afghanistan ended in the same chaos as in Iraq. On 2 May 2010 US forces killed Osama bin Laden in Abbottabad, named for an early Anglo-Scot involved in the Great Game. Terror hit Scotland in June 2007. Her month-old SNP government was faced with an attempt to blow up Glasgow airport by two Islamists driving a butane-packed jeep from London. Airport workers only just stopped them. People forgot.

But Kipling's other side, engineer MacAndrew's Scotland, persisted. The future status of the country remained unclear. A referendum on 18 September 2014 polled 55 per cent to 45 per cent in favour of the Union, and the 7 May UK election saw the SNP capture fifty-six of the country's fifty-nine seats. Such party change threatened Westminster's sovereignty as much as England's 'Europhobe' bugbear.

Sixteen-year-old Scots voted in the referendum: the overall turnout was 85 per cent and the quality of debate was praised. Nicola Sturgeon governed a country which had elected only nineteen women MPs between 1918 and 1999. Figures such as Rebecca West, Naomi Mitchison and Muriel Spark left their mark, but as late as 1975 no woman figured among the twenty-eight contributors to Gordon Brown's *Red Paper on Scotland*.

Even though its schools now sideline history as much as the 'women's work' of foreign languages, Scotland's industry, underestimated by an earlier Germany, had facilitated allied resilience in two world wars, perhaps too the oil boom that underwrote Margaret Thatcher's neo-liberalism, just before the oil bust in 1986 undermined Soviet power. The new elites would be flawed by a weak manufacture and the blurring of finance 'enterprise' into 'moral hazard'.

No Gods analysed the civil society created by economics within Unionism, then its upstaging by the drive to self-government: a peaceable process, though the parallel career of the first Scots colony, Northern Ireland (1968–98), was not. Containing that disorder enhanced a militarism that aided the UK's foreign intervention, first in the Balkans, then in the Middle East. The overreach implied by Gordon Brown's huge aircraft carriers building in Fife may connect Kipling's two twentieth-century worlds, yet kill: 'And worse than present jeopardy/May our forlorn tomorrow be?'

The book came out of the old 'generalist first year' of the Scottish universities. Ethics and economics meant reading the country's history after the turmoil of 1914–22 from the balance sheet. The fourth edition saw 'moral hazard' flare up in the headlong internationalisation of finance – its prime victims the Scottish banks in 2007–8. This has required a restructure of the post-1964 narrative in Chapters 6 to 8.

How to cram the 'vasty fields' of the Scottish century since August 1914 – starting and ending in melodrama – into 200 pages? The book has changed by more than a third since its first edition in 1981, but Hamish Henderson's salute to his 'Seven Good Germans', 'the dead of Cyrenaica' still seemed to work: their grand- and great-grandchildren have served well as Tübingen students and colleagues.

There are now four accounts of Scotland's twentieth century: from Richard Finlay, Catriona Macdonald and Tom Devine, besides this one: to measure against Joseph Lee's magisterial *Ireland 1912–1985* (1989) – though the speculation-chaos that succeeded his last chapter overwhelmed the boundaries of 'These Islands'. Against Thomas Hardy's 'Why load men's minds with more to bear?' to diagnose and warn remains important, as Chris Smout has shown in his 'Land and Sea' essay in the *Oxford Handbook of Modern Scottish History* (2012), on social-ecological as well as national grounds.

'Scottish politics and foreign cash' might have taken over, but can these be trusted to work synergically? John Watson, my publisher, compared this version to the Forth Railway Bridge, as its three complex towers – war, economic convulsion, divergent politics – still supported a remarkable continuity of civil society. Independent or not, Scots discourse, tolerance and pragmatism have prevailed. Can this persist and develop without the 'nuts and bolts' capability that built the bridge, or has commerce and the sheer weight of undifferentiated information burst the confines of state, law and morality, contributing to the grab-bag of 'moral hazard'? 'Administered Scotland', 1922–64 had to be examined through separate prisms: economy, society, politics, culture, each of which had its own social, corporate and intellectual criteria and power balances. Analysis had to come through reintegration, and tackling that led me to reorganise the 1964–99 sections in Chapters 6 and 7 and then in Chapter 8 attempt to follow, partly as a participant, the 'Holyrood' phase and its extraordinary climax.

Society has changed: women – moving from wife, much-missed, sister, daughter, students, editors and friends to the world of politics – have had analytic effect as well as increasing political roles. 'No Gods and Precious Few Women' wasn't just deserved: the critique forced a new approach to 1964–2015, and a critical assessment of the male record, underlined by the doubtful health of Scottish media at all levels. 'Meg Dods' and Marion Reid, 'Chris Caledonia' and Alice Munro have been, thankfully, 'more important than football itself'. The need to cut spectator sport down to size, along with stand-ins for proper community, has counted. Holyrood was educational and fun largely because of the characterful women who captured it. 'The problem with you, Chris, is that you're used to teaching students, so you say outrageous things to make them think, and then they go off and read.' That was Margo MacDonald. 'But ye cannae do that to the sensitive wee souls in this place.' Irreplaceable, yes, but almost immediately multiplied.

Housekeeping (1987), Bill Forsyth's all-woman film after a novel by Marilynne Robinson, set in a Scots-like community in the Rockies, raised themes about settlement, family and nature, John Ruskin's 'true economy', against which the new century will be judged. Well received in the US, it is scarcely known in Scotland, where masculine traumas, from *Braveheart* to *Trainspotting*, won out. No one living through 2005–8, from Gordon Brown and Alan Greenspan being lauded in Edinburgh to the catastrophic end of 'light touch' regulation, could rely on the wisdom of the markets or the honesty of professionals. Even Prof. Iain McLean's sympathetic study of Adam Smith reckoned the 'mercantile' approach of Sir James Steuart more influential – especially in areas of infrastructure and (broadly speaking) 'housekeeping' up to the 1830s, and the age of List, Marx – and indeed Ruskin, 'the Scot of Scots'.

After 1997, deindustrialisation, as Scotland's chief medical officer Sir Harry Burns wrote, destroyed the balance of work and life on which a true 'common weal' depended. The result brought Scottish finance low in the triumph (so far) of those old *roués* 'luxury and corruption'. This, and a two-thirds collapse in the oil price, imposed a darker question in days already grim – can we now steer our planet somewhere sensible in the time we've got, with what Thomas Carlyle called 'such intellect as comes to hand'?

Christopher Harvie
Melrose, January 2016

Acknowledgements

My thanks to daughter Alison, sister Jane and brother Steve, our extended family and carers, and Wilma Hewitt, our Mother Courage at Avenel, who have helped me to care for Isobel and George, and enabled a public life, teaching and the writing of books to continue. Tübingen brought Paddy Bort, Christine Frasch and Stefan Büttner to Edinburgh, and at Kirkcaldy Dave Torrance, Carol Lindsay, Bob Purdie, Ian and Di Chisholm, Tom and Eleanor Hubbard and many more confirmed the warmth of the Lang Toun – not to speak of Aileen Paterson and Chris and Anne-Marie Smout in 'greater Fife'. Jenny Wormald, Richard Findlay, Catriona Macdonald, Will Storrar, Robert McDowell and Terry Brotherstone have been an ideas exchange, and Paddy's *View from Zollernblick* (2013), my '*Festschrift*', has saved a lot of trips to libraries. Holyrood counted too, its MSPs and staff generating a memory and community in that strange but already historic building – what nearly-new Westminster must have been to Anthony Trollope in the 1860s. Borders Railway trains have replaced freezing buses rattling through the dark to Edinburgh, but their drivers on the twisting A7 deserve special thanks.

John Brown first suggested 'No Gods' as a title. His love for and documentation of our history writing will live on, as will Ian MacDougall's oral record of how Jock and Jean lived and logged what 1914–2015 threw at them. They too are winners of wars.

1

Finest Hour and After, 1911–22

'THE DARKNESS AND THE THUNDER AND THE RAIN'

In May 1915 young Captain Charles Sorley, born to an Aberdeen academic family, wrote to his mother from the front: 'There is no such thing as a just war. What we are doing is casting out Satan by Satan.' He left a vivid sonnet, *To Germany*

> You only saw your future bigly planned,
> And we the tapering paths of our own mind,
> And in each other's dearest ways we stand,
> And hiss and hate. And the blind fight the blind.

when a sniper killed him at Loos in the October of that year, and poems which influenced other dissident officers, trapped in 'the darkness and the thunder and the rain'. Loos was the greatest Scots slaughter since Flodden.

The German spy Lieutenant Carl Lody had been executed at the Tower a year before, after shaking hands with the firing squad. The staff of MI5 mourned a brave opponent, if an incompetent one. He had spent August in Scotland after war was declared – at 11pm on the 4th – observing ships and soldiers in and around Edinburgh, but he didn't visit Glasgow. Nor did any other agent, presumably because only about 10 per cent of Clydeside shipbuilding was naval. This indifference would lose Lody's chiefs at the *Generalstab* the war they had planned since 1895. Additional munitions outlay was projected at £1.6 million in 1914 by the British War Office. This might have covered half a morning's barrage in 1918. In a £6 billion outlay, the Clyde was the largest single unit.

The United Kingdom went to war for precise reasons: assisting the French and keeping the High Seas Fleet from breaking the 'distant blockade' of Germany. The first meant the common Golgotha of the Western Front, but the marine front lay off Scotland. The UK would fight in seven theatres: the Dardanelles, East Africa, Greece, Italy, Mesopotamia, Egypt/Palestine and Russia. Scotland's experiences must be seen in this world context – drawing on a specialised 'diaspora' involving a world network of docks, coaling stations, cables and freight forwarders, a third of the merchant fleet, with Edinburgh the major centre of mapmaking and systematised information. Besides the military, involved in various centres of the 'world crisis' were Scots *savants* – R. W. Seton-Watson, James Bryce, Arthur Balfour, Patrick Geddes, John Buchan, Sandy Hammerton, William Forbes-Sempill, Compton MacKenzie, even Hugh MacDiarmid – whose shadows would lie over the century to come.

To the editor and novelist Arnold Bennett 'the Clyde' stood for the real war of production led by Lloyd George. In his fly-on-the-wall political novel *Lord Raingo* (1926) he made him 'Andy Clyth', a Lancashire Scot. D. H. Lawrence's heroine of 'Ours is a tragic age' Constance Chatterley, was Glasgow-born, and reflected women's revolution in expectation – as well as Burns's delight in the 'life-force' of sex. Britain was *the* arsenal of World War I – it would be dwarfed by the USA and USSR in World War II – but without Scotland it would not have won. This world was where the story went: in Scotland, our concern, was only a part.

In August the government quickly passed the MI5-drafted Defence of the Realm Act (DORA), took over the railways, impounded ships and interned aliens. In countless drill halls the Territorial reserves mobilised: of their fourteen divisions Scotland supplied two and Captain John Reith (later of the BBC) recalled that they were cheered instead of catcalled in the Glasgow streets. Not all wanted abroad: the north-east was strong territorial country, but this was harvest time and the height of the fishing season. The socialist *Forward* found more enthusiasm for home defence than for avenging the wrongs of Belgium. Even Reith's battalion would only serve abroad as a unit.

Fears of attack if not invasion were legitimate and abounded. Troops guarded strategic viaducts, east coast towns put up barricades, police raided post offices. For the new Rosyth dockyard was incomplete, and there was no boom on the Forth, nor on Scapa Flow. Zeppelins appeared and on 22 September a German U-boat sank three 'old' cruisers (built 1902, but pre-turbine) off the Thames and First Sea Lord Jellicoe ordered the Grand Fleet from the Nore to Scapa, then to Lough Swilly. There, on 27 October, the new dreadnought *Audacious* hit a mine, sank and stuck, visible for four years and puzzling people. The big attack didn't come, but enough ships sank off the east coast for the Admiralty to take over its larger ports.

Similarly frenetic was the recruiting of the 'Kitchener Army' – what became in May 1915 Ian Hay's *First Hundred Thousand*. Of the 157 battalions of regulars from which the British Expeditionary Force was formed, Scottish regiments made up twenty-two, plus a seventh of the Territorials and almost a sixth of the 'first two hundred thousand'. Industrial districts and the Highlands alike responded enthusiastically, most employers promising to make up wages to peacetime levels. Attacks on football playing as 'next to treason' were answered by many taking the colours in 'K-1', notably Edinburgh's Hearts FC. Volunteering for the Scots version of the 'pals' battalions' broke British records, with James Dalrymple, their autocratic manager, turning Glasgow's famous trams into a giant recruiting office and furnishing a Highland Light Infantry battalion from his own staff.

Initially the Army waived height restrictions and created 'bantam battalions' of tiny *Giftzwerge*. Later it phased them out. Nine of the seventy divisions created by 1918 were nominally Scottish, although by then – their usual two battalions swollen to fifteen or sixteen – their local identity had dissolved. In fact two-thirds of the would-be K-1 volunteers never left the city, being found unfit. Others spent the autumn training in southern England, sometimes idyllic, more often squalid (no one could cook, and epidemics ran riot), though quite unlike Glasgow machine shops or the 'barras' of the famous ex-ned *Spud Tamson VC*. The boys of K-1 could not foresee the losses of Loos, a preface to the Somme in mid-1916 and Ypres in 1917. Were they consoled by a relative absence of caste differences between officers and men? Probably, for much of war *was* boredom, and in England commissions went almost entirely to public schoolboys, like young Captain Sorley.

A clever agent of the sort John Buchan later invented in *Mr Standfast* (1919) would have seen an exporting economy under threat. There was panic in Border tweed and Highland tourism, redundancies in the paper mills and much thrawnness when trade unions accused ladies knitting soldiers' socks of driving even more out of work. Hunting continued in the Tory shires 'to avoid adding to the ranks of the unemployed'. The Liberal Local Government Board proposed relief schemes of public works; a fund for the unemployed raised £20,000 from Edinburgh and £12,000 from Glasgow. Its peace-minded ex-provost, Sir Daniel Stevenson, brother-in-law of a Hamburg *Burgermeister*, urged fellow employers to fill vacancies caused by recruits, and the corporation to increase its expenditure.

Competitive patriotism moderated panic. In September Marshal Joffre broke the German *Schlieffenplan* on the Marne and the trench stalemate began, yet 'business as usual' would reign until the late 1915 offensives. At Hogmanay its tone was caught by the Tory MP Sir William Raeburn in the *Glasgow Herald*:

> The war has falsified almost every prophecy. Food was to be an enormous price, unemployment rife, revolution was to be feared. What are the facts? The freight market is now prosperous. Prices of food have risen very little, and the difficulty is to get sufficient labour, skilled and unskilled. We have not only maintained our own trades, but have been busy capturing our enemies.

War, it seemed, brought its own equilibrium. On the debit side, some raw materials and markets were cut off; enlistment reduced the labour force; government borrowing and purchasing pushed up inflation and insurance premiums. Investment, switched to war *matériel*, was hit by government control and enemy attack, but imports of enemy manufactures fell as did their competition in other markets. Substitutes were in demand, along with war contracts; there was less unemployment but also more opportunity for dilution and rationalisation, and a substantial rise in profits. The 'impact of total war' took over a year to hit home because the traumas it caused partly stemmed *from* this equilibrium, and the need to change it.

Few seemed to protest against the war, and once Belgium was invaded, the Liberal left, so nearly led by Lloyd George himself, was cleverly turned to activism by Charles Masterman at Wellington House off Whitehall. The veteran radical Viscount Bryce, a likely dissident, publicised 'German atrocities' in Belgium, whose Congo exploitation had made it a pariah in 1908. The papers and the Unionists rivalled the Liberal Party and its Free Kirk allies in being competitively pro-war. The socialist left, through *Forward*, its main organ, reflected a trade union-versus-socialist-internationalist conflict within the Labour Party. An articulate minority – some ministers in the Free Kirk, and Liberals of the Provost Stevenson sort – voiced Sorley-like views and founded in December 1914 the Union of Democratic Control, subsequently a meeting point for anti-war socialists and what A. J. P. Taylor called 'trouble-makers'.

The overall pattern wasn't only a flaring up of enthusiasm, but a pretty rational process of bidding for support with concessions or, as time went on, promotions: learning by mistakes. This was countered by executive performance, from brilliance to incompetence, 'lions led by donkeys', and so on, revolutionary reactions and their partial co-option. The year 1917 was a desperate one, ending with only the USA to play. But President Woodrow Wilson bore a name known to every Presbyterian, and the promise of a Covenant, while Earl Balfour promised the Diaspora its Jerusalem.

'BEFORE THE LAMPS WENT OUT', 1911–14

What would Lody the spy have found had he literally gone west? Glasgow's *fin-de-siècle* exhibitions of 1888 and 1901 had been cosmopolitan, in self-proclaimed 'Beaux-Arts' style, but that of 1911 planted pasteboard Scots vernacular in Kelvingrove Gardens, emphasising its 'patriotic and educational' aim of a Chair of Scottish History at the University. This displayed the new, very British, George V, feted in Wales, even in Ireland. A sort of 'disparate nationalism' was now affecting what Jim Bulpitt famously called 'low politics' – essentially civic but on the cusp of change. James Joyce in *Dubliners* (1914) borrowed a term from Ibsen's *Ghosts*: paralysed.

The Liberals, kept in power by Scottish votes after 1910, had emasculated the Lords and were about to pass Irish Home Rule; their Scottish Federation hoped 'all round'. The sixty-year schism in the Church had stopped hurting; the land system was

Table 1.1   Scotland: numbers employed in main industries, 1907–2012 (in thousands)

	1907	1935	1960	1995	2012
Agriculture, fisheries	237	203	167	30	60
Mining (oil)	132	94	120	4 (38)	(54)
Manufacturing (total)	622	420	767	608	
Iron, steel	231	{ 52	66	5	
Engineering		{ 98	293	135	
Textiles	141	114	123	35	196
Food, drink	71	66	96	91	
Other	179	90	56	179	
Construction	81	44	136	122	164
Service industries	341	609	1480	1480	1843
Total occupied	1,982	1,370	2,201	1,998	2,437*
Unemployment rate	3.7%	21.3%	3.2%	6.9%	5.9%

*Service employment in 2012
Trade and transport   493
Private sector commerce   328
State sector welfare   914
Arts and miscellaneous   141

being reformed. Gaelic culture was box office, from William Sharp aka Fiona MacLeod and Marjory Kennedy Fraser to Hugh Roberton's Orpheus Choir. Art and architecture, including C. R. Mackintosh, Sir J. J. Burnet, the Glasgow Boys (and Girls) and the Scottish Colourists, was distinctive and internationally respected.

But was there a spectre at the feast? Between 1906 and 1908 the Clyde's shipping output had slumped to half its 1905 tonnage. In 1910 and 1911 American competition cut the dividends of the North British Locomotive Company from 10 to 5 per cent. In 1913 German steel was being unloaded on the Clyde at under the cost of Scottish production; these were ominous developments for an economy in which eight staple industries – in order of numbers employed: agriculture, coal-mining, shipbuilding and engineering, textiles, building, steel and fishing – produced 60 per cent of its output.

The Scottish economy was more than a specialised sector of the UK. It was disproportionately large: with 10.5 per cent of the UK population, it produced 12.5 per cent of the UK's output. In consumer goods Scots still made distinctive furniture, pottery and footwear; English mass production and food processing had to contend with local markets and the factories of the Co-operative movement. Scottish housing, in two-roomed stone-built tenement flats, farm steadings or miners' rows, was different from the two-storey brick cottages of England and (as a Royal Commission was shortly to find out) much worse.

On paper, though, Scots workers led the UK, with unemployment much lower – 1.8 per cent of those insured in 1913, against 8.7 per cent in London. Skilled trades dominated: possibly 80 per cent in Glasgow, mainly in metalworking; large numbers in the printing, brewing, papermaking and rubber trades marked the second manufacturing centre, Edinburgh. Craft pride was reflected in 'men o' independent mind', among the 150,000 miners and an equal number of farmworkers. But things were changing. Aberdeen socialism had grown since the 1890s. Dundee, virtually a single-industry town, whose jute mills were migrating to India, returned a Labour MP in 1910 as well as Winston Churchill. In 1909 the Scottish miners' union became affiliated to the Labour Party, and in 1911 and 1912 severe strikes in the docks and mines and on the railways promised growing social polarisation.

Agriculture and fisheries

Agriculture had been the fulcrum of modernising Scottish society in the eighteenth century. Now it contributed 17.2 per cent of UK output. Highly capitalised mixed farms on the east coast contrasted with subsistence crofting in the Highlands. Rents had come down by 30 per cent between 1870 and 1910, but by diversifying into cattle and livestock, feedstuffs and pasture; in 1910 they grazed 15 per cent of Britain's cattle and 30 per cent of its sheep – Scottish farms were competitive. But neither lairds nor 'muckle fermers' liked Secretary Pentland's Agriculture (Scotland) Act, passed, after five years of struggle, in 1911, which set up a Board of Agriculture to grow the Liberal ideal of a free peasantry. The security of tenure and rent control enjoyed by 27,000 Highland crofters would go to a further 28,000 Lowland small farmers, promoting the creation of new holdings and consolidating existing ones.

Scottish fisheries had likewise become a major foodproducing industry. In 1905 their landings were £2.7m, or 25.5 per cent of the UK total (over 33 per cent if Scottish landings in England were included). In 1911 they employed 3,390, down a quarter on 1893, but more productive. Steam trawlers and drifters had replaced sailing boats, and new west coast railheads enabled efficient marketing. Up to 50,000 women gutted, salted and packed onshore, or followed the drifters to Lowestoft in pursuit of the herring shoals. Of their catch, 85 per cent went for export. 'Ecology? Conservation?' – 'Whit they?'

Textiles

Textiles had powered early industrialisation, but now had to cope with market changes and relative decline. In 1905 cotton was only 1.4 per cent of UK production, and woollens only 8.7. Linen, at 14 per cent, was established in small towns along the east coast, centred on Dundee and Dunfermline, while Dundee turned a third of the jute imported into Europe into the sacking that transformed a steam collier out into a grain ship home. After their peak in the 1870s, factories migrated, but Dundee magnates owned and managed their Calcutta plant. Foreign competition in other textiles was met by a variety of responses. In Paisley Coats and Clark amalgamated in 1896 to create a monopoly in thread spinning, drawn on by other firms to expand the machine-weaving of lace in North Ayrshire. Woollens – chiefly based in the Borders and the Ochil Hillfoots – tackled Yorkshire competition by concentrating on tartans and high-quality suitings, or carpetmaking in Glasgow, Bonnyrigg and Kilmarnock. All products were dominated by exports, chiefly to Europe and North America. The 1900s were dominated by a new boom in a fairly old industry: rubber. Established in Edinburgh by Americans in the 1840s, car and bike tyres boosted it and hundreds of Scots followed new railways to Malayan plantations. Welly boots were to prove Jock and Tommy's saviours in the mud of the trenches.

Heavy industry

Exports concentrated heavy industry – coal, iron and steel, ship-building, mechanical and structural engineering – in the Clyde basin and the Lanark and Ayr coalfields. But this rich mineral endowment – nearly two-thirds of Scottish coal production in 1913 – was dwindling, with growth switching to the large new mines of Fife and the Lothians, dominated by Sir Adam Nimmo's coal companies, and to a fast-growing trade – 10m out of 14m tons exported – with east Europe. This brought big port expansion at Leith in 1903, Grangemouth in 1906 and Methil in 1907. The Scottish miner was efficient, producing an eighth above the UK average, largely because of the electric coal cutter, pioneered by Anderson Boyes in Motherwell, and by 1913 accounting for 21.9 per cent of output.

Coal exports, though, reverted to primary production. Iron-smelting, their major market, declined along with reserves of Lanarkshire's 'blackband' ironstone. In 1913 this met only a quarter of Scottish demand, and, with elderly plant, pig-iron output fell. Scots firms had to use imported pig and scrap, lacking the modern equipment of Cleveland and South Wales, where 'hot metal' flowed from blast to steel furnace. In 1884 they had produced half of UK output; by 1913 only a third.

Shipbuilding, however, was at its zenith. The slump of 1906–8 shaken off, Clyde yards set a record of 757,000 tons and 1,111,000 horsepower of marine engines in 1913 (33.4 per cent and 49 per cent respectively of the UK total), when all of Germany produced only 646,000 tons and 776,000 horsepower. The naval race increased warship production, but this was only 10 per cent of total output. The Clyde had to catch up in new technology like turbines, diesel engines and welding, and was thirled to orders from Scottish shipowners, who controlled 4.5m tons, 27 per cent of the UK fleet.

Engineering, with an output valued in 1913 at £1.6m and a workforce of 78,000, ranged from locomotives and rolling stock (where Glasgow had about a third of total British capacity) to hydraulic equipment, steam engines for mine and mill, cranes, pumps, pre fabricated buildings and all sorts of structural work. The huge Singer sewing machine plant at Clydebank, which employed over 10,000, the Acme wringer factory, and Barr and Stroud optical instruments showed that it went beyond heavy industry, but the latter firms set the tone: low on capital, their individual orders small, reliant on skilled workers rather than on rationalised production. Innovation wasn't lacking – with Pilcher and Denny's work on aeronautics, Burt's invention of the sleeve-valve engine and mining electrics – but Scottish companies depended on exports. The North British Locomotive Company, sending half of its engines to the empire and 16 per cent 'abroad', was fairly typical. Increased foreign competition and glutted markets (improved efficiency cut replacement orders) were reflected in NB Loco's sagging dividends and the 'Beardmore problem'. The greatest engineering conglomerate on Clydeside, it had to be bailed out in 1903 by Vickers, yet its dynamic managaing director Sir William Beardmore continually broke loose from Sheffield, with attempts at diversification that were imaginative and innovative but rarely profitable, even after a boost from the post-dreadnought naval race. Financial and legal troubles bedevilled Scotland's pioneer volume car-production project, Argyll Motors. It went bust in 1912.

The free market was crucial to pre-war industry. Shipbuilders haggled with their workers, suppliers and customers; Glasgow iron dealers established world prices. Clydeside, and after it the whole Scottish economy, reacted sensitively to fluctuations in world trade and shipping freights. Its great firms were family or partnership concerns, their values usually artificially low. Weir Pumps of Cathcart were worth only £60,000 in 1913; Colvilles, the Lanarkshire steel giant, only £280,000 in 1918. Amalgamation and joint-stock companies were still fairly rare – railways accounted for 75 per cent of shares traded in Scottish industrial companies in 1908. The NB Loco, fused from the three family firms of Neilson Reid, Sharp Stewart and Dubs in 1903, with £2m capital, 10,000 workers and the second-largest locomotive-building capacity in the world, was a portent.

Power plays

In terms of power there were three Scotlands: the country-side where the gentry held sway; Edinburgh; and Glasgow – culturally further apart from one another than either was from London. Edinburgh, despite a wide range of industry, was still dominated by its 'castes' – the 'old professions' of law, religion and finance – parasitic on the gentry and increasingly on business, yet keeping the latter at arm's length (in the 1960s the New Club regarded Glasgow's takeover king Hugh Fraser as 'a mere draper'). More realistic, if flawed, were the plutocrats of the West and Dundee. Energetic, imaginative and a bit vulgar, they hung Corots alongside Faeds in their lobbies, and had steam yachts on the Clyde. Fathers had sacrificed everything to technical and economic success; their sons were ambivalent. They might stick on in the business and marry into other industrial dynasties, like the Bilslands, Colvilles, Weirs and Lithgows. Or shift from industry into finance, as did many a Dundee jute baron. Or sell out and move into genteel society, like the Tennants or the Clarks.

Sir Henry Campbell-Bannerman, prime minister from 1906 to 1908, was a rare parliamentarian from the mid-Victorian bourgeoisie, though industrialists often took to civic affairs, sometimes to the detriment of their enterprises. Was the 'London barrister MP' a result? Or did the rigidity of Edinburgh governance prevent the combination of finance and innovation needed to preserve the autonomy of Scottish capitalism?

Uncertainty affected the neighbours. The skilled craftsmen, capital as well as backbone of the heavy industrial workforce, were threatened by new machinery and an expanding labour force. More women were working, and more boys, who could be sacked when they grew up. Small-scale industries, facing mounting competition, groped for desperate remedies. In the yards and shops, pneumatic and self-acting tools intrigued employers who had seen German and American works, and noted where their nurseries' toy trains and teddy bears came from. Miners faced immigrant competition, after 1900 from the Baltic rather than from Ireland.

Parliamentary elections supplied Scots citizens, as John Vincent wrote of the English, with 'the circuses of their lives'. The country of Gladstone's Midlothian Campaign was more serious, but the idea of politics as social drama went even deeper. Elections were about status, citizenship, religious equality and, less sublimely, patronage. 'Constructive' legislation played a small part, but the cast was a high-grade one, and useful connections abounded. In 1910 a third of the Liberal cabinet was Scots or sat for Scots seats. Prime Minister Asquith, MP for East Fife, 1908–16, had married into the Tennant family of Scots chemical magnates. Arthur Balfour, 1901–5, as well as 'C-B' was Scots; so were the Unionist and Labour leaders Bonar Law and Keir Hardie, and Labour's ambitious secretary Ramsay MacDonald.

What connection was there between Scottish affairs and Westminster politics? 'Lads o'pairts', moving south to the civil service, passed Liberal frontbenchers returning to placid Scots seats. Although the split over Irish home rule in 1886 weakened the post-1832 Liberal dominance, it was restored in 1906, and extended at both elections of 1910, even though English Liberal seats fell from 309 to 189. In 1910 there were 779,000 ratepayer electors in seventy-two constituencies, plus three University seats. Sons living at home and most lodgers were effectively excluded, while businessmen had two votes. Such inequalities probably accounted for the sloth of Scottish politics; they allowed Unionism to survive – mainly in the south-west and a few suburbs. The lead it had briefly gained in the central belt, by recruiting the Orange vote, and (in 1900) the Catholics as well, dwindled with calls for disestablishment, which neutralised the Church of Scotland, and the unpopularity of protection in an exporting area.

The Liberals traditionally drew on east-coast burghs and counties and the 'incantations' of free trade, religious equality and land reform. Provosts and solicitors were still the powerbrokers, 'New Liberalism' seemed distant and there was no Lib–Lab pact in 1906. What, then, caused Liberalism's continued success? Hostility to the aristocracy explained the counties, loyal through the People's Budget, Parliament Act and Land Act. The towns? Sectarianism remained, but secularity was heating up under the ice. After 1909, with the miners on side, Labour won West Fife, Dundee and Glasgow Blackfriars in 1910. Much of the idealism which, in England, called itself New Liberal, passed into heterodox but interlinked radical groupings, from Young Scot home rulers to the 10,000-odd readers (mainly Independent Labour Party) of Tom Johnston's *Forward*, founded in 1906.

The activist part of government (Lloyd George, Churchill) conciliated the unions by reforming their legal status, set up Royal Commissions into housing and railways. By 1914, in response to union and woman suffragist pressure, a further reform bill was in prospect. Yet Scots issues receded: neither the home rule bills moved in 1913 and 1914, nor attempts to co-ordinate socialist activity, put the left on the offensive. Instead the Unionists won four out of fifteen byelections between 1910 and 1914. Propelled by the Ulster crisis, their revival seemed imminent.

Perhaps this upheaval reflected a more fundamental institutional shift. Until 1906 the politics which affected Scots folk's everyday lives had been civic: the affairs of the great cities (37 per cent of the population), the burghs and 900-odd parishes – traditional units which had since 1832 accumulated new powers. Still unrationalised, parishes not Poor Law Unions controlled welfare and, unlike England after 1902, education. The dominance of local elites remained: landowners, farmers, ministers and schoolmasters in the country; businessmen, rentiers and shopkeepers in the burghs. After the 1860s the elite had extended local government to contain the social pressures of industry and the urban workers. A 'civic consciousness' endorsed, both in the theory of Edward Caird and Patrick Geddes, and in practical bodies like the City of Glasgow Improvement Trust, extensive measures of 'municipal socialism', an ideology shared by the 'labour aristocracy' and even the socialist movement, but which stopped short of seriously altering the distribution of wealth and power. It was now under stress – from failure to tackle housing, the most obdurate social problem, from discontented skilled labour, from the developing power of the state.

The suture between parliament and civics was the Scottish administration. Scarcely 'Dublin Castle' – with no Viceroy or separate exchequer – this operated from offices at Dover House in Whitehall and in Edinburgh. The Secretary for Scotland, a lowly member of most cabinets since 1885, dealt with political organisation, patronage and a range of Home Office affairs; he presided over the Scotch Education Department, answered for the Boards (supposedly representing Scottish interests) of Agriculture and Fisheries, and Local Government, and – gingerly – over the Lord Advocate, who oversaw Scots Law.

The Secretary had usually been a peer, but Lord Pentland's Agriculture Act meant that his successors really had to sit in the Commons to handle questions and interventions, a third of which were on agriculture and about 10–12 per cent each on fisheries, housing and public health. Otherwise his portfolio was limited; his control was strong in education but weak in local government and industrial affairs, liaison with the Board of Trade being minimal. Much routine private bill legislation went to Commissioners in Edinburgh, and the Lord Advocate maintained a jealous control over it: the Secretary only gained official precedence over him in 1912.

Dover House was politically rather than administratively important: it reassured Scots MPs – organised since 1907 in their own Grand Committee for non-controversial legislation – that the Cabinet was aware of Scottish issues. After 1906 it kept an eye on the Scottish Liberal majority. Pentland was Campbell-Bannerman's confidant, MacKinnon Wood loyally Asquithian, H. J. Tennant Asquith's brother-in-law. Most of the Secretary's year was spent in London, with a trip around the Highland coast in the summer on a fishery cruiser. The 1914 trip did not take place.

INTO CLEANNESS LEAPING?

War affected Scottish 'low politics', so after 2 August Raeburn's 'business as usual' was understandable, before the 'Kitchener' battalions saw real action in mid-1915. Even then, casualties, though severe, were still only a fraction of what was to come. Armies had waited for business to adapt to war production, rather than forcing change. Such problems affected the main institutions of Scottish finance and some (though not all) industrial sectors, and were mainly caused by disruptions to imports, exports and finance. One result was comforting: the UK turned to Scottish banking practice. On 6 August 1914 pound notes, a fixture in the north, supplemented (and quickly replaced) gold sovereigns in England. But under the counter the City of London rapidly took over control.

The eight banks – the Bank of Scotland, the Royal Bank, the British Linen, the National, the Commercial, the Union, the Clydesdale and the North of Scotland – were still Scottish-owned. Their ruling conference of general managers got them to subscribe generously to the War Loans, and, in response to the Bank of England's real fear of the High Seas Fleet staging a 'gold raid', shifted their bullion south. The investment trusts used their huge stakes in American railroads, mining companies, farms and real estate as security for government loans in the US, or sold them to buy government stocks.

Textiles were hit immediately by a 30–40 per cent rise in freight and insurance charges, and by the invasion of Belgium, which knocked out Verviers, the chief source of yarn for Border tweeds. Substitute Yorkshire yarn wasn't good enough, and Border machinery found it difficult to handle khaki (which was 50 per cent shoddy). Its trade slumped and stayed down. The closure of the Baltic was disastrous for linen, pushing the price of flax up by 65–75 per cent. Jute was more complex: demand for sandbags was huge, while German commerce-raiders checked the supply of jute and the products of Calcutta. Dundee was hit by profiteering: spinners charged the inflated market price for yarn, but used jute bought at pre-war prices. Their profits soared to 56 per cent, while those of the weavers – subject to government price control – stuck around 10 per cent. The War Office had to organise the whole process, and did so on 1 June 1915. By 1918 a billion sandbags would be shipped to the fronts, and so this early crisis helped centralise state control.

War hit the coalfields immediately. The German market of 2.9m tons vanished, taking the Baltic market with it. New markets, formerly supplied from Belgium and northern France, were affected by a second disruption. Rosyth would not be ready until spring 1916, so the Admiralty requisitioned the Forth coal ports. By 1918 exports would fall to under 2.5m tons and although demand for steel for munitions kept the western coalfields active, the problems of the eastern fields spurred the enlistment of miners. Scotland had the highest miner recruitment in Britain: 26.5 per cent compared with 22.9 per cent in England and 22.5 per cent in Wales. But over 36.5 per cent of East Lothian miners were in uniform by August 1915, compared with only 20 per cent in Ayrshire. With the coalowners promising (at least initially) to make up the difference between

army and civilian earnings, the army seemed a good alternative
to parish relief, at least temporarily. Efficiency nosedived, as
the remaining miners were less skilled, older or less fit. By
November 1915 the government effectively shut off recruiting and in February 1916 set up its Coke and Coal Supplies
Committee to make Scotland self-sufficient.

This was achieved by September 1917, along with pooling
and regulation of railway wagons. Attempts to control home
prices failed. In July 1915 they simply provoked a switch to
exports. Regulation by local committees was achieved, but not
until late 1917. Fundamental disruption had been inflicted on
the industry, depleting manpower and starving the more productive eastern coalfield of capital and transport. Vital civilian
markets were lost – as matters turned out, for good.

For fishing the war was from the start disastrous. The herring
industry saw two-thirds of its market, in Germany and Russia,
vanish. Exports had reached Russia through Germany, and a
switch to Archangel largely failed. So, few fishermen refused
direction into the Royal Naval Reserve, and by 1918 about
25,000 fishermen out of nearly 40,000 were thus employed, with
302 steam trawlers, 838 steam drifters and 100 motor drifters.

The Highlands, neglected for so long, suddenly became
a scene of frenzied activity. Scapa Flow and Invergordon,
designated in 1912 as outstations to Rosyth, became fully
protected late in 1914. Their importance increased with the
Northern Barrage project of 1917 for a continuous minefield
between the Shetlands and neutral Norway. Over the single-
tracked Highland Railway thousands of special trains carried
coal, sailors, mines and ammunition; they returned south
with the trees of Highland plantations, chopped down by the
Canadian Forestry Corps. In mid-1916 the landmass north and
west of the Great Glen became a 'restricted area', which the
traveller needed a pass to enter. Behind this new frontier places
like Invergordon (population 1,110 in 1911) grew sevenfold.
The aluminium works at Kinlochleven and Foyers expanded;
Raasay's low-grade iron ore was mined, railways and blast
furnaces built.

'Business as usual' then dissolved. Commercial adjustment to war production proved impossible to square with machinery and goals quite alien to Scottish *laissez-faire*. This was dramatised by the Jacks case of June 1915. Partners of a Glasgow iron firm run by Andrew Bonar Law's brother were found guilty of supplying iron ore to (*inter alia*) Krupps in August 1914. The implication was that Lord Advocate Munro tactfully dropped charges against John Law, whose brother joined the government on 23 May (Andrew wrote that the firm's action would have been repeated by 99 out of 100 businessmen). Munro gave way to the Tory John Clyde: behind both was the far-sighted Lloyd George, Chancellor of the Exchequer in 1914, advocate of state power both in the industrial and social field. In 1915 this would transfer power both to the Scottish Office and to the business classes, via his new Ministry of Munitions, subverting many of the institutions of Scottish politics. A new challenger appeared, with new foreign allies.

RED RIVER

By 1917 a quarter of a million men and women were in war work in Scotland. Whitehall invested over £11m after late 1915, much of it in a vast explosives works at Gretna, while the Clyde had the biggest shell centre in the UK. 'Munitions' encompassed war *matériel*, from boots to battleships – but the heavy industries above all. The *Herald* reported in December, with one in seven shipbuilders enlisted, that the problem was 'obtaining sufficient labour, even at the high wages now ruling, and sufficient materials even at the equally high prices which are charged'. The Admiralty took over the yards fairly smoothly. Production, at an average of 520,000 tons, was below the peak of 1913, but warships needed powerful engines, so horsepower output rose 58 per cent by 1918.

Schlieffenplan kaputt! No encirclement of Paris. But in October 1914 Germany was also ready for a static war, with concrete dugouts. Cracking these demanded high-explosive (HE) shell fired from high-elevation guns with robust barrels. From

May 1915 this priority multiplied problems for engineering, as skilled labour was being lost to the front and to the shipyards. Government became determined on a drastic programme of expansion and rationalised production. A second stage happened after the Somme, the Kitchener army's real test, in summer 1916, and Germany responded, almost to the month. The new men were managers: in Germany Quartermaster-General Wilhelm Groener, in Britain Eric Geddes, the Scots head of the North Eastern Railway who became General in 1916 (military railways) and Admiral in 1917 (convoys).

Thus was created the 'Red Clyde', for left-wingers came to equate the pressure on Glasgow with the French army mutinies – both in late April 1917 – and the Bolshevik takeover in October, culminating in German mutiny and capitulation in autumn 1918. 'The rapids of revolution' – words of the Glasgow schoolteacher Marxist John Maclean, Lenin's consul perhaps echoed the 'broad and deep' river of Scott's *Waverley* – and would be revived in 1962, when lefties, disarmers and nationalists alike would sing Hamish Henderson's 'Freedom Come All Ye':

> When Maclean meets wi' freens in Springburn
> Aa the roses an geans will turn tae bloom,
> An the black boy frae yont Nyanga
> Dings the fell gallows o' the burghers doon.

The black boy was Mandela but there was serious Marxist politics here. The Clyde showed theory converging on industrial fact: crisis-ridden capitalism turning on skilled workers. Their 'actual humanity' engaged with their consciousness about how to use their power: the classic situation of 'praxis'. The Clyde, a key arms production region with skilled workers in a majority, should have levered revolution, and it has never lacked committed historians, who see in it lessons for contemporary struggles or a doctrinally wrong turning – a socialist and nationalist revolution betrayed by orthodox Labourism.

A revolutionary situation? This would have needed (1) capitalists determined to use the war to change the peacetime problems by 'dilution' – mechanising and deskilling work; (2) militant, class-conscious activists mobilising support among the widening workforce; (3) government losing control over public morale and public order. There was certainly evidence at times of all three: a serious industrial problem, government panic. Selective quotation can produce a scarlet ferment. In the troubles of early 1919 Secretary Munro, for example, told the cabinet that 'it was a misnomer to call the situation in Glasgow a strike – it was a Bolshevist rising', and blood-curdling reports found their way south from MI5's Sir Basil Thompson. The treatment of John Maclean looks like a witchhunt. But was there a developing pattern of organised working-class resistance? Actual conflicts were episodic, separated in time, occupying only a few months over eight years. They consisted of:

1. The 'tuppence an hour' engineers' strike of February 1915.
2. The Fairfield Strike of August 1915.
3. The rent strike of October–November 1915.
4. The imposition of dilution in Glasgow engineering shops, January–April 1916, culminating with the deportation of the shop stewards.
5. Then, after a three-year truce, with the Clyde tranquil, the Forty Hours strike of January–February 1919.
6. The election of November 1922, at which ten Labour MPs were returned in the fifteen Glasgow constituencies, of whom James Maxton and John Muir had been prominent in the wartime campaigns. These made up a socialist group in and out of Labour until 1946.

However, when such episodes of conflict are examined, even this limited consistency gives way. The situation becomes complex, individual crises and personalities become important. And the key figure was not from labour but management: William Weir (Viscount Weir, 1877–1959), the managing director of G. & J. Weir Pumps of Cathcart, who became munitions controller in Scotland on 13 July 1915.

Weir was young and innovative, but was he an appropriate appointment? Responding to engineering's problems, he was familiar with new American machinery and 'Taylorist' scientific management, wanted wholesale reconstruction and saw the war facilitating this via working women, even boys and girls: 'Whatever the unions may do, and notwithstanding any guarantee given, employment . . . never will be the same again.' The *Scots Law Courts Record* reflects his views but they were not shared by most Clydeside managers – even Beardmore, to whom periodic run-ins with workers were a fact of life. War gave innovators a chance, a degree of aggressive moral fervour – Weir gave all his firm's war profits to charity – of the sort that took Reith into the trenches. When engineers threatened to strike for tuppence an hour, his response, in a pamphlet entitled *Responsibility and Duty* of 30 January 1915, was scarcely tactful: 'Every hour lost by a workman COULD HAVE been worked, HAS been worked by a German workman, who in that time has produced, say, an additional shell . . . to kill the British workman's brother in arms.'

The engineers were now facing a 50 per cent rise in the cost of living. Co-op members to a man, they saw inflation caused by the profiteering of wholesalers, shippers and insurers, and Weir himself, who shipped in Americans paid well over Clydeside rates, triggering a strike that was to last from 15 February to 4 March. On 17–19 March both sides signed the 'Treasury Agreements' on wartime industry governance and on 30 April founded the Clyde Armaments Output Committee (CAOC).

But Weir persisted, using a report alleging poor productivity through absenteeism and drink: temperance propaganda which failed to consider enlistment and a less-skilled labour force, as Bonar Law pointed out in the Commons. By 15 May Weir was calling for martial law in the munitions districts. This served a political purpose. On 1 May Lloyd George became Minister of Munitions, dynamising production, and on 7 July the great Jacobin appointed Weir 'controller in Scotland of a miniature ministry of munitions'. On 30 August Weir replaced the CAOC with a nominal board dominated by management. As the *History of the Ministry of Munitions* comments: 'Just when these novel conditions called for free interchange of opinion between employers and workmen, mutual goodwill and readiness to adjust habits and prejudices, the round table was broken up.'

Weir had to set up a plant to supply the big offensives slated for mid-1916, spending and building before any full agreement with other firms or labour, and by August he had set up a co-operative production scheme for 28,500 HE shells a week. Firms drove hard bargains: Rowans the marine engineers wrangled until mid-October, 'determined to protect themselves at all costs against possible loss'. He was less tolerant with the unions. He had to gain dilution before production started, but the Amalgamated Society of Engineers fought its corner over its members' privileges and attempts to use the Munitions Act's leaving certificates to enforce discipline. Management kept its head down. In August Fairfields struck work over leaving certificates and shop stewards were jailed. Lord Balfour of Burleigh, the Conservative ex-Secretary whom the government asked to mediate, found the strikers to be pillars of the Kirk with sons at the front, livid about their rights being scorned. His and Bonar Law's tact contrasted with the inept MacKinnon Wood, who kept them in jail, but this, the one major shipyard strike, was settled . . .

. . . only to be followed by the Rent Strike. This was less industrial militancy than the culmination of Labour's pre-war campaign against the rigorous terms of Scottish house-letting and for subsidised public housing. Engineering management, eager to keep wages down, agreed with the men. So did government, expecting to legislate on Scottish housing anyway. It ended with the Rent Restrictions Act, to be passed in May 1916.

Dilution still remained a battlefield. On one side were Weir, Lloyd George and the developing Munitions Directorate in London under William Beveridge (in 1942 architect of the welfare state). Against them stood the Amalgamated Society of Engineers (ASE), London-based but locally run, facing an unprecedented clash with bosses wanting reorganisation and members sensitive to the threat yet solid with their mates in France. Both depended on the local union reps, the shop stewards, a minority of whom were radicals. Even these were split.

Some welcomed dilution (theoretically) as destroying internal barriers within the working class; others took a revolutionary anti-war stance. Some non-radicals were the toughest: resenting deeply *any* inroads made by women and the Irish into the domain of the skilled male Protestant.

The shop stewards now had the Clyde Workers' Committee (CWC), founded during the 'tuppence an hour' strike, and claiming to speak for the mass of munitions workers. Was it representative? Evidence to a Labour Party inquiry called it 'a heterogeneous crowd which had practically no constitution . . . you could represent a minority in the shop just the same as a majority, even though the minority was one'. The CWC gave the far left its opportunity, and brought to its meetings such as schoolteacher John MacLean MA, and others of Glasgow's rich collection of radicals from Christian pacifists to anarcho-syndicalists. This played into the Munitions Directorate's hands: to the industrial imperative they could add sedition and revolution, and there was no shortage of volunteer martyrs. The crisis came between December 1915 and April 1916. In December Lloyd George came north to win over the Clyde with his eloquence. He met the leaders of the shop stewards, but the planned rally was a disaster. The Lord Advocate seized the issue of *Forward* which reported it. The Clyde had now nominated itself as a test case, and Beveridge and Weir moved rapidly. On 28 January 1916 they appointed dilution commissioners, who quickly drafted agreements covering most engineering shops. A rear-guard strike at Beardmore's in late March was broken when Weir arrested assorted shop stewards – including David Kirkwood and William Gallacher – and deported them to Edinburgh.

Dilution had been smooth enough before the Commissioners; the March measures were a firebreak – what if there had been the same response the Dublin Rising of 24–30 April had received? The shell-forging and turning works were opened by May, when apparent naval defeat at Jutland (31 May–1 June) created new urgency, and reached full production by November and the last weeks of the Somme. By then Weir was in London (he became Air Minister) and the works employed equal numbers of men and women – by 1918 there were 30,000 women to 27,000 men. Even when severe strikes hit the English munitions areas in May 1917, shop-floor co-operation – now led by Kirkwood and Gallacher – became such that the *Herald*, earlier stridently anti-worker, opined that shop stewards 'may portend syndicalism . . . but they certainly mean that the actual workers will be in closer touch with the machinery of their unions, and also with their employers . . . Familiarity is more likely to breed friendship than enmity.'

By then Ireland was alienated, the Bolsheviks were Russian reality. In August 1917 a Glasgow Soviet worried Secretary Munro and even the War Cabinet; it folded when the Corporation didn't give it a school classroom to meet in. Were there vast meetings of revolutionary militants? Nan Milton, his daughter, wrote that to demand John Maclean's release from prison in May 1917 '70,000 or 80,000 marched in the procession, while 250,000 lined the streets'. But this was in fact May Day, and trade unionists were demanding a widened franchise, condemning the Munitions Act and discrimination against the Co-ops, and conscription in Ireland.

Pause and consider: this was bloodbath time. Over 7,000 Scots were killed out of 20,600 at Loos, a similar number on the Somme. The Nivelle offensives were about to provoke French mutinies, Passchendaele and Cambrai lay ahead. The year 1918 would be the worst of all. Yet the Clyde didn't erupt. John Buchan in *Mr Standfast* (May 1919) invented conspiracies unknown to MI5. So did the 'redness' of the Clyde stem from the same unsettlement as Ireland, and that surge of activism from the upheavals of 1905–6, now breaking? Mass trade unionism, worldwide political crisis, from the Rockies to the new Chinese republic? Right-wing scandals, Left governments, syndicalism, propaganda of the deed: the worlds of Henri Bergson and Georges Sorel, the *Futurismo* of Marinetti (or Orkney's Stanley Cursiter, one of the war's most remarkable talents) cinema-conveyed?

The USA declared war on Germany on 2 April 1917, but mobilisation would take months and didn't compensate for

Russia's collapse. President Woodrow Wilson's rhetoric (but lack of troops) didn't inspire his fellow presbyterian Haig, close to backing a negotiated peace in December 1917. Ludendorff's ability to concentrate on a single-front assault after peace with the Bolsheviks on 3 March 1918 had Haig's forces with their 'backs to the wall' on 11 April, but a Scotland won for 'the justice of our cause . . . and the freedom of Mankind' played well in Wilson's USA; her Catholics were given educational self-government. The Pope's peace efforts were frustrated; Covenant ideology helped to subvert Austria. The shipyards were working flat out to repair U-boat losses; trench survivors were making guns for GIs whose first major success came as late as September 1918. Austria and Turkey collapsed; on 4 October Berlin requested an armistice, terms of which were handed over on 7 November to Allied C in C Marshal Foch, and Naval C in C Admiral Sir Rosslyn Wemyss, of an old Fife family. A remarkable outcome for a small country.

By November 1918 war enthusiasm had joined the Clyde conflict and the CWC in vegetating. When more trouble came, in the Forty Hours strike of January–February 1919, this was more a portent of the future disunity of the left. On 14 March 1918 the Scottish Trades Union Congress (STUC) had called for a post-war forty-hour week in order to prevent mass unemployment among demobilised men. After the 1918 election – in which the Unionists won ten out of fifteen Glasgow seats – this demand was echoed by a special conference in Glasgow on 27–8 December. The CWC revived itself to demand a thirty-hour week. The strike actually took place in co-ordination with the Orange workers of Belfast, and on 27 January 40,000 came out, rising to 70,000 on the 28th. On the 30th, the Carters' Union settled for a forty-eight-hour week, and Lloyd George called a conference on this basis but, under pressure from Munro, despatched 12,000 troops, 100 lorries and six tanks to Glasgow. The climax came when a huge crowd – not wholly composed of strikers or even the unemployed – assembled in George Square on Friday 31 January to hear the government's decision on the conference. Suddenly the police (staging strikes elsewhere) charged the crowd: the leaders, Gallacher and Manny Shinwell of the Trades Council, calmed things down, although at the cost of their own freedom. Glasgow was momentarily alive with troops, but the strike ended on news of a conference and continuing regulation of wages and rents. A few 'ringleaders' were tried for sabotage and given short prison sentences: a truce compared with1848, when soldiers shot six in food riots; the suffragettes had been more destructive, Sinn Féiners would later sabotage and run guns but this had no connection with industrial unrest. Pending the 1922 election, the Red Clyde was over.

The outcome was a draw between management and labour. Weir's 'scientific management' (impractical anyway) was pigeonholed; the world of the ASE restored. Peace, and reconstruction, made even labour unrest seem a sign of life. Lord Leverhulme, the Merseyside soap king poised for ambitious Scottish projects, told the Herald in 1917 that it was 'the healthiest sign we have got today'. He – and other Coalition Liberals who confirmed Lloyd George in December 1918 – thought enormous investment in war production, and reparations from Germany, could diversify Scottish industry. The munitions drive depended on electricity; there would be new schemes to tap hydro power. Lorries and cars, mass-produced, might restart the motor industry; Beardmore's 'enormous resources' would enable them to put 'mass production' into practice. Yet left-wing distrust had good grounds. For all Weir's high-mindedness, the History of the Ministry of Munitions put shell profits at 'a somewhat high rate' – in 1916 clearing 40 per cent.

Little of this money went to industry. The Scottish banks in 1919 were glutted with huge capital balances, while the portraitist Sir James Gunn remembered forty years later that 'painters . . . benefited from the desire of war profiteers to translate their gains. There was a boom in etchings: prints soared to fantastic prices. One of MacBey's reached the peak at 500 guineas.'

Where else could the money have gone? Much war investment could only serve war purposes – like vastly extended engine-works for naval escorts. With inflation unchecked until 1921, it carried penal interest, as Beardmore's found. Scottish capitalists sold their own shares, bought land or invested abroad or in the south. The revolution myth obscures the real loss on the Clyde: co-operative decision-making over innovation was possible. The shop stewards, representing something wider than a 'Labour aristocracy', could revere as well as flay their bosses. Intellectually, MacLean's 'Tramp Trust' were management's equals, still convincing in 1960s interviews. Weir and the munitions directors were tactless and footloose; after the 1921 slump they threw their chances away, confirming the workers' distrust of management and new technology. The Red Clyde and the range of its impact, from literature and psychology to the cinema and social policy – MacDiarmid, A. S. Neill, John Grierson retailed by later generations, masked a confusion: consciousness-gain as well as political defeat.

'A LAND FIT FOR HEROES'?

For the Scots, the supreme sacrifice hurt. How to explain the exhilaration? For Siegfried Sassoon, recuperated at Edinburgh, working for the Labour *Daily Herald*, 'Everyone was a bird; and the song was wordless; the singing will never be done.' The great map of the Amiens front – 'Backs to the Wall' – would go on show at Earl Haig's Bemersyde. On 14 June 1919 a Vimy bomber with a Scots engineer crossed the Atlantic to Ireland. Valhalla sank: the *Hochseeflotte* was scuttled on 21 June in Orkney. On 2–6 July the Glasgow-built airship R 34 crossed from East Fortune to New York, returning after the ticker tape on 10–13 July. John Buchan published a causerie, *The Island of Sheep*, in which all parties talked up reconstruction, Parliaments of Man, Federations of the World, and so on. From Clyde-built convoy to Wilson's Covenant, the Scots had been there; without them things would have gone otherwise.

The *Parliamentary Return* of 1921 simply divided 745,000 British dead by 10 to produce a toll of 74,000, but most Scots probably agreed with the National War Memorial white paper of 1920, which estimated 100,000, or over 13 per cent of Britain's dead. Scots territorials, at 5 per cent of the male population, nearly double the British average, suffered early at Loos in October 1915 and disasters like Gallipoli and Iraq. Men were retained by war industry and mines, and casualties in urban areas were the UK average – Glasgow's 18,000 dead is close to the UK's 1 in 54 – but in the counties it could be twice as severe. Selkirk (5,000) lost 240 dead, only forty-five in 1939–45. They were nearly all infantry privates; one officer died for every thirteen men. Few Scottish working-class families escaped, or lacked ex-soldiers who emigrated rather than face the *anomie* and poverty of the post-war years.

During and after the war both wages and prices escalated but, between 1914 and 1920, real wages grew by around 25 per cent, though redistributed among working folk in a way that penalised Scotland. From a 1914 index of 100, a skilled shipwright's wage only rose to 223 in 1920, an engineer's labourer's wage to 309, women's wages to about 250. Welfare aided real wages through rent control and national insurance, extended in 1920 to nearly all manual occupations. Despite the depression, primary poverty was lower than in the 1900s.

Even in the euphoria of 1919 Scottish businessmen worried about takeovers and government action. The Ministry of Munitions ended dealing in iron on the Glasgow Exchange on 31 May 1916. Banking control stayed south: Barclays and the Midland 'affiliated' the British Linen and Clydesdale banks in 1918, and in 1923 the North of Scotland, so three out of seven were under London while the others invested in government stocks or London commerce; even the Unionist *Herald* saw 'the commercial community . . . sighing for a banking William Wallace to free them from Southern oppression'.

Because the Scottish economy was more complex, and export-oriented, government intervention struck deeper than in north-east England or Wales. No major industry escaped. Besides coal and jute, heavy linen (another Dundee speciality), wool purchases, hides, leather and meat, all important Scottish agriculture-based industries, were controlled through ad hoc mixtures of local supervision, compulsory purchase and price-fixing. In agriculture and fisheries control went even further, using existing Scottish machinery.

In response to soaring shipping losses, government in 1917 introduced a measure of food rationing and demanded the conversion of grassland (which had a low calorie yield per acre) into arable. The Board of Agriculture worked through county production committees with paid executives and in 1918 grew Scots arable acreage by over 30 per cent. As elsewhere, recruitment and later conscription forced wages up fast: the War Office plucked labourers from the farms, and the Board tried to bring them back for ploughing and harvest. The Corn Production Act of 1917 established minimum wages, slightly lower than in England, to be fixed by joint negotiating committees. For Joe Duncan, the farmworkers' leader, this confirmed the workers as skilled experts, not the Liberal ideal of peasant smallholders. But the promise of land for crofter soldiers remained, and was to prove troublesome. Although the Board of Agriculture admired its new system, 'Axeman Geddes' did for it in 1922, along with guaranteed prices and minimum wages. Scottish agriculture reverted to livestock, though declined less than the wheat-producing south.

The case was worse in fishing. With boats absorbed in Admiralty service, as minesweepers, patrol boats and tenders, the loss of markets was not immediately noticeable. Indeed, the fishing fleet modernised its operations in the parts of the North Sea not covered by naval operations. Eight hundred sailing vessels were motorised; 4,614 boats (just over 50 per cent of the fleet in 1914) made 1918 'the most lucrative season ever experienced', in the opinion of the Fisheries Board. It had co-ordinated wartime purchasing and saw canning and increased fresh fish consumption as post-war options, but the big deal was resuming herring exports. No: the Russian civil war and Britain's hostility to Bolshevism gave way to German hyperinflation 1923, and competition from neutral, efficient Norway. The boats netted a money income of £4.1m in 1922, against £3.3m in 1918 and £4.0m in 1913, but real income was down 53 per cent. Old equipment and boats offered fishermen only bare subsistence, derived largely from dumping herring at fishmeal factories.

To the Highlands the war brought a new desolation. Forests were felled, fishing boats rotted on the strands where their owners had left them in 1914 – often never to return. Deaths and emigration ended such industries as slate quarrying in Lorne and Caithness; prohibition and liquor control closed down distilleries. The Haldane Report of 1919 promised 250 miles of new railways (with equipment salvaged from the western front), roads, bridges and piers, and extensive replanting under the new Forestry Commissioners. Lord Leverhulme, who had bought Lewis in 1917, planned the industrialisation of the islands on the Scandinavian pattern, around tweed and deep-sea fisheries. But all of this depended on British economic prosperity. The returning servicemen, maimed by the tragic loss of 205 on the *Iolaire* within sight of Stornoway on Hogmanay 1918, mistrusted this new world and demanded their own land. The resulting friction hamstrung Leverhulme, and the downturn swept his and the government's plans away. Population had held up in the 1911–21 decade, because war inhibited emigration and peace promised prosperity. In the 1920s it fell by 10 per cent.

Support had grown for collectivist 'reconstruction', but with Lloyd George the hostage of the Conservatives, the retreat was rapid, even if the Scots needed positive policy to remedy state-induced distortions of economy and society. Without this, they tended to surrender economic responsibility. Railway reorganisation was the test case. In 1919 Geddes, as first Minister of Transport, proposed nationalisation, with an autonomous Scottish region. Conservatives shrank this in February 1921 into the 'grouping' of lines into five private regional monopolies. But a Scottish Railway alarmed the business community, burghs, MPs and trade unions. War strategy had upgraded maintenance and wages, with costs up 291 per cent on 1913, compared with 227 per cent in England. A separate Scottish company would have to maintain these standards, while carrying only 45,000 tons of traffic per annum per route mile, compared with 82,000 in England. It would close rural lines and reduce wage levels. So a cross-party campaign used the rhetoric of nationalism to secure the amalgamation of the five Scottish companies 'longitudinally'. The London Midland and Scottish (Caledonian, Highland, and Glasgow and South Western) and London and North Eastern Railways (North British and Great North of Scotland) came into being in 1923. Little then happened in thirty years that saw dramatic modernisation – especially electrification – in Europe.

RECONSTRUCTION AND REACTION

Reconstruction showed the challenge to traditional Scottish government, and its failure. There was certainly, in the Kirk, local government, law and education, a settled will to reform. The Kirk's Commission on the social and moral issues of the war (1919) admitted that it hadn't 'explained either to the few or to the masses the urgency of social justice and Christian brotherhood'. The Free Church shifted from the Charity Organisation Society-style individualism of its 1911 conference. School boards and teachers pressed for a comprehensive educational settlement. Urban reform was given a huge shove by the Housing Commission. It had been suspended from February 1915 to October 1916. Its indictment, in its 1917 *Report*, of landlords, burghs and counties, and Dover House, was as pungent as its description of the state of the country's dwellings:

> unspeakably filthy privy-middens in many of the mining areas, badly constructed, incurably damp labourers' cottages on farms, whole townships unfit for human occupation in the crofting counties and islands . . . gross overcrowding and huddling of the sexes together in the congested industrial villages and towns, occupation of one-room houses by large families, groups of lightless and unventilated houses in the older burghs, clotted masses of slums in the great cities.

Its demand that a renewed Local Government Board ensure minimum standards forecast a revolution in the Scottish Office. The responsibility was taken on by the new Board of Health of 1919, but it took until 1939 for the Scottish Office to integrate its social, agricultural and industrial responsibilities. The 1919

Act was carried by Dr Christopher Addison, the Whitehall Minister of Health, almost certainly because of the Spanish flu pandemic which, carried rapidly to Europe by migrant workers and US troops in April 1918, killed 250,000 in the UK and up to 33,000 Scots, half in the country and half among servicemen.

This did nothing to aid governmental coherence and Whitehall scarcely helped. After 1915 Tory Lord Advocate Clyde and Liberal Robert Munro at Dover House restored the 'Parliament House rule' that the Scottish Office of 1885 was supposed to replace. Munro aggravated the Forty Hours strike, and frustrated Leverhulme in the Hebrides; but his Education Act, though it lasted only ten years, incorporated Catholics in government and stymied Sinn Féin. Tom Johnston would show in World War II the value of personalising the Secretary's powers. For now, Dover House's lights burned dim.

In Britain the 1922 election saw the destruction of the old Liberals and the rise of Labour. Scotland returned twenty-nine MPs (plus a prohibitionist and a Communist) out of Labour's 142; and the Clydesiders imposed Ramsay MacDonald as leader, respected for his anti-war stance. He became the governing option, with 191 seats, late in 1923. But was war the motor of change? Arthur Marwick and Jay Winter argued that it grew trade unionism and collectivist ideas, discredited New Liberalism and, in its 1918 Constitution, courted mass support. Arthur Henderson's entry into the war cabinet (1915) legitimated it, and his later conflict with the coalition over conscription, Russia, and a negotiated peace drew disillusioned radicals to what became, in MacDonald's words, 'a party of the people', not of a class.

Against this Ross McKibbin maintained that pre-war tendencies were already building a trade unionist, collectivist Labour – but not socialist – party. The unions used their growing power, and the game-changer was the Reform Act of 1918, expanding UK voters from 7.7m in 1910 to 21.4m, with the addition of women over the age of thirty as well as an enlarged male electorate. This would have happened anyway. War destroyed the Liberals' ability to control the situation, but couldn't slow the rise of a working-class party out of one wing of their alliance. From this stemmed a decade of tensions, sapping the ideological and constitutional liveliness of both radicals and socialists.

Scotland's wartime politics resembled the rest of Britain. Opinion at by-elections – four out of eleven were contested – seemed loyal. On two occasions (Glasgow Central, 28 May 1915 and Aberdeen South, 3 April 1917) the contender was more warlike than the successful coalition candidate. A 'negotiated peace' man got 15 per cent on 10 October 1916 in North Ayrshire, against the laird and Somme General Aylmer Hunter-Weston, despite the slaughter. Eddie Scrymgeour, Churchill's prohibitionist, pacifist critic, got 21.8 per cent on 30 July 1917 at Dundee. Consider the future electorate and neither was negligible.

The Unionists continued their pre-war recovery in the election of 14 December 1918. Liberals won forty-three seats, but half of them were 'Lloyd Georgeites', and this, with twenty-twoTory gains, mainly in the west, aggravated organisational weaknesses. Of the seven Labour MPs, two had gained mining seats, South Ayrshire and Hamilton, and the other three gains were in Aberdeen, Govan and Edinburgh Central. Dundee and West Fife were retained. The Clyde didn't show Red, and the 'collaborator' Coalition–Labour minister George Barnes was returned for Tradeston. Polls were low, as most servicemen had yet to be demobilised, although high in mining areas, where many were already back home. But neither the war nor the 1918 Act seemed to have caused a major shift. In 1910 the average Labour constituency vote was 4,926; in 1918 it rose 28 per cent to 6,813, but the electorate had, over this period, risen 183 per cent from 779,000 to 2,205,000.

However, some loyalties had changed – notably in the Cooperative movement. The creation of the labour aristocracy between 1860 and 1914, it was strong in textile areas, like Angus and the Scottish Borders, and in the coalfields, most families having multiple members: 10 per cent of the population against a UK figure of 7 per cent. It began the war jingoistically, its 1915 Congress refusing to aid German and Austrian co-operators interned in Britain. But through low prices and no profiteering by 1918 its membership grew by a third, notably in Lanarkshire and Edinburgh. It was hit by the advantages that Lloyd George's policies of food control gave to its old enemies, the private wholesalers and retailers, and in 1917, led by Sir William Maxwell, of Edinburgh's St Cuthbert's Co-operative Society, it switched to Labour. In demonstrations its problems came second only to the iniquities of the Munitions Act. In December 1918 three Co-op candidates nearly got elected; elsewhere its shift gave Labour a major boost, and formal alliance in 1926.

Left to itself, war would have enhanced Labour: some eighteen to twenty MPs might have been elected, mainly in the coalfields, a few more in the cities. But economic circumstances were changing. In mid-1919 there were already danger signs; by 1920 definite alarm. Shipbuilding on the Clyde had gone above 650,000 tons in 1919 and 1920; in 1921 it dropped to 510,000 and in 1922 to under 400,000. The prospects for 1923 were dismal (less than 170,000 tons was actually built). The same applied to heavy industry and construction. NB Loco production fell by two-thirds between 1920 and 1921. The government's 'homes fit for heroes' programme, started only a year after the report of the Royal Commission, and after a big pre-war building backlog, failed. Only 2,000 houses were built in 1920, compared with 48,000 in England; in 1921 there were 6,000 against 120,000. Costs were inflated, labour was scarce and expensive, and local authorities dragged their feet. Landlords, battered by the Rent Restrictions Act, were falling to Labour's shrewd handling of the issue.

This information reached Dover House. The new Board of Health's 'Industrial Unemployment and Distress' report of 1921 registered angst:

It is difficult to pick out any industrial occupation as being principally affected by unemployment; almost all are in bad condition ... those engaged in export trade and the means of export are worse than those engaged in the home trade ... Very inflammable elements which, while subjected during ordinary times to damping down by the saner and much larger section of the community, will not improbably be fanned into activity as the endurance of that more sober section is broken by the continued tightening of waist belts around empty bellies.

In 1917 the Housing Commission had welcomed social discontent; now government feared it. Extremist agitation – after the spring of 1920 directed by the Moscow-organised Communist Party – was giving new focus to the discontents of slum-dwellers and the unemployed, while Sinn Féin supported the campaign against the British. Labour, ably organised on Clydeside by Patrick Dollan, scooped most of this agitation by a positive policy on rents and housing, and the Catholic Church and *ci-devant* Irish National Party switched its support and Labour won Bothwell and Kirkcaldy at by-elections.

The 1922 election, on 15 November, set a qualified seal on this shift. The *Scotsman* found it 'vague and confused', since Lloyd George's forces acted in unison with the Unionists who had ditched him in July of that year. There were four four-cornered and nineteen three-cornered contests, but in another forty-three the twenty-four 'National Liberals' and eighteen Unionists acted together. Beyond Clydeside little changed from 1918. Labour maintained an 'armed neutrality' with the Asquithian Liberals, and didn't get beyond the eleven coalfield seats, where nine of the MPs returned were miners' agents. The left in general scored in Dundee, where Labour pacifist E. D. Morel and prohibitionist Scrymgeour beat Winston Churchill, but it stood pat in Edinburgh and Aberdeen. The rural socialist vote of 1918 didn't grow, after a setback to Joe Duncan's Farm Servant's Union.

But in Glasgow there was a real turnaround. Labour captured ten of the fifteen city seats, and Dumbarton, East and West Renfrew, and Rutherglen. A Communist (Walton Newbold) got in for Motherwell. A red river? Many elected had been prominent in industrial unrest and anti-war action, but success came from the depression, housing problems and the alienation of Catholics from the coalition because of the Irish troubles.

The right-wing press blamed Labour's appeal to working-class women: a House of Lords decision that, due to a technical formality, all rent increases since 1916 were illegal was 'worked upon by base appeals and . . . used to the utmost to stimulate the virus of Socialism in the community'. Catholic voters, some 75,000 in Glasgow, were instructed by the *Glasgow Observer* to vote Labour: their vote supposedly 'organised from the top . . . recorded the dictates of their leaders with the authority of automata'.

Such cynicism was far from the minds of the 8,000 who packed the St Andrew's Halls to send off the new MPs. With a fervour that recalled the Covenant of 1638 or Gladstone in Midlothian in 1879, the Clydesiders pledged themselves to lofty ideals then took the train south. At Westminster Kirkwood said to Wheatley, 'John, we'll soon change all this', yet they proved that parliament could tame revolutionary fervour and soothe even fierce reactions to the brutal changes which had narrowed industrial Scotland's future.

By 1922 Scottish capitalism had changed profoundly. Markets were no longer expanding, nor did the free market promote industrial co-operation. Near-monopolies ruled in heavy industry – or mergers. Whisky was consolidated by the Distillers' Company. Most Scottish shipowners sold out to to the 'big four' (Ellerman, Furness Withy, Peninsular and Oriental, and the Royal Mail Line). Imperial Chemical Industries (ICI) and Anglo-Iranian Oils took over oil and oil-based chemical industries.

The remaining Scots-based firms had a difficult future: distilling, its profits low through wartime liquor control, faced prohibition in America; shipping faced a dwindling freight market, and jute stronger competition from a semi-autonomous India. Many magnates quit while the going was good, vaulting during the boom to head British consortia. Was there an age factor behind this? Were the sons of entrepreneurs born and based in Scotland less secure through southern education, less confident of their stake in a Scottish future?

Collectivism had expanded in two areas: economic

co-ordination and social policy. Scots entrepreneurs re-educated the traditional civil service, coordinated business and government. In Weir's wake came the industrialists Andrew Duncan, James Lithgow and John Craig, the shipping controllers Lords Maclay, Inverforth and Inchcape, the remarkable Geddes family, Eric, Auckland and Mona, who had created auxiliary military services. No way socialist, they used the state to mould economic change, control the terms of trade, regulate supplies and keep workers in order – mapped out by the grand Fabian Lord Haldane in his *Machinery of Government* (1918).

This state was London-directed, its Scottish side a 'welfarism' that constrained business. The *émigrés* used their wartime experience to modify capitalism, through cartels, ententes with government and new consumer bodies like the Empire Marketing Board. Their own Scottish capitalism was weakened by defections, rent control, public housing and the civic emancipation of Catholics, once of low status but now flexing new powers. Liberalism faced a fifty-year eclipse, through splits and local anti-socialist coalitions. 'Civic reform' was crushed between economic crisis and working-class organisation, yet the latter – the hierarchy of skilled men – was weakened. Miners and fishermen had twenty years of decline before them. Agriculture recovered, the Liberal dream of a free peasantry dissolved. The Marxian Lewis Grassic Gibbon would bury it in the last lines of *Sunset Song*, in 1933, within a stone circle above the Mearns: 'They died for a world that is past, these men, but they did not die for this that we seem to inherit.'

2

A Troubled Economy, 1922–64

WHAT HAPPENED TO ECONOMIC HISTORY?

In 1976 the Scottish Council for Development and Industry created a 'Scottish Input–Output Diagram'. A marvel of early computing, it showed in colour-coded statistics where investment and materials came from and where manufactured goods or services went. It loomed over the desk in Tübingen where I wrote the first edition of this book, and outside there was a rather similar economy, with nearly 40 per cent of GDP in manufacture. It would be possible to replicate it in 2015 for Baden-Württemberg, but not for Scotland. The years after 1960 brought accelerated growth and fairer distribution, but the collapse of traditional Scottish manufacturing took such models – and 'economic history' – with it.

Economic history's great days started just before 1914: on the left as part of the Labour College movement, expounding *Das Kapital*, and on the right owing less to Adam Smith than to the 'housekeeping' or 'protectionist' tradition of Sir James Steuart or William Cunningham. Writing 'business history' became a trade, until firms shut or were taken over, when academics turned to Scottish finance – a change from declining manufacture, hollowed-out employment, emigration, and social and political instability. Its scandalous end in 2008 was left to another threatened species: journalists.

Table 2.1, based on the censuses of production and other official statistics, tries to sketch long-term trends over the

Table 2.1   Scottish gross output, 1907–2012, in million £s (at current prices)

	1907	1935	1960	1995	2012
Agriculture, fisheries	26	42	113	1646	2500
Mining (oil, gas)	25	34	62	4,845	11,712
Manufacturing (total)	159	275	708	10,173	11,900
Iron, steel	62 {	26	70	838 }	3,966
Engineering		41	281	3,930	
Textiles	29	39	67	767	240
Food, drink	31	65	125	1,975	3,720
Other	37	49	165	2,663	3,980
Construction	13	15	125	3,310	5,800
Service sector	42	133	956	34,397	43,100
Scottish 'narrow' GDP	263	431	1,964	60,313	86,896*
UK 'global' GDP	2,230	4,902	22,560	1,005,050*	1,504,777*
(as % of UK 'narrow' GDP)	11.8%	8.8%	8.7%	8.5%	11.3%*

*Includes value of offshore oil and gas production after 1995
The 1907–60 statistics show data based on successive Censuses of Production. 1995 and 2012 don't just show the oil factor but at a UK level the 'light-touch' banking boom and 'asset-backed securities' and after the Crash of 2008 'quantitative easing' of the money supply. Current UK 'global' figures are based on the complex relationships of finance (however obscure), not on industrial widgets. A computer game can be claimed as 'bigger than North Sea oil' . . . 'Aye Right.'

century: rather paradoxical ones. The 'real output' of the Scottish economy, allowing for inflation, grew by only sixty points between 1907 and 1960, but by 101 points from 1960 to 1976. A male manual worker's average wage rose by 108 points between 1907 and 1960, and by 101 points from 1960 to 1976, but unemployment rose from 3.6 to 6.4 per cent. Emigration (see Table 3.1) reflected people's expectations: it was 15 per cent higher in 1951–78 compared with 1921–51. Natural population growth was negative by the 1970s.

In a similar economic structure, West German real wages rose by 174 points between 1960 and 1976; it would do better than Scotland out of North Sea oil. So, how much of Scotland's parlous condition after 1960 was 'legacy' from previous events and decisions? And why was this accompanied – until 2008 – not by poverty but by affluence?

This means analysing the industrial structure which was fundamental before 1939. Economic historians of the 1970s had tried to assess the effectiveness of the responses of the 1930s, before they were superseded by 'war economics' and Whitehall-imposed 'demand-management' and 'planning'. There was a risk in this. What use was it to compare Scotland with Finland or Sweden if no one in the 1930s actually thought in those terms? Roy Campbell, through wide reading in Scottish business papers, argued that its fatalism – given constraints of international demand and Scottish resources – was inevitable.

But the problem was broader. International demand after 1945 was much greater than in 1922–39, as well as economic 'planning' in the private as well as the state sector. Scottish failures stemmed from missed opportunities as well as over-commitment, and from the absence of intelligent steering mechanisms. How much was this a legacy from the 1930s, when there was a general conviction in the wider civic society that 'planning for pluralism' was necessary, an aim also shared by nationalists and socialists?

The National Government's Commissioner for the Scottish Special Area had a £4m budget (1935–8). His Economic Committee made *The Case for Planned Development* (1938) to the Barlow Commission but its scheme for a Development Agency stayed on paper. Goals of planning and diversification were pursued after 1945, but heavy industry, disrupted by contradictory policies from Whitehall, was left to decline. It figured little in the revived 'planning' of Prof. Tom Burns' Toothill Report of 1961. By 1974 and the Economic Planning Enquiry which created the Scottish Development Agency (SDA), it could supply only 10 per cent of the engineering needed by North Sea oil.

What influence did Scotland have on the UK economy? In the 1960s, Richardson and Aldcroft recorded faster growth between 1922 and 1938 than before 1914. New industries – motor vehicles, electrical goods, chemicals, artificial fibres – along with house-building grew in southern England. Investment shifted from capital goods to this domestic market, after 1932 safeguarded by Whitehall through tariffs that reduced unemployment benefit and favoured the employed. The 'regional problem' was the price to be paid – but in UK terms this was not unbearable. Such historical interpretations argued that early regional policy was a fruitless shot at reversing the inevitable, retarding the growing areas of the UK economy.

But was the drift south inevitable? Were its new industries optimally sited, highly productive, well managed? Or did lack of planning mean that the underused resources of the north were paralleled by congestion and duplication of facilities? Were service industries and white-collar occupations – with no great degree of, or criteria for, productivity – absorbing money and skills needed for proper industrial development?

THE STRUCTURE OF INDUSTRY

As a percentage of total output, the traditional staples suffered a steep decline between 1907 and 1935, which then levelled off. In 1960 they still accounted for about a third, but by 1976 this had fallen to under a fifth. Was there room for change?

More serious for Scotland was the post-1930s decline of 'other manufactures' – clothing, food and drink, paper, chemicals, timber and leather goods – frequently through competition from the expanding south. Growth in services (always too vaguely defined) was a compensation, but the manufacturing base was narrowed by the 1950s. It was still largely Scots-owned and dominated by small- to medium-sized concerns. Large factories (common in the new industries of the south) were almost wholly

Table 2.2 Trends in major outputs

	1907	1935	1960	1996	2012
Staples*	53	39	30 ⎫	30	12
Other manufactures	26	27	15 ⎭		
Construction	5	3	6	8	6
Services	16	31	49	62	82

*Staples include agriculture/fisheries, mining, metals, engineering and textiles

confined to the heavy industries. Forty-nine factories employed more than 1,500 workers, two-thirds in the Glasgow area, and more than half in metallurgy, engineering and shipbuilding.

Shipbuilding

The health of Scottish manufacture depended on international trade. Any fall in this meant overcapacity in shipping and a fall in owners' profits: fewer ships were ordered and depression spread from shipyards to steel and coal. In 1921 not only did the naval market vanish, but the post-war boom collapsed, carrying with it the UK's share. Shipping was glutted by the products of American shipyards, the confiscation of German ships and the selling-off of government steamers. The evidence was there for years, silently anchored in the Clyde's sea lochs.

The river's strength in passenger-cargo liners and specialised ships, for which high grades of craftsmanship and finish were required, provided partial compensation. But the yards were constrained by old equipment and the restoration of pre-1914 working practices, while modernisation was inhibited by post-war inflation. Beardmore's reconstruction ruined them – and their old machinery was eagerly bought up by their rivals!

But rivalry hadn't been the rule: shipowners reserved berths or bought shares in shipbuilding firms, which had coped with wartime shortages by taking over steelworks in a tight system of vertical cartelisation. In the early 1920s Lord Pirrie presided over a 'dominator' of Royal Mail Lines, Harland and Wolff, Lithgow, Colvilles Steel and coal mines. This was probably inevitable, but checked innovation and diversification.

Until 1929 a booming American economy sustained the 'Atlantic Ferry' for five-day trips by *nouveau riche* and immigrant alike and paid for passenger liners. In 1930 Cunard laid down a £4.8m 81,000-ton supership at Clydebank. But the Wall Street crash ended work on 'No. 534' and orders vanished; by 1933 total Scottish output, at 74,000 tons, was lower than in the 1850s. In February 1930 James Lithgow and the Bank of England had set up the National Shipbuilders' Security

Corporation to 'rationalise' the industry by buying up and 'sterilising' under-used yards. It cut capacity 15–20 per cent by 1935 – at the cost of great unpopularity – but by then work resumed on No. 534, the *Queen Mary*, completed in 1936. Cunard laid down a sister ship, and the government started subsidising cargo steamer construction. Overshadowing everything, rearmament brought, between 1935 and 1939, £80m worth of orders. The underlying problems of the industry remained as far from solution as ever, though in 1941–2 it saved the country.

Heavy engineering

Heavy engineering, the other main export staple, was hit even harder. The fall in raw material prices cheapened imports but meant that underdeveloped countries, with less to spend, switched to Japan. UK exports to India fell by 90 per cent between 1913 and 1935 and exports through Scottish ports fell by 42 per cent from 1913 to 1937, hitting railway rolling stock, mineral handling gear, sugar-cane crushers, and so on. Between 1904 and 1914 NB Loco built about 400 engines a year, mainly for overseas; between 1921 and 1931 output averaged 150. Their size and value had increased, but annual income was halved. In 1932 the market collapsed completely, and never recovered. The same went for other heavy engineering products: boiler exports and machine tools halved between 1913 and 1935, though heavy electrics – notably mining machinery – were some compensation.

Coal

Coal had complex, if more soluble, problems. In 1913 it had produced a record 42.5m tons; between the wars it averaged 30m, with growing power station demand but much-reduced exports: the 1935 figure was 20 per cent lower than 1913, aggravated by oil-firing at sea, hydro-electrics in Ireland and Europe, and the exhaustion of the great Lanarkshire coalfield, down from 17.5m tons in 1913 to 9m tons in 1937. But the labour force fell even faster, from 139,500 in 1913 to 86,500 in

1937. Large collieries (20 out of 400) now produced 75 per cent of the coal, output per man increased and coal cut by machine rose from 22 per cent in 1913 to 80 per cent by 1938. Such were the spoils of the coalowners after 1926.

Scottish production per man *vis-à-vis* Britain had already been 112:100 in 1913; by 1938 it was 141:118, despite the problems of exploiting the growing Fife coalfield – chiefly a shortage of houses. A tight partnership between the state and owners was created by Labour's Mines Act of 1930 which set regional production quotas; international agreement cut exports but aided profits. Mining royalties were nationalised in 1938, but shares in coal companies had by then risen by 300 per cent. The losers were the miners: although they got pithead baths and welfare institutions, their real wages fell by 4.5 per cent from 1913 to 1938, and unionisation declined until, in the Fife of the 'Little Moscows' in 1934, it was less than 30 per cent. The Fife miners elected Willie Gallacher as Communist MP in 1935, but morale fell away. In 1942 a Ministry of Information report found talk about 'we would be as well off under Hitler' disturbingly widespread.

Steel

Sixty per cent of Scottish steel (itself about 11 per cent of UK production in 1935) usually went to shipyards and heavy engineering, so it was a perilous business. Dwindling local ore, under-capitalisation and foreign competition, followed by arbitrary wartime expansion and shipyard control, meant this no longer worked. Was the industry to be reorganised as a Scottish monopoly, or allied with English concerns? Little happened during the 1920s, because of the rivalry of the Pirrie Combine and local firms, and unhelpful banks. In 1929 the American consultants, Brasserts, recommended concentration on a single large works using imported ore at Erskine on the Clyde, but it was 1934 before amalgamations gave a steel-only Colvilles about 95 per cent of capacity. Stewarts and Lloyds of Mossend followed another Brassert suggestion and sent machines and men to Corby, in the Northants ironstone fields, in 1932, taking with them most Scottish tube-making. Rearmament brought vastly increased profits, helped by doubling productivity between 1924 and 1937. It also meant that the resiting of the industry was postponed *sine die*.

Textiles

Textiles scarcely fared better than the heavy industries, the number of employees falling from 137,000 in 1924 to 113,600 in 1935. In wool, changing fashion (willowy flappers used a quarter of the cloth needed for an Edwardian lady) and an extra, mid-1920s slump after the UK's return to the gold standard, closed many small mills. Cotton thread survived through a cartel with Mussolini's Italy: Cantinieri Coats of Lucca and Paisley. Some recovery came in the 1930s, with the semi-mechanised production of Harris Tweed after 1934, feeding a growing leisure market and chain-store Yorkshire tailors like Burton and Jackson. Retail growth expanded knitwear in the Hillfoots and Borders, while Shetland hand-knitting, thanks to Coco Chanel, marked *haute couture*. Michael Powell's film *The Edge of the World* (1938) dramatised the evacuation of St Kilda (1930) but, consolingly, bosoms were back! In carpets, too, Scotland, with a third of the UK industry, grew through the English building boom, not to mention the invention of the vacuum cleaner. This also boosted the hard-pressed jute industry, in Calcutta and Dundee, though by 1938 this seemed on the edge of a precipice as the English economy faltered. 'Happy as a sandbag' had real meaning in 1939.

Aircraft and motor vehicles

Scotland had developed substantial aircraft and vehicle industries during World War I, but in the 1920s, when passenger planes were rare and military orders subject to government defence and purchasing policy, aircraft production vanished. Beardmore's experimented with heavy bombers and Weir's with autogiros, but to no avail. Only when defence expenditure went up by 25 per cent after 1937 did production come north. Rolls-Royce established their 'Merlin' engine plant at Hillington, and Blackburn an airframe works at Dumbarton.

Motor manufacture was more complex and more tragic. Before 1914 more than forty firms had applied Scots engineering, coach- and bicycle-building skills to the problem. With a big landed and sporting clientele, the Scots 'heavy car' – the Argyll or Arrol-Johnston – up to three tons and 30 horsepower, was famous for finish and reliability. Albion logically changed it into a lorry, and survived. Argyll struggled back after the failure of 1912. Reconstructed as a niche producer, it and a few other firms lasted into the 1920s.

Why did the industry then founder? Distance from southern markets and the West Midlands smallware industry? Possibly. Failure to develop motorcycles, as popular as cars until the early 1930s, anticipating the small car in terms of market, technology and maintenance? A large American plant might also have turned the tide. But the move to Dagenham and Luton by Ford and General Motors in the late 1920s, the impact of their output and the 1929 slump all brought the death blow. In 1935 Scotland contributed only 1.5 per cent of UK production.

Chemicals

Scots chemical output was worth £19m in 1924 and £15m in 1935; it had fallen from 10.2 per cent of UK output to 7.7 per cent. The reason was a combination of obsolescence, wholesale corporate reorganisation in the likes of ICI and Unilever, and international cartels. The dyestuff and bleach industries crumbled rapidly under the new technologies of Cheshire and Teeside, while compensating developments by the new combines were restricted to petroleum products at Grangemouth and explosives at Ardeer. The state did not get involved; rather sinister cartels (notably with IG Farben in Nazi Germany) moved in. This specialisation frustrated applied science in general. Despite Scotland's medical tradition pharmaceuticals, for example, remained a tiny sector until World War II.

Food and drink

Industrial sector problems hit consumer goods, although Edinburgh, as a food-processing and brewing centre, enjoyed almost southern prosperity. But British drinkers downed a third less beer and two-thirds less whisky between the wars, and American drinkers didn't legally exist – until 1933. Mergers produced the Distillers' Company in 1923, McEwan Younger in1931. Prohibition was good for Scotland; it hit bourbon harder than scotch (creating a remarkable trade via Canada, the Caribbean and the Mob, unlikely to figure in company histories). When the temperance movement in Scotland made itself felt in veto polls after 1913 and through wartime controls, the 'alternative' of soft drinks, sweeties and cigarettes increased. Large factories for canning and biscuit-making opened. Using modern techniques, however, the 'sugar hit' was achieved with a smaller workforce. Diabetes and cancer increased, unquantified. False teeth figured as wedding presents.

Furniture and fittings

High family expenditure on food was not repeated in consumer durables. There was no mass-production furniture industry, and the cable cartels that dominated the London electrical goods sector had no desire to move their factories north. In 1935 only 2 per cent of electrical goods output came from Scotland, largely in the heavy machinery sector. Weir and Lithgow's attempt to set up British National Electric's household goods factory at Carfin met with little success. Small houses made for a small market, and one already saturated from the south.

Agriculture and fisheries

Agriculture was still Scotland's major industry, but between 1921 and 1938 its labour force declined from 126,900 to 105,300, and its output fell from £48m to £40m (in UK terms from 17.2 per cent to 14.4 per cent). This stemmed partly from a growth in English productivity, partly from structural changes and partly from government policy. Lorries and tractors cut demand for horses by a quarter; whisky decline pulled barley production down. More seriously, government's first subsidies – for beet (1925) and wheat (1932) – designed to safeguard English arable farming, penalised Scottish mixed farms (although these were inherently much more profitable). In fact of the total subsidies of £68.25m paid by 1935–6, only £4.2m (6 per cent) went to Scotland. With the introduction of cattle subsidies in 1934 things started to change, but by then many Scots 'marginal' farmers had left for the richer lands of East Anglia, like those whom Ronald Blythe recorded in *Akenfield*:

> It was the land of Goshen compared with Scotland. A better climate, easier working soil, with no damn great lumps of granite pushing out of it. It was, 'Come on Wully, come doon here! Send home for brother Angus and sister Mary and her man!'

Fisheries were so bad that even the Cabinet used the word 'tragedy' in 1934. East European markets were dead and Norwegian competition increased. Catches held up with more efficient motor-boats, but their masters' real income increased by only 3 per cent between 1913 and 1937. Louis MacNeice's comment was icy and apposite: 'His brother caught three hundred cran when the seas were lavish/Threw the bleeders back in the sea and went upon the parish'.

Only in 1935 was the Herring Industry Board established by the government to maintain minimum prices and assist re-equipment, but shortly afterwards overfishing brought the white-fish industry, centred in Granton and Aberdeen, into peril. By the time legislation was drafted to aid it, its old trawlers had largely been drafted for war service.

Transport

Economic decline meant contraction on the railways, intensified by 'rationalisation': the transfer south of locomotive building. Staff fell by over 18 per cent between 1924 and 1935. Since less than 8 per cent of mileage was closed down, there were productivity gains, but modernisation was delayed until the financial structure of the railways had been safeguarded by the Transport Act of 1933. Both the LMS and the LNER then introduced fast 'shop-window' services to and from London (with useful publicity from Alfred Hitchcock's *The 39 Steps* of 1935) using powerful passenger and freight engines, but few orders for these came to Scotland, and government-subsidised electrification served only London and Liverpool. Grievances over high freight rates were authoritatively endorsed by the Scottish Economic Committee (SEC) in 1939.

Ramifying bus services slowed the drift from the countryside, and opened it to coach tours. Started in the early 1920s, often by exservicemen converting old army lorries, these services quickly became dominated by Sir William Thompson's Scottish Motor Traction Company (1906). The railways took a 25 per cent interest in 1928 and increased this to 50 per cent by 1939. Although the trams remained 'gondolas of the people' in the four cities, the bus firms took over and closed down the smaller systems. The lorry and delivery van became familiar in the villages, but commercial road haulage was restricted by the sluggish development of light industry, and the rise of the private car by the small size of the middle class. In 1935 there was one car for every twenty-five people in England, but only one for every thirty-six in Scotland.

The railways, along with Coast Lines of Liverpool (who took over Burns and Laird's Irish steamers in 1921), also oversaw the reconstruction in 1925 of David MacBrayne's. In return for a government subsidy of £40,000 per annum, freight and passenger rates were controlled and elderly steamers replaced by diesel 'pocket liners' and linked to new bus services. Coastal shipping was still important, with regular passenger and freight services to many smallish Scottish ports from England, as well as from Leith and Glasgow. After 1932 its top end had competition. The SMT started Scotland's first internal air service. In 1933 Highland Airways began flying from Aberdeen and Inverness to Wick and Orkney. In 1936, as with the buses, regional monopolies took over. Railway Air Services flew Anson mono-planes to Liverpool and Belfast; Scottish Airways flew Rapide biplanes to the west coast and the Highlands. By 1939 the enduring pattern of Scottish internal services had been created.

Electricity

The provision of adequate electricity by Glasgow Corporation had been crucial to munitions production, and William Weir himself took a leading part in the creation of the state–private enterprise partnership of the national grid. An act was passed in 1926; construction started in 1927, and the Central Scottish Grid, stretching from Aberdeenshire to Carlisle, was complete by 1931. It cost £3.4m, about 20 per cent of the UK total, and thus subsidised Scottish industry, yet only 18.5 per cent of the work went north. Between 1924 and 1929 the British Aluminium Company spent a further £5m on a huge hydro-electric scheme to produce aluminium at Fort William, and in the 1930s three further schemes, purely for power supply, followed – in the Tummel area, at the Falls of Clyde and in Galloway.

Yet by 1935 Scottish electricity consumption was only 8 per cent of a UK figure boosted by new industries in the south-east. Electricity charges were higher than in the south, few electric manufacturers moved north. Scots developments pumped electricity into the English grid, or produced semi-finished materials, and anger at this underlay the parliamentary defeat of the Caledonian power bills of 1936–8 – the only Scottish issue in the inter-war period that absorbed the attention of the Cabinet.

THE PROBLEM DEFINED

The multifaceted nature of Scotland's crisis marked it off from the other 'depressed areas'. Unemployment (25 per cent in 1932) was less than in Wales (40 per cent) or the north-east (33 per cent), but it accompanied structural upheavals across all industrial sectors, aggravated by the policy changes of firms, financial institutions and governments. Falling demand for

Scottish capital goods coincided with foreign tariffs against Scottish luxury goods. Declining landed wealth and (until 1936) inappropriate government subsidies hit farming. Foreign unrest, autarkic policies and loosening imperial ties menaced traditional markets. If revaluation in 1925 was bad, welfare cuts and protection after 1931, aiding the southern 'home market' at the expense of exporting areas, were worse. To all of this the relief offered to coal by government aid, to steel by protection and rearmament after 1935, while magical for harried entrepreneurs (whose share values shot up), could only be a palliative.

Scottish unemployment averaged 14 per cent in 1923–30, against the UK's 11.4 per cent. But from 1931 to 1938 this percentage ratio rose to 21.9:16.4. Numbers on poor relief in the 1929–36 period climbed from 192,000 to 341,000, an increase of 76 per cent against a UK increase of 13 per cent. The contrast with London was even starker: there unemployment hit its worst at 13 per cent in 1932, and fell to 6.3 per cent by 1936, when even prosperous Edinburgh still had 12.3 per cent, Greenock had 20 per cent and Airdrie 30 per cent.

Only in 1930 did Labour's J. H. Thomas order the first regional surveys. Professor W. R. Scott and his Glasgow economists identified some 100,000 men in west central Scotland alone as 'permanently surplus'. Traditionally, they had migrated; an average of 147,000 had left Scotland each decade from 1861 to 1911, but between then and 1930 this more than doubled. From 1931 to 1939 migration fell to under 100,000. It had swelled the proportions of the old and very young in the 1920s; in the next decade those in employment became victims themselves.

Unemployment was not a function of industrial decadence. In some 'traditional' sectors it resulted from advance. Between 1931 and 1935, for example, Scots productivity increased by 8 per cent, against 5.6 per cent in the UK. Unemployment hit family incomes and cut demand for consumer goods, so female labour in such industries fell, making matters worse. The middle class did well enough; rarely were more than 5.5 per cent of them unemployed. They suffered pay cuts, but their employment actually grew faster than in England between 1921 and 1931, by 20 per cent against 14 per cent – although there, too, emigration continued to operate as a safety valve. Scotland's demography aggravated unemployment: a rate of natural increase about 30 per cent greater than that of England meant that a larger working population met a declining job market. In Scotland in 1923–38 the labour force stuck at 22 to 24 per cent of the population. In England it went from 26 to 33 per cent, boosted by growth in women's jobs and the service industries. So there was 20 per cent less earning capacity in a Scottish family, increasing the period when families risked poverty (chiefly when they had children under earning age).

PLANNING A WAY OUT

Government was not inactive, but scarcely helpful. Faced with overextended heavy industries (which could be of military importance) and a labour surplus, Lloyd George and later the Unionists handed the former over to the Bank of England, and tackled the latter by assisted migration schemes, enacted in 1920 and 1928. By 1939 these had shifted 250,000 men and women, largely to the south of England.

Labour in 1924 was more positive; continuing Lloyd George's Trade Facilities Act of 1921, loaning £5m at low interest to foreign buyers of heavy engineering products, until Churchill ended it in 1926. In 1929–31 its public works programme built the three-lane Edinburgh–Glasgow A8, the 'Boulevard'. No Labourite or Unionist questioned the 'balanced budget' – defending it against Keynes's and Lloyd George's *Yellow Book* plan for reflation by deficit financing of roadbuilding and elec-trification, paid for in the long term by 'multiplier' growth in the general taxpaying capacity of the country. However negative such reactions, the central issue remained: could such schemes succeed in an economy that lacked the 'new' industries it pro-posed to stimulate?

In such situations the banking system played in Europe a criti-cal role. Not in Scotland, where the strength and sophistication of its financial institutions – a virtue during industrialisation – now channelled investment *away* from the country, a flow driven by the need to service the debts of heavy industry. Although innovative financiers like J. Gibson Jarvie, the founder of hire purchase, struggled to set up a Scottish industrial investment trust, the banks were unbudging and only in 1938 did his scheme get off the ground. The Scots-American trusts were battered in 1929; the survivors were unadventurous. In fact, most interest in Scottish affairs was taken by the Clydesdale, whose owner, the Midland Bank, was a lone unorthodox voice in the financial world. The banks seemed there to soothe the middle class, not only as clients but by 'white-collar' jobs in constantly multiplying branches.

Self-help

Labour, in a purely cosmetic move, had encouraged regional groups for industrial development. Partly stimulated by this, on 7 May 1930 the Convention of Royal Burghs set up the Scottish National Development Council (SNDC), after resolutions moved by Sir Alexander McEwen of Inverness and the Duke of Montrose, both later of the Scottish Party. Despite its nationalist origins, by late 1931 the SNDC had the support of Sir James Lithgow and of William Elger of the Scottish Trade Union Congress; in 1932 it got a grudging measure of government funding. It took on full-time staff and two years later had produced several reports on economic problems, and a glossy quarterly magazine, *Scotland*.

Lithgow was the SNDC's key figure. He had many of William Weir's strengths and weaknesses: talented, hardworking but undiplomatic, he had a logical case for backing it. Only by cutting capacity and manpower would the heavy industries live; new enterprises could absorb the surplus. But he had little expertise in consumer goods. As the SNDC gained momentum, so did factory closures. Between 1932 and 1934 fifty-eight factories opened in Scotland, while eighty-eight closed.

Government action

Government began to move. In 1932 and 1933 Walter Elliot, as Minister of Agriculture, started inquiries into health and nutrition in areas of high unemployment, prompted by his friend John Boyd Orr of the Rowett Research Institute, Aberdeen. MacDonald's Cabinet on 28 March 1934 agreed to 'informal' investigation of central Scotland, south Wales, north-east England, parts of Cumberland and Lancashire, partly to smooth the path of the new Unemployment Assistance Act. On 24 October the Cabinet suggested a 'Special Areas' Commissioner, with four regional agents. But Sir Godfrey Collins, Scottish Secretary, gained a separate appointment – responding to pressure from Lithgow and the Unionists for administrative devolution. The original investigator, Sir Hugh Rose, an Edinburgh paint manufacturer and head of the Organisation for the Maintenance of Supplies during the General Strike, became the first (unpaid) Scottish Commissioner.

Rose's 'Special Area' covered the counties of Lanark, Renfrew, Dumbarton, Fife and West Lothian, and parts of Ayr and Stirling. Not Glasgow: to declare the 'Second City' a 'distressed area' was too much. Between 1934 and 1939 Rose and his successors Sir David Allan Hay and Lord Nigel Douglas-Hamilton spent some £4m. Initially they could only aid public works, but after 1937 they assisted small firms through the Special Areas Reconstruction Association. There were failures: some doomed, eccentric smallholding experiments; several ailing firms, bailed out, going to the wall; but the Commissioners did co-operate imaginatively with the SNDC. Rose recommended in his first report, November 1935, 'An authoritative Scots body ... financed by the government to explore industrial conditions, and in general aim at introducing into our economic structure ... [an] element of orderly and planned development'. These proposals went far beyond his local remit, but from Dover House Collins backed them against the interdepartmental Special Areas Committee and in March 1936 authorised the SEC, only six months before his sudden death.

The Scottish Economic Committee

The Economic Committee under Sir William Goodchild was formally a sub-committee of the SNDC but the Commissioner paid for it and it co-operated with Elliot, Secretary of State 1935–7: timely, as in March 1937 Baldwin announced the Barlow Commission into the Distribution of the Industrial Population. The SEC reported to it on the Highlands, light industries and rearmament policy, published as *Scotland's Economic Future.* It helped promote the Empire Exhibition, Scottish Industrial Estates, Films of Scotland and the Scottish Special Housing Association.

When war broke out, the SEC was suspended. Whitehall viewed it with suspicion, and its advocacy of autonomy was, outside Scotland, replaced by the policy of 'direction of industry' advocated by a Labour Party inquiry of 1937 under Hugh Dalton, which underlay his 1945 Distribution of Industry Act. But it had focused Scottish 'middle opinion' on economic and social reconstruction. It drew the agricultural research of Boyd Orr into welfare, science policy and propaganda, involved Empire Marketing Board staff like John Grierson and Elliot. It rejected the neo-classic economics of Sir William Scott in Glasgow for the Keynesian ideas of James Bowie, director since 1931 of the new Dundee School of Economics. Finally, it linked up with the planning movement inaugurated by Sir Patrick Geddes, strengthened by the creation of the National Trust for Scotland in 1931 and of the Saltire Society in 1936 by William Power, Boyd Orr, Bowie and Thomas Johnston, influential advocates of economic and physical planning.

Elliot made the Empire Exhibition of 1938 in Bellahouston Park, Glasgow, the climax of these developments. Costing £11m, it drew on his many connections in science, publicity and the arts. Art Deco in spirit – its architect, Thomas Tait, brought in the young Basil Spence and Jack Coia – it was to draw, besides 13m visitors, light industries to the new industrial estates. The year 1938 was the summer of Munich – and it rained! – but it showed a real advance in analysing the Scottish problem. The

SEC, the Clydesdale Bank's report and Bowie's *The Future of Scotland* (1939) gave the issue a new social dimension. When Bowie, for instance, costed an average town at £10m, he questioned the accounting which could close a local industry as unprofitable. But such analyses were of an economy expanded by rearmament, while 'underlying' factors – stagnant international trade and an English demographic decline – seemed temporary. Ideas and personalities of the 1930s remained prominent after the war. But were they still relevant?

WORLD WAR II

Between 1939 and 1945, in contrast to 1914–18, war production was subject to centralised control. An embryo organisation had existed since 1924, and in December 1933, with Hitler in power, a small, mainly Scottish, advisory group – Weir, Lithgow and Sir Arthur Balfour – assessed potential wartime demand. Detailed planning began in 1936 but until 1939 organisation was constrained by peacetime finance and facilities: only RAF outlay was on a potential war footing.

After World War I armaments production had been cut back to the Royal Dockyards and Ordnance Factories and a few outside firms. It had also changed to concentrate on the internal combustion engine and its derivatives: Lithgow tried vainly to interest Scottish firms as, with the most suitable factories being in the south of England, skilled labour moved south to fill them. Only in Admiralty orders – to the shipyards and Beardmore's – did Scotland do well. When war broke out again Beardmore's once more acted as the nucleus of gun and armour production, expanding into factories at Dalmuir, Germiston and Linwood, and Clyde shipyards turned out an average of 400,000 tons of shipping a year – five ships a week by 1943 – not much under their 1914–18 levels.

This time there was conscription from the outbreak of war on 3 September 1939. Unemployment fell to 20,000 (1.6 per cent). But 'concentration' of non-munitions production closed many Scottish factories, often permanently ('other manufacturing industry' fell from 26 per cent of output in 1935 to 14 per cent in 1951), and until late 1941, 90 per cent of requisitioned factory space was used for storage. Thirteen thousand girls were drafted to the Midlands, causing some outcry. By July 1942, under pressure from Scottish MPs, Tom Johnston at the Scottish Office and the SNDC (now the Scottish Council on Industry), storage was down to 57 per cent, and by 1945 some 7,000 war-connected projects – 13.5 per cent of the UK total – had been set up, including 119 complete plants: a total investment of £12m. Of these the twenty-six under the Ministry of Aircraft Production were the largest, employing 100,000 workers by 1945. Scotland became the main staging post both for convoys and for aircraft; Prestwick in 1944 was the busiest international airport in the world.

The workforce changed radically; from 80 per cent male in 1939 to only 60 per cent in 1944. Agriculture expanded: arable acreage increased 15 per cent to its 1918 level through revived Agricultural Executives, 75 per cent subsidies, guaranteed prices and a state holding of 227,000 acres. Wheat and barley acreage doubled, potatoes increased by 75 per cent. Yields – because of well-fertilised former grazing land – exceeded England and Wales in practically every crop, sometimes by over 30 per cent. The number of tractors more than doubled, from 6,250 to over 16,000. The fishing fleet shrank from 5,000 to only 936 boats but, as fishing in English waters was effectively banned, it did creditably, although much of it remained obsolescent.

The apparent unity of 'the people's war' masked disturbing trends. Although Johnston claimed economic gains, such as the birth of the North of Scotland Hydro-Electric Board, and exorcised any 'Red Clyde' repeat, citing a strike record of only 0.7 per cent of working days lost, productivity was bad in munitions factories and worse in the mines. The Ministry of Information reported an undercurrent of discontent, which expressed itself in volatile politics. Although the fighting itself claimed only 40 per cent of the casualties of World War I, deaths in the RAF were twelve times greater and in the

Merchant Navy almost two-and-a-half times greater. As deaths among officers and NCOs doubled, Scotland, with 15 per cent of UK secondary pupils, sacrificed too many from a generation in which more had been invested than in the men of Flanders. Their losses would echo in subsequent inadequacies of management and innovation.

World War II drastically changed economic and social policy. Labour's 1945 victory made this explicit, but the 'managed' economy, achieved through fiscal policy, really dates from May 1940, when Churchill replaced Chamberlain and Keynes moved to the Treasury. Chamberlain had started the Barlow inquiry – but *executive* 'middle opinion' exemplified by the Beveridge Report (December 1942) integrated the new economics with the 'right' to full employment and health care. This was reinforced by trade union power in the coalition, personified by Labour minister Ernest Bevin, and the Attlee government continued with wartime practice. Dalton's Distribution of Industry Act, 1945 (carried by Churchill's brief caretaker ministry) applied consensus to regional policy, rejecting the SEC's Development Authority for centralisation under the Board of Trade. The Council on Industry became the Scottish Council: Development and Industry (SCDI) in 1946, with representation from local authorities, unions and business (or at least parts of it). Joint bodies linked the Scottish Office to other ministries with industry remits, but the semi-autonomy of the SEC was lost – tragically – at a time when decisions increasingly ended up in the hands of less-than-expert Whitehall mandarins.

INDIAN SUMMER

Was 1940–51 an economic watershed, as Labour claimed – at least until the late 1960s? Had nationalisation of 'the commanding heights', centralised allocation of factory space, investment incentives and physical planning checked the drift south and promoted diversification? Or did the managed economy, by masking fundamental industrial continuities, make readjustment more difficult?

Financial assistance was limited (in real terms it was only about 56 per cent above the resources allocated to the pre-war Commissioner). The main weapon, compulsion, wasn't needed because of the lack of factories and housing in southern England. American companies feared losing European markets through possible tariff increases and shipping shortages, and would open factories wherever the British government allowed them. Even so, the finance crisis of 1947 curbed regional assistance by a third, the export drive checked diversification, while in the heavy industries controls on investment and profits, and lack of state assistance, deferred re-equipment.

In the 1950s government assistance was, in real terms, less than in the 1930s. New industrial building in Scotland ran at 12.2 per cent of the UK figure from 1945 to 1951. It fell to 6.5 per cent by 1958. Regional policy was close to Labour's heart but in 1951 the SCDI's Committee on Local Development noted that 'the disappearance of large-scale unemployment has by no means been due entirely, or even principally, to the new policy'. The wartime decline in the range of Scottish manufacturing wasn't reversed, and by 1953 Alec Cairncross reported that 'dependence on the heavy industries has grown rather than diminished'.

Shipbuilding

The need to restore wartime destruction – allied losses alone came to 23.3m tons, compared with *total* losses in World War I of 15m tons – and the bombing of enemy docks and shipyards brought an Indian summer to the Clyde. But Cairncross noted the 'comparative indifference' of the heavy industries 'to new equipment, new knowledge, and new opportunities for development'. They had been granted a reprieve, but they didn't try to reverse the verdict.

Their slump in 1957–8 turned out to be terminal. It started with a drop in demand – against a world trend of booming orders. In 1954 world shipping totalled 97m tons, freighters averaged 6,000 tons and the world's largest ship was the

Queen Elizabeth at 83,000 tons. By 1973 world tonnage was 289 million, the largest ship, the tanker *Globtik Tokyo*, grossed 239,000 tons and the combination of containers and 'inter-modal' transport had transformed freight handling. The closure of the Suez Canal in 1956 focused attention both on oil consumption (Britain's grew 200 per cent between 1950 and 1960) and on its transport. The Cape of Good Hope route both demanded and permitted huge ships; their pattern influenced other cargos and dock design. Scots had experimented with the new technology for years – Brassert's proposed waterside steelworks in 1929, Denny's first modern car ferry in 1939 (sunk in 1940), the Finnart oil-discharging port in 1952. These innovations were not developed. Why?

There was no simple reason. Development failures beset car ferries: Scotland's early lead was hit by the 1939–55 decline in motoring, and by the sinking of the roll-on, roll-off *Princess Victoria* off Stranraer in the devastating storm of 31 January 1953 with 130 drowned. Economically a worse disaster than the *Titanic*, years passed before another attempt was made, and by 1964 the Germans and Swedes had cornered the market. As the airlines took their toll, vehicle ferries were the only way that the 'hotel-ship' yards would survive, yet Denny's, the major short-sea builders, closed in 1961. They were soon followed by other specialist firms, like Simons Lobnitz of Renfrew and the Grangemouth Dockyard Company.

The tragedy was that these yards had near-Scandinavian standards of innovation and tranquil labour relations, while the great Clydeside concerns were a mess. Their family dynasties were conservative, in design, marketing, research and labour relations. Their equipment was depreciating by £9m per annum: only half that sum was being re-invested. Research and development ran on peanuts – £250,000. Rationalisation was badly needed – in Japan five engineering works served eighteen main shipyards, on the Clyde nine works served sixteen yards – but it was seldom even discussed, management rivalries and union bloody-mindedness ruling out even joint consultation.

Engineering

Heavy engineering initially benefited from its semi-monopoly position. Until 1950 railway orders were almost at the 1920 level, and in 1947 Pressed Steel Fisher built a huge waggon plant at Linwood, near Paisley. Yet diesel and electric locomotives were taking over. Reprieved by the £1bn British Railways re-equipment programme of 1955, which brought orders for 34,000 out of 46,000 new waggons to Linwood, *and* the Glasgow electric 'Blue Trains', NB Loco failed to adapt and closed in 1961. In 1962 Linwood was turned over to the motor industry.

It was not all loss, however. Many of the techniques of heavy industry were equally applicable to 'industrial building' – a 1960s mantra, and the reservoir of skilled manpower was indispensable for installing and maintaining the second wave of light engineering 'transplants' – Westclox, IBM, Hoover – after 1962 motors at Linwood and Bathgate. What had been lost, however, was the link between skill and innovation: something which not even the National Engineering Laboratory at East Kilbride in 1947 could remedy.

Steel

Scottish steelworks largely provided plates and castings for heavy industry: in 1950 15 per cent of their output went to mechanical engineering, 15 per cent to constructional engineering and 20 per cent to shipbuilding. Only 0.3 per cent went to vehicles (against 12 per cent in the UK). Although a 'hot-metal' works was built at Clydebridge in 1938, Motherwell, Hallside, Glengarnock and Parkhead still used Siemens open-hearth furnaces to smelt a mixture of scrap and imported pig-iron. After 1945 scrap and coking coal were scarce and steel imports grew, but political uncertainty inhibited planning: Labour had nationalisation on its 1945 manifesto, but didn't legislate until 1948. Delayed by the Lords, the takeover only came in January 1951, ten months before Churchill's Tories came back. In 1953 they returned the industry to private hands, subject to overall control by a state board. The nationalised board favoured reviving Brassert's scheme, but its successor in 1954 let Colvilles build a new integrated iron-and-steel works at Ravenscraig, near Motherwell, served by an ore-discharging plant at Glasgow's General Terminus Quay. This opened in 1960, and alongside it in 1962 the company started a steel strip mill to serve the motor industry. Economists had favoured a shore site in south Wales, but mounting government unpopularity in Scotland made Harold Macmillan split the scheme and loan Colvilles £50m. In 1967, when Labour renationalised the industry, Scotland's output of strip steel had risen sixfold, but overall production continued to decline. Providing 20 per cent of UK output in 1920, it had fallen to 12 per cent by 1960. The industry was badly sited, technically conservative; its wide product range was dictated by a predominantly local market: all aspects that the corporate planning of the new British Steel Corporation announced itself ready to remedy.

Energy

Labour nationalised the mines in 1948, and shortly announced an expansion intended to double output to 30.6m tons by 1965: centred on the Fife coalfield and centralised production in thirteen large mines, of which the greatest, Rothes, would cost £15m. But the expenses of mine-sinking, with miners still working old pits, meant productivity didn't rise and the Scottish region of the National Coal Board slid into deficit. The complete failure of Rothes in 1960 led to rapid contraction. By 1970 production was down to 12.7m tons with 29,700 men. It wasn't helped by the Hydro Board. By 1961 its construction programme was virtually complete and it supplied over a third of Scottish electricity. Before the war, socialist and environmentalist critics of Highland water power had stressed this consequence. Johnston had sold it successfully as an agency for regenerating the Highlands, a national investment and a triumph for Scots autonomy – and it was rarely criticised. But it was none of these things; and without it, coal might not have hit the trough of the early 1960s. By 1965 the Hydro Board's contribution was plainly inadequate, and a programme of large steam generators – coal, oil and nuclear – was announced. Power generated, about 1,900 megawatt hours in 1939, rose to 2,208 MW in 1950, 3,017 MW in 1961 and 10,378 MW in 1978.

Agriculture

War and Labour government completed the reconstruction of agriculture. After 1947 the state guaranteed prices for farm produce, injecting 20 per cent of UK agricultural expenditure into Scottish farming, against 6 per cent in 1939. Scotland had only 11 per cent of UK output but, as livestock received higher subsidies than arable produce, her dependence on it increased. By 1964 she reared 15.2 per cent of UK livestock, compared with only 9.5 per cent of livestock produce (milk, eggs, and so on) and 7.5 per cent of arable crops. Farms were consolidated and sophisticated equipment bought, as rural electrification was extended. Land workers, 120,000 in 1945, tumbled to under 40,000 in 1964. Although they were better off and could now afford a car, freezer and television, the differential between their income and that of the farmers widened. It now made sense for landowners to farm their own land, so the 'gentleman farmers', whom the sociologist James Littlejohn had noticed filtering into *Westrigg*, proliferated.

Agricultural-based industry also flourished. Meat- and fruit-canning expanded in Fraserburgh, Dundee and Fochabers, supplemented by freezing and vacuum-packing. Brewing and distilling grew spectacularly. Breweries, increasingly English-controlled, pushed up output from 1.2m barrels in 1939 to over 2m barrels in 1960, soaring to over 5m barrels in 1980, although many resented the abandonment of traditional ales for lager-type beers for a UK market. Distilling's post-prohibition upswing was checked by the war, but it subsequently became Scotland's leading export industry. In 1975 its output was valued at £312m. Shipbuilding brought in only £215m.

The service sector

After World War II services (vaguely defined, and it lasted) rose to dominate the economy. In 1936 their components – transport and distribution, business and commerce, and public service – made up about 32 per cent of output, against 36 per cent in the UK. By 1958 Scotland had almost reached the UK level of 49 per cent; in the 1960s she went ahead. Given the size of the country, transport was always important; likewise the public services. But business and commerce lagged: in 1958 income from these was still 28 per cent below the UK level, while in 1961 Scotland had only 7 per cent of UK administrators and managers. Retailing was checked by low expenditure per head, which actually *fell* from 92 to 90 per cent of the UK level between 1953 and 1962, and remained fairly low until the mid 1960s: few public markets, a strong but stagnant Co-op movement and enough future in high street department stores to encourage tycoons like Isaac Wolfson and Hugh Fraser. Self-service came late, around 1960, and only then did growing consumer expenditure attract the English multiples. By 1978 Scottish consumers were spending slightly over the UK level, but the incomers would change the face of the Scottish high streets completely.

Transport

Transport changed slowly in the 1950s. Tramcars dwindled, and finally vanished from Glasgow in 1962. Cars were still relatively rare outside country districts, because of dense and cheap bus services, and the sheer difficulty of accommodating them in the narrow tenemented streets of the big towns. The railways had changed little. Only five trains a day ran from Glasgow to London in 1957; the fastest one took 7 hours 40 minutes, 70 minutes longer than 1939. There were still 3,208 miles of track. New roads were few, save in new towns and housing schemes, but by 1960 even local lanes had been surfaced, although in the Highlands single-tracked roads were still the rule. MacBrayne's steamers still loaded goods, cattle and cars 'over the side'; puffers still chugged through the Forth and Clyde and Crinan Canals, out to the beaches of the Western Isles. Change began in 1955, with the start of the Forth Road Bridge. By the time it opened in 1964, a Tay Road Bridge was also under construction (opened 1966) and road expenditure had risen from £2.6m to £34m, or in real terms by 1,000 per cent. This was at the expense of the railways, which were drastically rationalised, both by Conservative and Labour governments. This process benefited some areas – intercity passenger, container and bulk traffic – but the division of responsibility between the Ministry of Transport (railways) and the Scottish Development Department (roads, ferries and buses) frustrated coordination. The fruit of the vast expenditure of 1960–75 was a railway system reduced by 42 per cent and a fall of 50 per cent in bus passengers.

Tourism

Tourism was equally impeded by poor planning. Boosted by holidays with pay after 1938 (the Loch Ness Monster arrived on cue) it roughly doubled in size between then and 1958, to earn about £50m a year. But it remained unsure of its aim: a mass market or a wealthy one? Although the government set up a Scottish Tourist Board in 1946, it gave it only £20,000 in 1958, and by then the mass market was going: the rainy Clyde was losing out to the sunny, sexy Costa Brava. When the state did intervene, stimulated by the Irish example, in the 1960s, it perpetrated some horrid developments like the Aviemore centre and squandered assets like the Clyde steamers. Business had doubled again by 1970, but grew only a third as fast as the rest of Britain. The Highlands and Islands Development Board, though, served its area well, and also boosted the quality of crafts and souvenirs. In the 1950s families toured the Highlands in Morris Oxfords and complained about Japanese knick-knacks. In the 1970s they could buy quality pottery and handweaves to take home in their Datsuns.

PLANNING REDUX

Scotland's economic problems in the late 1950s were difficult to unravel. Structural changes in the heavy industries were fundamental, but government actions aggravated them. Deflation in late 1957 – the consequence of an overambitious defence programme – coincided with the phasing out of National Service. Civilian jobs were shed, while the potential labour force swelled. The government stopped subsidising shale and jute and cut back on the coal industry. So unemployment doubled between 1958 and 1959 from 58,000 to 116,000, while the outlook in the heavy industries, mines and railways seemed even worse. Tory losses in the general election of October 1959 made Scottish apprehension explicit.

'The spectre of the 1930s' or the result of labour fractiousness? There were grounds for both views. Productivity was poor: in the mines scarcely higher than thirty years earlier. Incoming American firms put Scotland, with Italy, at the bottom of their productivity scale, but the memory of what that had meant in the 1930s went deep. 'Hostile suspicion', Cairncross noted in 1952, 'often flares up in reaction to proposals in which there is any hint of labour redundancy'. With reason: agriculture saw a 300 per cent productivity gain between 1939 and 1960, but the winners were the farmer or the consumer, not the weakly organised farmworkers or the local community. Other unions were more grimly defensive.

Management was indifferent. As Tom Burns showed in *The Management of Innovation* (1961), the 'mechanical' relationships between departments in Scottish firms lacked the strength of the 'organic' corporate identity of American firms. Scots managers eluded difficult organisational problems either by blaming others or by assuming 'irreconcilable differences of attitudes and codes of rational conduct'. Scottish inventiveness could still produce the marine stabiliser, fibreglass, ultrasonics, but long-term planning, state or private, was missing. Responsibility had drifted south, and too much ability had followed it. The successors of flawed giants like Weir or Lithgow were, as advocates of 'planning', more diplomatic, but also less original and less energetic. Consensus was preferred to abrasiveness, even if the resulting cosiness masked failure. There were exceptions: Sir William Lithgow realised in the mid-1960s huge ships would be built on greenfield sites near where they were needed, but that design and research could be carried out in Inverclyde, Scotland. He helped create Hyundai in Korea. But his second part, *Oceanspan*, a rejuvenated Clyde, remained unrealised.

The Unionists froze out the planners, the SCDI and the trade unions. The Council had attracted many Americans, but could foresee stiffer opposition – both from the EEC (founded in 1957) and from Eire after the Whitaker Report (1958). The grand regional plans of Mears, Payne and Abercrombie had been pigeonholed for a decade; as the backlog of war-delayed building was made up by the mid-1950s, the architects and planners feared a repetition of the 1920s, and were echoed by property men, the construction industry and an increasingly vocal road lobby. The STUC, having helped attract American firms by sweetheart deals, now worried that militancy would grow with unemployment.

But the spectre of economic decline was not the only motive for 'planning'. Britain changed sharply in the mid-1950s; TV, rock, anger, a bit of hedonism propelled the country out of the 'Victorian straitjacket'. As usual this reached Scotland late, but by 1959 Scots lumped smaller houses, fewer cars, worse food and more restrictions alongside worries about mounting unemployment. Gavin McCrone's detailed survey *Scotland's Economic Progress* came out in 1965; it showed growth (9 per cent between 1954 and 1960) running at half the UK level, and income per head 13 per cent lower – political factors as (if not more) important than industrial reconstruction.

In 1960 Macmillan's Local Employment Act resumed a regional policy, and the Scottish Office, acting through the SCDI and Tom Burns, began its 'Inquiry into the Scottish Economy'. The resulting 'Toothill Report' (November 1961) was politically crucial: reviving he notion of planning and gaining it consensus support. As economic diagnosis it was more suspect. The central problem remained that of the heavy industries. Before 1939 their productivity grew but their market stagnated; after 1950 the opposite was the case. Yet was their decline inevitable? Cheap labour and raw material might have gone, but skills, adaptiveness and a valuable range of ancillary industries remained. Could specialised types of production be maintained, or should heavy industry gradually be phased out in such a way that its ancillary industries became self-standing and its skills were preserved? Toothill unhelpfully ignored heavy industry in favour of 'new industry' growth points, infrastructural improvement and industrial incentives. By dismissing economic devolution, it also handicapped a planned adaption from old industries to new. Compared to the Scottish Economic Committee's realism in 1938, Toothill ended indeterminate, even if the Scottish Development Department (1962) and the Central Scottish plan (1963) stemmed directly from it, and Labour was quick to use it as a stick to whack 'stop-go' Unionism. But after 1964 it dropped its positive 'growth points' for a broad Scottish Development Area – and found itself giving first aid to the rapidly ailing heavy industries. The SCDI itself also switched and in 1970 adopted Lithgow's *Oceanspan*, using the Clyde as a breakbulk port for western Europe. Sensible enough, but for two things: (1) 'To lose traditional industries with comparative international advantages', as the economist Peter Jay told it in 1974, was to court 'a perpetual dynamic of decay'; and (2) heavy industry had in North Sea oil the prospect of revival – *but on the wrong coast.*

3

The Pillars of Society, 1922–64

'UNION SCOTLAND'

'A separate society', according to Tom Bottomore in *Sociology*, the word of the decade when it came out in 1962, implies 'political independence along with distinct economic, religious, and familial institutions'. Scotland before 1999 didn't meet that bill. Until about 1974 its politics and economy seemed clearly British, with important if *declining* variations. Yet Bottomore's list of the 'functional prerequisites' of society suggests a more complicated picture, stressing systems of communication: centred on family, welfare and education 'for the socialisation of new generations and systems of ritual, to maintain or increase social cohesion'.

Commercial communications and culture – certainly distinctive – come in Chapter 5. Socialisation, ritual and social stratification start here, but such categories overlap rather than exclude. Different interpretations have seen inherent structure and system as crucial or, with Marxism, regard the central motive of human action inhering in one part – the economy – which steers the rest. But in 'Union Scotland' education, religion and law had functions that were political as well as social. They legitimated Scottish distinctiveness and required the adaptation of British legislation. As there was no Scottish legislature, their own politics was about maintaining their status – and that of their members – in a pluralist society.

Interpreting this causes problems. The history of Scottish institutions, written 'from the inside', tended to stress their distinctiveness over their actual function, while studies of British society rooted in (or challenging) a class analysis usually either excluded Scotland or aggregated its data into 'British' patterns then treated as norms. Parochial complacency and metropolitan sloth meant that no real attempt was made to relate Scottish distinctiveness to class or capital.

Scotland substantially originated the study of 'man in society' in the eighteenth century, and produced Sir J. G. Frazer and Sir Patrick Geddes in the nineteenth, but twentieth- century Scottish sociology was marginal. Unlike inter-war Europe, where it was central to Liberal or social-democratic social planning, the Scots produced only a handful of research papers, and the *Third Statistical Account of Scotland* (which began ambitiously in 1943) showed a decline from Sir John Sinclair's *Account* in the 1790s and the Kirk's *Second Account* in the 1830s – a failure reflected in the planning mistakes of the 1960s. Was this down to the plight of the inter-war Scots universities, and their lack of investment in research? Possibly, but there were good social scientists, some of whom taught in the universities. If the study of Scottish society idled, was this aggravated by the *power* of Scottish institutions?

THE PEOPLE

Between 1921 and 1961 the number of Scots increased by only 6 per cent. Despite lower rates of natural increase the English and Welsh grew in number by 21 per cent. Out-migration was the main reason, but not simply due to economic deterioration. It was higher in 1900–14 and in the Indian summer of the 1950s than in the stricken 1930s, when the world slump cut it by half, contributing to Scotland's high unemployment. An 'emigration ideology' was certainly present – especially after 1945 when overseas settlement outran 'drifting south'. As *Scotland* reported in 1956, 90 per cent of emigrants were under forty-five and 'drawn from the most important industrial groups'. Family ambitions, rather than direct economic circumstances, prevailed as motive. In the

1960s losses were 94 per cent of natural increase; in the 1970s they were 163 per cent.

Regional population distribution changed little after 1870. The Scots of the central Lowlands increased from 61 per cent of the total in 1871 to 76 per cent in 1961, but the percentage dwelling in the four cities and twenty large burghs – fifty-one in 1901 – scarcely changed. The drift from the northern counties – 8 per cent between 1911 and 1931 – dropped to 2 per cent by 1951. Some industrial growth and better communications (especially cars, buses and delivery vans) countered farm mechanisation and fishing decline, until hydro-electricity, oil and the Highlands and Islands Development Board between 1951 and 1974 pushed population up by 15 per cent. Lacking such inputs, the Southern Uplands, stable until 1951, dropped by 6 per cent.

But buses, council housing and lack of long-term planning also 'froze' in the central belt many old industrial settlements, an unlovely 'third Scotland' sprawled from South Ayrshire to Fife. Merging with outlying city housing schemes, speculative developments and new towns, it wasn't much liked or visited: without city facilities or country traditions (devoid even of sociologists). But as the population of Glasgow plunged 25 per cent between 1951 and 1980, it steadily grew. Its political volatility in the 1960s hinted that the pragmatic SNP might provide a substitute for an absent community identity.

One absent ingredient of 1960s UK politics was racial tension. The post-war labour surplus meant little inward migration. As the Irish inflow slackened after the 1920s, most incomers were English (5 per cent of the population by the 1960s, 8 per cent by 2000) usually in somewhat temporary armed service or management roles. They found Scottish education and housing strange and made government office transfers tricky – hence Toothill's attempts to reassure. The tension that the Irish had aroused in inter-war Scotland, and that New Commonwealth immigration provoked in England in the 1950s and the 1960s, was absent. 'Ethnics' made up only 0.2 per cent of the 1966 population, compared with 1.1 per cent in the UK: no more salient than Jews, Italians, Poles and foreign students in the larger

Table 3.1 Population, 1911–2014 (in thousands)

	Scotland (% of UK)	Natural increase	Net migration	
			To rest of UK	Overseas
1911	4,760 (10.5)			
1911–21		360.2	–238.6	
1921	4,882 (10.4)			
1921–31		352.4	–330	–60
1931	4,842 (10.5)			
1931–51		502.3	–210	–10
1951	5,096 (10.1)			
1951–61		339.3	–140	–142
1961	5,179 (9.8)			
1961–71		346.3	–196	–157.5
1971	5,228 (9.2)			
1971–81		55.9	–54.1	–92.1
1981	5,180 (8.9)			
1981–91		21.0	–22.0	–77.0
1991	5,083 (8.4)			
1991–2001		–0.1	–11.0	–22.0
2001	5,062 (8.4)			
2001–11		–1.7	+69.5	+135.3
2011	5,295 (8.3)			
2014	5,347.6 (highest-ever level)			

Table 3.2 Scottish new town populations

	Actual (2011)	Planned
East Kilbride (1947)	75,000	95,000
Glenrothes (1948)	32,000	70,000
Cumbernauld (1956)	50,000	70,000
Livingston (1962)	56,300	100,000
Irvine (1969)	39,500	120,000

towns. Immigrants (with a substantial African-Asian middle class) either integrated well or were unobtrusive; working-class racialism was absent. Were the Scots more tolerant? Possibly: despite much anti-Irish propaganda in the 1920s, the Catholic community had become 'established' and there *seemed* few echoes from the Ulster troubles (1968–98). Immigrant numbers were never sufficient to put this to the test, but rose to 4 per cent by 2010.

FAMILY AND HOUSEHOLD

Families, as in the rest of the UK, fell in size, though were still comparatively large in 1961. This increased the non-earning population – and thus the poverty figures – in the 1930s. More babies survived: thanks largely to antisepsis, infant mortality fell from 1 in 6 in the 1890s to 1 in 8 by 1911 (below the UK figure of 1 in 7). This improvement didn't last. In 1938 it was 1 in 11, but England had improved to 1 in 16, and Holland stood at 1 in 30; this was largely due to Scotland's industrial depression and poor housing, although possibly aggravated by later marriage and inferior antenatal facilities. In the 1930s government and local authorities started to shift confinements to maternity homes, and this accelerated under the National Health Service. Angus, for example, got its first maternity hospital in 1939; by 1948 60 per cent of births were in such hospitals, and by 1966 97.8 per cent. By then infant mortality had fallen to 1 in 66. In 2011 it was 1 in 270.

Large families were due in part to the large Catholic population: 15 per cent in 1961, against 10 per cent in the UK. In the Protestant middle classes, attitudes changed. In 1918 Dr Marie Stopes, from an Edinburgh liberal background, published *Married Love*, praising sexual pleasure and, logically, contraception. She was attacked by all the churches – the Kirk grudgingly retreated in the 1940s – but family planning clinics were opened in the cities, and in the 1930s Aberdeen formulated one of the most advanced family planning and maternity services in Europe, under its Medical Officer of Health, Sir Dugald Baird. 'Artificial' contraception was less important than *coitus interruptus* or abstention until the 1940s, but family size dropped from around five to two children. Reduced drinking must have helped, and a growing if tardy valuation of the wife's role as wage-earner and housekeeper.

In its turn, this exposed marriage to greater stress. Divorces, while more available than in pre-1914 England, were prohibitively expensive, and reform was delayed until 1938. Thereafter the number increased to 2,000 in 1951, 3,700 in 1966 and 13,000 in 2006 (falling to 10,000 in 2011) reflecting both growing instability and male irresponsibility; the number of single-parent families, 4,000 in 1947, grew to over 25,000 in 1972 (and 163,000 in 2011) – although this also testified to a disinclination among Scotswomen to tolerate semi-servitude.

Before World War I, and for long afterwards in heavy industry areas, women were housekeepers: usually to more than one worker per household. But they became a quarter of the labour force in 1921, a third by 1961. Their wages were still poor, rising from under 40 per cent of male wages in 1921 to 50 per cent in 1961. But they were more socially mobile than men; Littlejohn, in *Westrigg*, noted that farmworkers' daughters could marry farmers without the latter losing caste. They would often move into towns, in search of better partners. The same applied to miners' daughters, escaping male-dominated pit villages. Even before post-1945 light industries set out to attract them, women became the majority in Scottish towns. This was true of textile communities, but as women usually outlived their menfolk and then moved near to relatives this meant that in the 1950s (within an overall ratio of 101 men to 109 women) a large burgh showed 88 single men to 124 widows, while a country parish would show 110 single men to only 81 widows.

Surveys, like Willmott and Young's of East London, stressed the shift from 'extended' to 'nuclear' families. The Scottish case was less straightforward, as farmworkers moved around almost like nomads – although minimum wages and national insurance (1935) were ending this. The extended family – with relatives living close to one another – was urban and quite recent. A 1960s survey of north Edinburgh housing estates found that in Wardieburn, a 1930s slum-clearance scheme, 83 per cent of families had relatives in the city, over a third within a mile, while only 35 per cent of families in owner-occupied Silverknowes had Edinburgh relatives. Ideal for bringing up children and running households – unthinkable for men – the working-class 'hive' of interlocking activities differed from the middle-class 'network' of optional acquaintances, and was run by wives, grannies, aunts. It was also being sapped both by growing numbers of working women and by rehousing. There were three responses to this: *escalators* aimed at an affluent nuclear family, buying more consumer goods – though not housing or private schools. Fathers played a greater part in family life and DIY: 'the contrasting wallpaper, the television set in one corner, and the budgie in another'. They were like the 'affluent workers' of John Goldthorpe's Luton (maybe in electronics or motors) but there was another group, more characteristically Scots: *locals* originally from the same area, aiming to recreate the interdependent working-class community. Success often depended on the 'stairheid wifie', such as the one who organised a fry-up on Granton foreshore. Where these weren't around, Wardieburn *mourners* regretted the 'paradise lost' of their old communities, and found it difficult to integrate unruly kids or problem families that got dumped there.

Their resilience diminished with income, and found paying costs of fuel and furniture, set against young earners moving out, difficult. Working-class community required some degree of affluence because it gave even the extended family a new lease of life. Car ownership rose from 1 in 7 people in 1961 to 1 in 5 in 1978, 1 in 3 in 1990 and 1 in 2 in 2013. Telephones multiplied even faster, also owned by 1 in 7 in 1961 but 1 in 2 in 1978. With 81 per cent of homes connected in 1990 and 90 per cent of individual Scots with mobiles by 2014, families could theoretically remain 'extended' – though they now lacked the instant community that once lurked in the crabbed type of the 'phone book', and got the unwanted pest of the cold call.

Family life preserved accents, although broadcasting and 'talkies' (1923, 1928) and school suppression of the 'speech of the street' emasculated the old dialects. 'Speaking broad' marked working-class identity, but leaders – either inarticulate (like William Adamson MP) or else of 'plum in the mooth' precision (Hugh MacDiarmid) – bore out some of Edwin Muir's notions about the effect of having to be literate in a foreign tongue. In London, however, Scots was less socially crippling than provincial English. Sean Connery's Edinburgh accent established him as a very potent James Bond: not a part for a Brummie.

HOUSING

Family life was literally 'cabined and confined'. In 1911, 8 per cent of the English and Welsh lived in one- and two-roomed houses: 50 per cent of Scots did the same. Blame high land values, legal peculiarities, rapid urbanisation, a tradition of multi-storey living and relatively low rents. Despite the Royal Commission's report, after 1918 the situation became, if anything, worse. One- or two-room households had dropped by about 3 per cent per decade, between 1871 and 1911; the fall to 1931 was only to 44 per cent. The target was 250,000 new homes (rather over a quarter of the existing housing stock). Between 1919 and 1939, 300,000 were built, but in 1935–6 the first survey to use common criteria throughout the UK found that 22.5 per cent were overcrowded, compared with 3.8 per cent in England. The best Scots case – Edinburgh with 17 per cent – nearly matched the worst English one: Sunderland with 20.6 per cent. Clydeside towns reached over 40 per cent and even council houses (12 per cent of stock) were as overcrowded as the national average. Almost half of Scottish housing stock was reckoned inadequate.

Success in winning rent control was double-edged. As private renting was now uneconomic, landlords wouldn't alter, enlarge or repair. Even after 1918, new building per head of population was only 60 per cent that of England, and there was nothing like the 'Metroland' boom of the 1930s. Growing industries, cheap mortgages, building societies, raw materials, incoming skilled labour, potential customers – all were lacking.

Local authorities and the state were both inexperienced. The first had, before 1914, rehoused only 1 per cent of families, but the Housing (Scotland) Act of 1919 made them the main instrument. This, without a proper advisory staff or effective cost controls, led to overpricing, and the 'Addison Act' was a virtual dead letter by the time of the Geddes axe: only 25,000 houses were built between 1919 and 1923. The Chamberlain Act of 1923 subsidised privately built houses for rent by £4 per annum, and built over 50,000. John Wheatley's Act of 1924, however, was Scottish in conception and execution, the work of the brainiest Clydesider. Government paid an annual subsidy of £9 per house per year to the local authority. Passed to the tenants, this meant a cut of between a third and quarter in weekly rent, or an extra room. Houses built 1925–9 went up by 140 per cent.

The theory was that council houses would suit better-off tenants (like my grandfather, an electrical engineer), their rented houses then passing to the less well-off. Lower down the ladder slums would steadily be cleared. However, this needed economic growth, otherwise it would subsidise the better-off while slums stayed full. In 1930 Labour shifted to wholesale slum clearance and rehousing on new higher-density estates, while the Act of 1935 concentrated on the 'intolerable overcrowding' revealed by the report of that year. Secretary Elliot attained an inter-war best of nearly 20,000 completions in 1938, and formed the Scottish Special Areas Housing Association, a state-owned group to develop new construction systems. It would play a remarkable role – but after 1945. Council houses of the 1920s were roomy and elegant, often in stone and if well-sited worth maybe £200,000 today. The 'clearance schemes' of the 1930s were cheap and looked it. Wardieburn and Craigmillar in Edinburgh and Blackhill in Glasgow, with grim rows of three- and four-storey tenements, had three or four rooms, a kitchen and a bathroom, but were far from pubs and shops. They separated 'extended families' whose small but closely grouped room-and-kitchens had been a sort of federative house. They were already seen as centres of social dislocation by the 1940s.

Housing remained an acute problem after 1945. 'Prefabs', mass-produced in former aircraft factories, were imaginative (I lived in one, 1946–9), but exports had priority over housing, while town-planning schemes provoked head-to-head tension between the planners and the municipalities, particularly

Glasgow. Anxious about green belt, the drift to new towns and overspill schemes, the cities turned to technology. Glasgow's first multi-storey scheme, in Partick, was completed in 1952. The Unionists, inspired by Harold Macmillan, boosted the rate by over a third. In 1954 they built over 38,000 houses, 12.5 per cent of the UK total where, in 1938, Elliot got only 8 per cent. The drawback, though, was in size and quality: slum-clearance dimensions persisted.

The Unionists stuck to Elliot's pre-war concentration on public rented housing. A comparison between 1921 and 1961 shows a fall in private renting common to both countries, from over 80 per cent of households to under 25 per cent. Scots owner-occupied building trebled, to 20 per cent of completions, between 1954 and 1964, but this was far behind the English rate of 62 per cent. In Scotland the main change was to council tenancy (42 per cent compared with 24 per cent in England). Because of rent control, low council rents and no building boom, only 25 per cent of Scots households were owner-occupiers, compared with over 42 per cent in England. In contrast to other areas of social policy, state intervention actually differentiated between Scottish and English society, and in an area that affected political behaviour.

FOOD

Reports on Scots nutrition are plentiful pre-1914 but less so for 1918–39, despite the research of the Scottish agriculturalist John (Lord) Boyd Orr in his *Food, Health and Income* of 1936, which concentrated attention on the effect of malnutrition on between a third and half of the population. The pre-1914 reports claimed an apparent paradox: diet deteriorated as the population got wealthier and more urbanised. The oatmeal and milk of the farm 'hinds' was boring, but high in protein and roughage, unlike the trend to meat, tea, white bread and liquor. In 1938 the Ministry of Labour found that reductions in the cost of imports increased the variety of food with a greater amount of meat, poultry products and fruit, but its unhealthiness persisted.

Sugar – short-term energy at the cost of tooth decay and diabetes – was 5.4 per cent (against 4. 9 per cent in an English family's food budget); the Scots were also low on fresh vegetables (11.8 per cent against 12.8 per cent). For those in industries and areas afflicted with unemployment and low wages, standards may even have fallen since the 1890s.

To this end, in the 1930s, the programme of free milk in schools and of domestic science classes tried to cope with the 'secondary' malnutrition of about 20 per cent of the population; but for the bottom 30 per cent nothing short of increased income would work. World War II brought this about: D. J. Robertson, in 1953, calculated that Scots food expenditure indices rose from 110 in 1939 to 244 in 1951, while the UK figures rose 109 to 228. Yet peculiarities persisted: more cash went on cereals and sugar, less on fruit. Tight-lipped, he found 'Scots housekeeping . . . definitely urban and determinedly in the tradition of the working class.'

The Scotland of the 1950s remained austere. The booze culture of pre-1914 had fallen away. In 1953 the Scots spent 18.4 per cent less than the UK average on drink, and little on eating out, because of strict licensing and few good restaurants (big problems for the Edinburgh Festival). They made up for this by 'smoking like lums', spending 11 per cent more than the UK average. 'Can there be life after dark?' others besides Arthur Marwick asked in the early 1960s, but matters soon changed.

HEALTH

Scots ate amply, if not wisely. They also grew taller and lived longer. A Glasgow boy born in 1910 would on average be 4ft 7in tall at 13 and weigh 75lb; a thirteen year old in 1954 would be nearly 4 in taller and 15lb heavier. Was this the result of the National Health Service in 1948, of rationing, of better general health care or of growing affluence? The research shows that the NHS improved rather than revolutionised health care – as with maternal provision. The conquest of tuberculosis and infection helped. Before World War I the mortality rate from TB was

20.8 per 10,000. Isolation of cases, better public health, inspection of milk products and X-rays cut this to 10.8 per 10,000, even before antibiotics – a retiring Scots inventor, Alexander Fleming, boosted by Lord Beaverbrook of the *Daily Express* – ended the menace . . . for the moment. Fever cases also subsided, for similar reasons. Angus had 231 per annum in 1908, eighty-one by 1965, though a decrease in such 'young people's diseases' meant an increase in the death rate from heart disease and cancer, which struck after the age of sixty.

Hospital provision and treatment was aided by the National Insurance Acts of 1911 and 1920. Hospitals divided both by type and organisation: a large number of voluntary hospitals, staffed by consultants and residents, served the larger burghs, and there were the county hospitals, often cottage or isolation hospitals under the local GPs. The two types gradually converged: many voluntary 'infirmaries' were subsidised by trade unions, while bodies like the county nursing associations set up after 1918 removed the 'poor law' stigma from the county hospitals. In 1938–9 came the construction of four large 'Emergency Medical Service' hospitals in rural areas – Law and Strathyre, Peel and Stracathro – designed to cope with bombing raids on the main cities. When these did not materialise, Tom Johnston used them to improve civilian medical services, a factor that eased the switch in 1947 to the five regional hospital boards of the NHS. These directed sixty-five management committees; parallel Health Executive Councils governed the GP services. The counties and large burghs rounded up the rest, as Local Health Authorities covering infectious diseases, school medical and dental services, midwifery, and public health.

The NHS soon eased the worst problems. An integrated maternity service reduced infant mortality – in Glasgow from 1 in 13 in 1947 to 1 in 28 in 1953 – and there were overdue improvements in eye treatment and dentistry, and in preventive medicine insofar as it affected the schools. But, though the NHS was carried by Aneurin Bevan, leader of the left, friend of Dr A. J. Cronin in his Tredegar days, and urged on by Dr Stark Murray of Paisley and the Socialist Medical Association and 'evidence-based' Dr Archie Cochrane of Gala, efforts at preventive, workplace-based medicine hit the reef of the British Medical Association. With the Highlands Medical Service (1913) and the depression in mind, the struggle among the tenements and schemes went on, but by the 1960s (when the BBC's *Dr Finlay's Casebook* looked back) inadequate expenditure and an ageing population were taking their toll. Would things get better? No: said heroin, alcohol and Aids.

UNEMPLOYMENT AND POVERTY

Many Scottish institutions anticipated their own reform, or rendered the result distinctive. With the poor law, however, regional differentials were eliminated wholesale. Few regretted a system which before 1914 denied outdoor relief to the able-bodied, though this qualification was rarely observed. Nine-tenths of relief granted was outdoor; even Beatrice Webb commended the professionalism of the parish relieving officer, usually the local teacher. After the war the old poor law could not face down endemic industrial depression: in 1921 the unemployed at last got outdoor relief. But, while this remained local, rates varied and depression-struck parishes imposed crippling burdens on local industries, accelerating closures.

In 1929 Walter Elliot's Local Government (Scotland) Act transferred relief to the counties, sustained by big block grants from Dover House. National Insurance, funded by stamps paid by workers and employers alike, had been introduced in 1911 and after 1919 was extended to cover most workers (except farmhands or earners of more than £250 per annum). As unemployment spiralled after 1929 the Scottish Insurance Commissioners went into deficit. Cuts in benefit would be a condition of the loan from foreign bankers in 1931 which split the Labour cabinet and brought about the National Government.

Cuts were prompt. They affected women, the long-term unemployed (whose benefit was cut to twenty-six weeks) and those with only a few months' contributions. Workers no longer on insurance benefit now got a 'transitional benefit' from

the state, their 'hardship' assessed by a 'means test' by local
Public Assistance Committees, examining all family circumstances, like working sons and daughters, savings, and so on.
National Insurance was regarded as a right honourably paid
for. Transitional benefit, and the poor law to which it was an
overture, was a stigma, accepted only under duress, unwelcome
through the inquisition involved. Bitterness about the 'means
test' remains.

Government got its way. By 1932 about 50 per cent of
benefits were means-tested. As a last resort, the poor law was
by 1935 relieving 59,000 workpeople and 101,000 dependents,
trebling the 1930 figure. Scales of relief still varied and Scotland
was penalised by the freezing of the block grant. Expenditure
increased by £1,800,000 (19 per cent), while the block grant
only increased by £100,000 (4.7 per cent); so Scotland's rates
were 6 per cent higher than England's, additional discourage-
ment to industrial development. Even after the Unemployment
Act of 1934 made relief a UK duty under the Unemployment
Assistance Board (UAB), Scottish local authorities still had to
raise £800,000 (28.5 per cent) of the £2,800,000 (or 5 per cent
of total unemployment relief) not covered by the UAB, a burden
not removed until 1937.

The UAB was to fix national standards of relief and combat
the anomalies of the awards made by the local Public Assistance
Committees: but it found itself sanctioning such variations and
voicing general disquiet about Scottish working and living conditions. Left-wingers alleged that the UAB was an instrument
for policing the working class, and cited the grim work camps
that it operated in Argyllshire, but its rates were reasonable
and its reports helped wake government to the need for further
expenditure on relief works and housing.

Before the UAB came into action, those on the dole in
Scotland, in 1935, totalled a staggering 1.16 million, or nearly
250 in every 1,000. After World War II, and the adoption of
a full employment policy, the UAB's successor, the National
Assistance Board (1948), had to deal with about a tenth of that
number, who fell through the pensions and insurance 'net'.

The NAB's chairman was George Buchanan, twenty years earlier an unruly Clydesider MP. This was a new left attitude to Westminster. In 1922 it had cited Scotland's comparative poverty in the case for home rule: as James Maxton said in 1923: 'They can do what they like about English children but that they are not going to suffer Scottish children to die'. Now, with Scotland relatively poorer, equal entitlement to benefit was an argument for the Union.

Without economic control, the welfare state lessened poverty, but couldn't eradicate it. Numbers on assistance increased, from 20 per 1,000 in 1947 to 38 per 1,000 in 1961 and 62 per 1,000 in 1972 (2014 statistics show 158 per 1,000 in poverty, which cast back to those 1930s figures). The result of deindustrialisation was 'multiple deprivation': a growing number of old people, casualties of social fragility like unmarried mothers and deserted wives, drugs and endemic ill health. Moreover, those entitled to benefit frequently either did not claim it, or mis-spent it, with results apparent in family breakdown and juvenile crime. This provided the background to the Kilbrandon inquiry children's courts (1964), the children's panel system and, in 1968, the the Social Work (Scotland) Act. This integrated child care, home helps, mental health, probation and, later on, prisoner welfare and hospital social services. The Act advanced on previous practice, but still differed from England. Even in an 'integrated' area, Scottish distinctiveness crept back.

EDUCATION

Scots showed the gulf between groups that marked an upwardly mobile society. They prided themselves on furthering the bright but badly off, but recruitment patterns narrowed before World War I, and the universities had become steadily more middle-class oriented. Such relationships were altered by the war, and the 'Fisher Act' of 1918 aimed to remedy the effects of four years of disruption.

Subsequent retrenchment frustrated it. The leaving age of fifteen, for instance, was not enacted until 1939, in time to be postponed 'for the duration'. Although Scotland continued to receive about 14 per cent of British educational expenditure, her relative performance declined. She had 18 per cent of secondary pupils in 1913, 15.3 per cent in 1938. Moreover, the day of the all-ability local school was ending. Anticipating the recommendations of the English Hadow Report, the new secondary schools were after 1923 divided into 'junior' and 'senior' secondaries, only the latter being academic. Although this made little difference in many country districts, it created a serious social gulf in the larger towns, and also increased the propensity of the gifted to move out once they had their qualifications. Jennie Lee, who left a Fife mining community for university and politics, was saddened that most of those who used this stepladder then abandoned the community that had originally given them their chance. Oral history in the 'Little Moscows' has shown the quality of their leadership: Lawrence Daly, future miners' leader, corrected the historian E. P. Thompson's proofs down Beath Pit.

Higher education fared badly between the wars. Full-time students fell from 10,400 in 1924 to 9,900 in 1937, while in England they rose by nearly 19 per cent. The decline was worse among female (26 per cent) than male students, but the latter suffered from the lack of jobs in areas where the Scottish universities had traditionally excelled: engineering, metallurgy and naval architecture. This curtailed research and investment: English university expenditure rose 90 per cent, the equivalent Scottish figure by scarcely a third, so able Scots moved south as postgraduates, slowing the development of new subject areas. Worst of all was vocational and further education, which the 1918 Act stressed; in 1955 only eight local authorities had technical colleges, and barely a tenth of school leavers attended them full time. Day release certainly grew, from 900 students in 1939 to 24,000 in 1955: still only a fraction of the potential. If *Scotland* condemned the 'sheer ignorance' of eighteen year olds in 1961 as 'a bleak omen for the future', it was scarcely the fault of the youngsters themselves.

Three major reorganisations in as many decades hadn't helped: the Local Education Authorities of 1918 were swept away by the Local Government (Scotland) Act. Neither they nor the school management committees which replaced the old School Boards had been particularly successful; perhaps they had simply not been given enough time. The professional organisations fought defensively over redundancies, wage cuts and threatened status: an intensely 'political' spirit which still avoided real discussion of policy or indeed philosophy. A. S. Neill fled to Dresden, then Summerhill in Suffolk; more mechanistic innovation came through the Scottish Education Department (SED), since 1921 situated in Edinburgh, and its inspectorate. Could either substitute for the 'great working academy' of the shipyard or the machine shop? Looking back from 2014 at 'deindustrialisation' Sir Harry Burns, chief medical officer, thought not.

The 1944 Act was anticipated by the re-establishment of the Advisory Council on Education, created by the Council of State. After 1945 there were notable innovations in curricula and methods, aided by direction from the inspectorate and increased expenditure on school building. This benefited the academically inclined; as Scotland lacked English O-levels until 1961, 93.4 per cent of pupils left school at fifteen without any qualification. By 1978, 58.3 per cent of pupils gained at least one O-level, and 17.2 per cent gained three or more Higher-level passes. As only 3.7 per cent reached this stage in 1951, the wastage of talent was palpable.

LAW AND ORDER

As far as statistics go – and *they* are suspect for a start, varying between constabularies, let alone between Scotland and England – the Scots were losing their lead over the English. In 1938 'crimes known to the police' were 11 per 1,000 of the total population; in England 7 per 1,000. By 1951 both countries were 14 per 1,000. The 1938 figure improved on 1913: a reduction of almost two-thirds in alcohol-related offences; these fell to only one-fifth. Did types of crime vary with levels of affluence? Most criminologists argue that economic recessions see a rise in crimes against property while affluence breeds crimes against persons. Yet violent crime in late 1930s Scotland was six times that of the south. It subsequently declined. The two world wars weren't uniform: crime slumped in 1914–18, stayed flat in the peace but revived after 1939.

Crime, in 1981 a neglected aspect of Scottish society, surely offered huge rewards to a Scots Richard Cobb who could use the courts to explore its pathology. It was urban, masculine and relatively unorganised – at least in a commercial sense. Glasgow gangs, devoted to fighting and drinking, used petty theft and protection rackets as a means to this end, with two major waves of gang warfare sweeping over Glasgow in the 1930s and 1960s. Yet the Western Isles, statistically awash with booze, were almost crime-free. And connections between crime and religious confession? Before 1900 two-thirds of the Scottish jail population was Catholic, disproportionate for the whole of society, if not for its poorest part. Was this the result of poverty, or of discrimination by Protestant bailies? It fell to 25 per cent by the 1920s, when the Catholic minority had legitimised its position. Irish political violence figured only briefly in 1920–1, less than pre-war suffragette acts of violence which outdid anything the Red Clyde got up to. As a rule, Scotswomen – truly the country's most oppressed group – were law-abiding, and became even more so. The ratio of male to female crime was 4 to 1 in 1913, 12 to 1 in 1951.

Violent crime was working class; murder a family affair. Fraud, tax evasion and embezzlement were middle class, but corruption was relatively new. It happened where business met local government, from the 1930s increasingly run by inexperienced men on low incomes, and played an important if tragic role in councils, 'quangos', trade unions and the Co-ops, swelling with complex organisations and investment drives. The old grandees blamed the extinction of civic politics and the rise of Labour, but it was surely also the result of remote, secretive administration and finance.

Scottish police forces, like those of England but unlike the Metropolitan Police or the Royal Ulster Constabulary, were local concerns. There were in 1920 thirty-two 'joint-county' or 'county-burgh' authorities – Glasgow was the largest in Britain. They found it difficult to cope with political disturbances (see 1919 in Glasgow), urban violence and growing traffic problems. Sir Percy Sillitoe, in Glasgow from 1933, found elderly officers, a decrepit CID and (it later turned out) corrupt political leadership. His reforms – from policemen's checked cap-bands to police boxes and radio-controlled cars – soon spread to other forces.

Was there innovation in the prison service? Until 1950 Scottish prison admissions consistently declined, from 50,000 to under 9,000. There was little pressure to modernise big 'bastilles' from the 1860s. On the other hand, as crime rose during the 1950s, these became increasingly overcrowded. Admissions were over 12,000 in 1961, and peaked at 18,773 in 1975. While readers of the *Sunday Post* were reassured to see old lags behind bars and scandalised at the privileges they were alleged to enjoy, being banged up in ancient, crowded buildings could scarcely diminish the anti-social tendencies of the inmates.

Law had civic and economic as well as criminal functions. It was as central a part of Edinburgh's caste system as investment trusts, and before 1914 was judiciously assimilating to the south. When economics tightened after 1918, there were two responses. Lord Macmillan (Unionist Lord Advocate in the 1924 Labour government) moved south to the English bar and became legal handyman to successive governments. Andrew Dewar Gibb, also a Unionist and Professor of Scots Law at Glasgow, went from defending his subject to the chairmanship of the SNP. In the 1940s another Unionist, Lord Cooper, revived Scots legal theory, and under his disciple, Professor T. B. Smith, Scots lawyers claimed an almost Savigny-like identification between Scots law and the national *Geist*. They were still over-influenced by party patronage, but after 1945 took a prouder line, stressing how close Scots Law was to the codes of the European nations. Solicitors, with academic qualifications absent in England, became active businessmen, estate agents as well as conveyancers. The legislation of the 1960s strengthened internal pressure for reform. The new Scots Law Commission under a leading innovator, Lord Kilbrandon, in 1965 appeared to confirm this, and the difficulty of transferring its recommendations to the statute book subsequently became a major argument for devolution.

RELIGION

The disestablishment of the Church of Wales was carried by parliament in 1913. Because of the war, it did not become law until 1920. In 1921, however, the Church of Scotland Act permitted an 'established Presbyterianism' to remain, and ended the sectarian rivalries of 1843. In 1929 the United Free Church fused with the Kirk. Feelings for unity grew after the Free Church merged with the United Presbyterians in 1900 (litigation was so labyrinthine that both got bored with disestablishing the Church of Scotland). There was little divergence over World War I, something more complicated over tithes, but the upshot was a Presbyterian Church more united than it had been for over a century, although no longer reaching the 36 per cent of the population the three churches had reached in 1886.

Formally, Scotland was still religious, although the actual balance was changing. In 1930 the Kirk claimed 1,271,095 members, 26.2 per cent of the population; the Catholics claimed 560,000, or 11.2 per cent (up from 9 per cent in 1886). To the south the Church of England had only 11.0 per cent. By 1960 decline even seemed to have been halted, with the Kirk on 25 per cent, but the Catholics had risen to 14.9; the evidence of ministers' reports in the *Third Statistical Account*, however, is of a general drift from regular religious participation from World War I on.

The Kirk's secular role withered, notably with the end of the parish councils in 1929 (ministers tended to sit as if of right), slum clearance and rehousing, and secular alternatives in education and entertainment. The Catholic Church, on the other hand, was strengthened by the 1918 Education Act's incorporation of its schools within the state system along with their religious distinctiveness, and through further immigration from the Free State and Ulster after 1921. This spurred a racist movement within the 'uniting' Kirk and some conservative nationalists; its later influence on 'Protestant' parties in the 1930s dissipated this. In the united Kirk two tendencies, Catholic and Evangelical, competed. The Iona Community, founded in 1938 by the war hero turned pacifist George MacLeod, sought a mystical and ritualistic religion, as well as strong social commitment. Funded substantially by James Lithgow, it devoted itself to work in the slums of Clydeside as well as to the reconstruction of the medieval abbey of Iona. A decade later, after 1947, the Rev. Tom Allan's 'Tell Scotland' movement, which culminated with the Rev. Billy Graham's 1954–5 Glasgow Crusade, reinstated the Evangelical tradition. The two clashed in 1961, when a committee of the General Assembly, including MacLeod, recommended the reintroduction of bishops in the Kirk, only to have its report rejected by the Assembly in session, after an energetic campaign by Beaverbrook's *Scottish Daily Express*. With an ultramontane dogmatism not far behind that of Eire, Scottish Catholicism could gain communicants until the mid-1960s, with distinguished converts – Muriel Spark, George Mackay Brown – in literature and the arts.

The political choice of Protestants broadly followed class lines; Catholics, including middle-class Catholics, voted overwhelmingly for Labour. This derived from traditional Irish resentment of Unionism, and partly because Scottish Labour was careful to protect the Church's educational privileges. This had its bizarre side. In 1931 the Catholic *Glasgow Observer* simultaneously anathematised socialism and commanded the faithful to vote for Jimmie Maxton! But, given the weakness of Labour organisation along the Clyde, the Catholic lobby was a conservative influence. On the Protestant side traditional links between the Kirk, the Orange Order and the Unionists flared up in the mid-1920s, overshadowing the predominantly Liberal U.F. Church, then fell back. As its membership fell in the 1960s, the politics of the laity and its monthly, *Life and Work* – seemed to settle to the right.

CLASS

The institutions of Scottish social life variably, sometimes contradictorily, assimilated to UK norms. Few New Commonwealth immigrants, larger families, rented public-sector housing, different eating and drinking patterns, more pervasive religion: these guaranteed distinctiveness. The economy had, of course, steadily been taken over by the south, and social welfare; but in law, education and housing, Scotland still radically diverged, unilluminated by London authorities such as Professor Peter Hall – 'We get the same morning papers, we see the same television programmes, we buy the same goods in identical supermarkets, lured by the same advertising'. Where, then, does class come in?

Any treatment of institutions distorts if it fails to relate them to the economic structure through class relationships and the distribution of economic power. Socialists who attacked the SNP during the 1960s argued that 'real divide' lay along class lines, and that class consciousness was the common property of British working people. Bearing in mind the subsequent career of Scottish nationalism, that argument still has to be met.

This approach is not proved by notions that Scotland was more working class than England. There were other marks of divergence. Mark Abrams' calculations of income distribution for *The Home Market* show a Scottish upper class, largely based in Edinburgh, strengthening its position over 1934–49, which also showed a growing percentage of 'working-class' incomes. Extremes of the social scale grew in numbers, while the middle class declined from 21.8 per cent to 18.9 per cent. Its English counterpart grew from 21.3 to 26 per cent.

This shows a more proletarian, class-conscious country. Even if we accept that the educational system enabled social mobility, the corollary of this is increased tension *between* classes. From the sociological research – and little matches James Littlejohn's *Westrigg*, which goes far wider than the 'Cheviot Parish' (actually Dumfriesshire's Eskdalemuir) it surveyed – class consciousness seems *pathological*: working people who were, in Marx's phrase, 'of a class, but not for a class'. Penetrating social and recreational life as well as work, this related to masculine dominance. Women were more mobile, could manoeuvre to exercise a greater degree of responsibility, but this conformed to the 'managerial' or 'problem-solving' skills of the upper classes as a whole. As a result, 'on any issue the working class is sharply divided while the middle classes are more unanimous, though with a difference of emphasis between property owners and professionals'. Even *within* working-class organisations the move of someone to a leadership role could be resented as a breach of class solidarity.

Applying this to Scottish politics shows an analogous development, with the leadership of Scottish working-class organisations recruited from the middle class, or deferring to middle-class ideologies. How had this come about? By destroying the Lowland peasantry, 'improvement' had also removed local relationships of kin and community, out of which an 'organic' society, with demotic leadership structures, emerged on the continent and in Ireland. The Scottish alternative was the consciousness of the skilled industrial worker, but this both lacked realistic political expression and depended on industrial changes that the workers could not control. World War I speeded the rise of the Labour Party; it also saw the frustration of its bid for political leadership, and the start of its decline.

Socialists welcomed the broader working-class solidarity of the time. As its president, William Leonard MP, told the STUC in 1925:

> the gulf which divided the skilled from the unskilled is fast disappearing, and, as a craftsman, I welcome the change ... our forefathers dexterity and fine points of craftsmanship are no longer needed by our present methods, and the same tendency is bringing up to our level those who at one time were dubbed 'only labourers'. Unemployment is with us until we dismiss Capitalism. I care not what type of government we have, if it tries to work this lack of system – the problem will remain.

This was a view sanguine to the point of self-deception. In 1935 the UAB thought an 'unfortunate feature' was 'the number of skilled workmen of various kinds who cannot be absorbed into their own industries and who are gradually drift-, ing into the general labouring class, a section which is already over-crowded'.

The skilled working class had supplied the labour and co-operative movement with most of its leadership, yet its own identity was ambiguous. Its culture, for instance, was almost wholly derived from the middle class. Thus, as it broke up, the educated element of the younger generation shifted into the middle class, through education, or emigration, rather than try to politicise the unskilled. The two sons of Willie Gallacher, Communist MP, went to university, and were killed flying for the RAF. Mrs Gallacher mourned her 'poor, clever bairns'. Neither she nor her husband would have denied them the chance to leave their class.

Although economic change increased class polarisation, Scottish institutions inhibited the development of active class consciousness. They provided means of 'spiralling' out of manual labour, but they also created, by public intervention, intermediaries – schoolteachers, doctors, local officials, councillors and MPs, social workers – what Stephen Maxwell called 'a state-sector middle class'. In the 1960s, after the eclipse of indigenous capitalism and the capture of Unionism by the agricultural interest, this class effectively dominated most of Scottish society.

4

Polit   ернment, 1922–64

(handwritten annotation)

THE ACCUSING EYE

The wife of a 'Glasgow Boy', Lady Hazel Lavery, as Cathleen ni Houlihan, stares from the pound note of *Saorstat Eireann*, 1928. The Union too far of 1801 created the Irish Question in British politics. Obsessive after 1880, it continued long after the setting-up of the Free State in 1921. Did it end at Good Friday 1998, in the British-Irish agreement, only months after the Scots and Welsh had endorsed home rule? No Scottish Question had existed before the 1960s, although the Speaker's Conference of early 1917 had recommended, besides female suffrage, a form of home rule all round *and* proportional representation. Dismissed by Lloyd George as 'a device to defeat democracy' this might have enabled a federal settlement. Between 1922 and 1964 Scottish issues occupied the Commons for no more than a few hours, or cabinet for as many minutes, even at the pit of the depression: the Caledonian Power Bill of 1936–8 excepted, which had defence implications.

A partial explanation? Before 1945 'high politics' meant foreign affairs, the empire and the armed forces. The Irish took the constitution as an issue away with them in 1921; the subtraction of their seventy-odd anti-Tory votes helped the Conservatives until 1945 and prolonged Westminster's restricted agenda. The Government of India Bill, not the UK slump, took up 84 per cent of legislative time in 1934–5.

Things changed by 1964: in real terms public expenditure was up three times on 1914: from 28 per cent of the 1914 budget of £207m it had risen to 77 per cent out of £6,727m. Plainly, only when government's weight shifted to social policy, after 1945, could Scottish issues feature – unless they were constitutional. But no 'Scottish' movement was strong enough to create these.

Scottish politics had patently changed after 1918 and its Reform Act, but what were they about? Old Liberalism viewed new electorate, new politicians with vast distrust. To Asquith his Paisley voters in 1920 were 'for the most part hopelessly ignorant of politics, credulous to the last degree, and flickering with gusts of sentiment like a candle in the wind'. Did they want socialism, or even know much about it? His Scots wife Margot nailed Rosslyn Mitchell, who beat him in 1924, after drafting the Clydesiders' declaration of 1922, as 'highly educated and no more Labour than you'. In 1931 Scottish loyalties to Labour would be shown to be thin: its inter-war record was neither consistent nor imaginative. It may have replaced Liberalism on the left of the two-party system, but the latter's collapse, sudden and still to be explained, left a vacuum not filled until 1945.

What filled it? A class-based loyalty to Labour's welfare state? This may have fitted the 1950s, but the years to 1979 suggested complexity: class politics skewed by distinctive local government and its close relation to the Scottish Office. Scots voters made 'secular' political choices in an increasingly Scottish context, but how had this evolved? The work of Unionists as much as of Labour, and of movements within Scottish administration itself?

LABOUR CONTAINED, 1922–35

Unionists and Liberals

November 1922 inaugurated a brief period of three-party politics, but by December 1924 the Unionists were dominant. In the UK their breach with Lloyd George had preserved their independence. They had 335 seats in 1918, 345 after November 1922. In Scotland, however, they lost seventeen seats in 1922 and gained only one in 1923. Only in 1924 did the party sweep forward to thirty-eight seats. But in 1935 it still held thirty-seven; not till 1964 did this drop below thirty.

Unionist success resulted from organisational rather than social change; its vote kept steady from 1924 to 1955. The Scottish Unionist Party of 1911 linked rural Tories to right-wing urban Liberals, nominally under five regional councils, but actually controlled by the Westminster leadership and Conservative Central Office. This was strengthened by a near-unbroken line of Scots who chaired the UK party: Arthur Steel-Maitland from 1911 to 1917, George Younger from 1917 to 1923, J. C. C. Davidson from 1926 to 1930 and John Baird from 1931 to 1940. Steel-Maitland and Davidson modernised local party organisation, with regular subscriptions and (at least nominally) elective committees, efficient agents and greatly increased income from businessmen, often former Liberals. Membership rose: in Glasgow up from 7,000 in 1913 to 20,000 in 1922 and 32,000 in 1929: almost double the non-trade union Labour Party *and* the Independent Labour Party (ILP) for the whole of Scotland.

This cohesion trumped the disorder of the Scottish Liberal Federation. Formerly policed by frontbench MPs and local managers – usually solicitors – the wartime split between Asquithians and Lloyd Georgites was fatal. Even the rallying-call of 'free trade in danger', which kept unity in 1923 – along with the mysterious Lloyd George fund – brought no recovery. In 1924 organisation collapsed, with *one* candidate nominated for Glasgow on the eve of the October election. Only eight MPs survived it, mainly in rural seats. Lloyd George took over from Asquith in 1926, but all but Archie Sinclair in far Caithness disowned him. In 1929 it was farmers' discontent about falling prices, not Lloyd George's imaginative 'Yellow Book' programme that brought five gains, in a performance almost 30 per cent worse than in the UK. The rise of urban Labour forced, more swiftly than in England, an 'anti-socialist' *entente* with the Unionists. The year 1929 saw what proved to be the last

Table 4.1   Westminster MPs elected for Scottish constituencies, 1900–2015 (number of MPs and % of vote)

	Unionist		Liberal		Labour		Other/SNP	
	MPs	%	MPs	%	MPs	%	MPs	%
1900	38	(49.0)	34	50.2	–		–	–
1906	12	(38.2)	58	(56.4)	2	(2.3)	–	3.1
1910	11	(39.6)	59	(54.2)	2	(5.1)	–	1.1
1910	11	(42.6)	58	(53.6)	3	(3.6)	–	(0.2)

1918 Reform Act: All men over 21 and women over 31 enfranchised

	Unionist		Liberal		Labour		Other/SNP	
1918	51	(49.9)	15	(15.0)	7	(22.9)	1	(12.2)
1922	37	(42.8)	16	(21.5)	29	(32.2)	2	(3.5)
1923	16	(31.6)	23	(28.4)	34	(35.9)	1	(4.1)
1924	38	(40.8)	9	(16.5)	26	(41.1)	1	(1.6)

1928 Women over 21 enfranchised

	Unionist		Liberal		Labour		Other/SNP	
1929	22	(35.9)	14	(18.1)	36	(42.4)	1	(3.6)
1931	58	(54.3)	8	(8.6)	7	(32.6)	–	(4.5)
1935	45	(44.8)	3	(6.7)	24	(41.8)	2	(1.7)
1945	30	(41.1)	–	(5.0)	40	(49.4)	4	(4.5)

1948 Scottish universities seat abolished

	Unionist		Liberal		Labour		Other/SNP	
1950	31	(44.8)	2	(6.6)	39	(46.2)	1	(2.4)
1951	35	(38.6)	1	(2.7)	35	(47.9)	1	(0.8)
1955	36	(50.1)	1	(1.9)	34	(46.7)	–	(1.3)
1959	31	(47.2)	1	(4.1)	38	(46.7)	–	(2.0)
1964	24	(40.6)	4	(7.6)	43	(48.7)	– SNP	(2.4)
1966	20	(37.7)	5	(6.8)	46	(49.9)	–	(5.6)

1969 Voting age lowered to 18

	Unionist		Liberal		Labour		Other/SNP	
1970	23	(38.0)	3	(5.5)	44	(44.5)	1	(12.0)
1974 (Feb.)	21	(32.9)	3	(8.0)	40	(36.6)	7	(22.5)
1974 (Oct.)	16	(24.7)	3	(8.3)	41	(36.3)	11	(30.7)
1979	22	(30.0)	3	(10.0)	44	(42.0)	2	(18.0)
1983	21	(28.4)	8	(24.5)	41	(35.1)	2	(12.1)
1987	10	(24.0)	9	(19.2)	50	(42.4)	3	(14.3)
1992	11	(25.7)	9	(13.1)	49	(39.0)	3	(22.2)
1997	–	(17.5)	10	(13.0)	56	(45.6)	6	(24.0)
2001	1	(15.6)	10	(16.4)	56	(43.9)	5	(24.0)

Table 4.1 (*cont.*)

	Unionist		Liberal		Labour		Other/SNP	
	MPs	%	MPs	%	MPs	%	MPs	%
2004 Scottish Westminster constituencies reduced to 59								
2005	1	(15.8)	11	(22.6)	**41**	(39.5)	6	(17.7)
2010	1	(16.7)	**11**	(18.9)	41	(42.0)	6	(19.9)
2015	1	(14.9)	1	(7.5)	1	(24.3)	56	(50.0)

'Unionist' column includes Liberal Unionist to 1912; 'Coalition Liberal' 1918–22; 'National Liberal' 1931–64.
Bold type indicates government.
Seventy-two constituency seats 1900–2001, thereafter fifty-nine.

rally, as party discipline dissolved and Lloyd George fell sick. In the 1931 crisis Scots Liberals would support the National Government overwhelmingly.

Labour

The Liberals' killer had been the first Labour government. In December 1923 Ramsay MacDonald formed a minority administration. Scots were a quarter of his cabinet, and provided its major successes, with MacDonald's conciliatory foreign policy and Wheatley's Housing Act. Little else could be achieved – save proof that Labour could govern and the Liberals couldn't: hence their October *débâcle*. But even in Scotland Labour lost eight seats, and by the time it recovered in 1929 poor organisation and the setback of the General Strike had taken their toll.

Labour was stuck somewhere between Unionist integration and Liberal autonomy, its structure an awkward compromise between federation and mass movement. The executive of its Scottish Council had six union representatives, four from constituency parties and trades councils (often more or less the same thing), four from women's sections, two from the ILP, and one apiece from the moribund Social Democrat Federation (SDF) and the Fabians.

Less than half of the eighty-odd unions affiliated to the STUC sent delegates to Scottish Conference – only thirty-one, for example, in 1930. These represented just 42 per cent of engineers, 39.5 per cent of textile workers and 45.5 per cent from the distributive trades. Strongly affiliated unions, like the miners (89 per cent) and railwaymen (83 per cent) had been hit by the depression; only five of the thirty-six Scots-based unions sent delegates. Were they represented through the trades councils, or simply uninterested in politics? Labour was less nationalist than the STUC, also weaker at the grass roots; individual membership per head of population was only a third of that in London in 1929. This was partly due to the strength of the ILP, and partly to trades council representation – which also opened them to Communist influence.

In 1922 the Clydesiders had been kingmakers for MacDonald, but they faced competition. The Cambridge-educated former conscientious objector Clifford Allen became ILP chairman and moved the party to a left-Liberal position, appealing to middle-class reformers as the intellectual powerhouse of the left. With success: membership increased from 25,000 in 1922 to 60,000 in 1926. But Allen's aims conflicted with the Glasgow MPs' concern with unemployment and, to a lesser extent, with their nationalist inclinations.

At the industrial grass roots, moreover, the ILP had to face the Comintern. The Communist Party of Great Britain (CPGB), founded in July 1920, had some Clydesiders on board, but

Table 4.2 The backgrounds of Scottish MPs at selected elections
1911, 1945, 1979 = MPs at Westminster; 2011 = MSPs at Holyrood

1911 (72)	%	1945 (72)	%	1979 (72)	%	2011 (129)	%
Liberal/Asquith		Labour/Attlee		Tory/Thatcher		SNP/Salmond	
n/a		Women 4/72		Women 1/72		Women 45/129 b	
Business	35	Workforce	31	Workforce	19	Business	18
Law	28	Other prof.	24	Business	16	Politics	16
Other prof.	18	Business	16	Law	15	Law	8.5
Land/farming	13	Land	8	Teaching	15	Teaching	8.5

its structure implied obedience to Russian directives. Leaders who survived tended to be former Scots Catholics, accustomed to ultramontane control; less docile radicals followed the example of John Maclean and retreated into uncompromising sects. The CPGB had some electoral success before 1924, while its relationship with Labour remained undefined. Walton Newbold held Motherwell from 1922 to 1923; James Geddes came second in both years at Greenock. Its housing agitation helped increase Labour's vote but attempts to affiliate in 1924 were rebuffed. Then it tried to penetrate the unions through the Moscow-funded National Minority Movement which helped to raise the political temperature in the months before the General Strike of 4–12 May 1926.

The General Strike

The strike – Hugh MacDiarmid's 'Camsteerie Rose' – reacted to the decline of the coal industry and the attempts of mine owners to force wage reductions. The vacillations of the General Council of the Trades Union Congress (TUC), pledged to support the National Union of Mineworkers (NUM), were reflected by the leaders of the STUC and the 'first-line' unions – in transport, mining, docks and printing. Preparations were sketchy, save in some coalfield areas where the Minority Movement organised 'Councils of Action' to enforce picketing and control food supplies, while Baldwin used plans prepared in 1919. The Lord Advocate activated an emergency administration planned for the confrontation with the 'Triple Alliance' unions in 1921, with Scotland divided into five regions; their officials could call on the forces and the Organisation for the Maintenance of Supplies, a private body of volunteers – some from the far right.

The initial impact was on transport. Dock work stopped, as did trains, even on remote branch lines. But the government got supplies moved by sea and lorry, while student-manned trams (easy to drive) kept going in the cities. There were many confrontations: working-class solidarity went far beyond the unions, with Orange flute bands joining picket lines (even if the

Grand Masters were as hostile as the Catholic hierarchy). On 11 May the 'second line' unions came out, and the TUC General Council in London backed down: 'The thistle like a rocket soared, An' cam' doon like the stick!'

'Demoralised by the utter and absolute capitulation' – in the words of a young participant, Jennie Lee – the strikers resumed work. Many were sacked, demoted or victimised. Locked-out miners endured until November when, driven by hunger and the approach of winter, they surrendered. For a former elite, it was a terrible defeat, with wages and status reduced to a level little above that of the unemployed.

Political Labour benefited, as working-class loyalty to Liberalism vanished. Asquith was as hostile as Churchill, now a Tory. Liberal bailies acted with Unionists to assist the government and penalise strikers. The Communists gained during the lockout, but lost when it ended, and Labour recovered in local politics – in Edinburgh's November elections its seats rose from six to fourteen. The strike enhanced 'British' class politics, at the cost of the nationalist element in Labour: local power, in the eyes of astute managers like Patrick Dollan, was within grasp.

Unionist reform

Baldwin remained in power until 1929. Because of Churchill's orthodoxy as chancellor, his government only aggravated Scotland's economic plight, a reaction uncomprehended through the drift of frontbenchers away from Scotland (with only one exception, no premier, chancellor or foreign secretary sat for a Scottish seat between 1922 and 1963, against five between 1900 and 1922). The place was relatively unstable (Unionists consistently held only 45 per cent of Scottish seats between 1918 and 1939, compared with 65 per cent in the English Midlands); Scots businessmen were also reluctant to stand. Unionist MPs, drawn from groups like advocates and landowners, were dull and remote from Scotland's economic and social problems. There were a few exceptions, and fortunately one played a key role in the Scottish Office for many inter-war years.

Walter Elliot, the son of a wealthy auctioneer, and the only 'professional' Fellow of the Royal Society ever to become a cabinet minister, had been a Fabian while at Glasgow University, out of a brilliant generation including James Maxton, Tom Johnston and James Bridie. He entered parliament in 1918 – 'Will stand, which party?' had been his (apocryphal) response to nomination – and advocated collectivist, if somewhat paternalist, social reform. He was no nationalist but, as Under-Secretary for Scotland, 1923–9, secured two major changes in Scottish administration: the reorganisation of Scottish central administration and the Local Government Act of 1929.

The first measure, carried in 1928, converted the system of nominated boards, only indirectly responsible to parliament, into an orthodox civil service on the lines of the Scottish Education Department. Criticised by William Adamson, Scottish Secretary under Labour, for subordinating administration to Whitehall 'to a far greater extent than has ever been the case', in fact it coincided with a physical decentralisation of government *from* Whitehall. In 1936 1,333 out of 1,416 civil servants working for the Scottish departments were to be based in St Andrew's House, the new government headquarters in Edinburgh, planned in 1929 and built, to the design of T. S. Tait, between 1932 and 1937. But the departments of agriculture, education and health, and the Scottish Office, were only linked by being subject to the Secretary of State. 'Organic' co-ordination still had to be achieved.

Much more drastic was intervention in local government, which provoked persistent 'national' agitation. Without the usual preliminary of a royal commission, and going further than Neville Chamberlain in England, the 1929 Act swept away the parish councils, the Local Education Authorities and many of the powers of the smaller burghs. The new system consisted of four counties of cities, twenty 'large burghs' (over 20,000 inhabitants) and thirty-one county councils which divided between them responsibility for most local authority services. A further 171 'small burghs' held onto limited public health and housing; in the 'landward areas' of counties somewhat nominal 'district councils' got what was left. The historic Scottish parish was now a religious and registration area: nothing more.

The nemesis of Labour

The act attracted vocal opposition from Scottish local authorities, from the infant National Party and from Labour, which pledged repeal. MacDonald's failure to do so, when he formed his 1929 administration, was the first pratfall in a disastrous career. Labour had gained strength but not unity after 1926. In the ILP Maxton had supplanted Allen and tried to win over industrial militants; but this caused a divergence with the Glasgow grass roots which Dollan cultivated zealously. Some of the party's home rulers, like R. E. Muirhead and C. M. Grieve, moved to the Nationalists. Wheatley, its one real statesman, was in the toils of an expensive and embarrassing lawsuit. MacDonald excluded him from his government. Ill and embittered, he flayed Jimmy Thomas's inept attempts to cope with unemployment until, worn out, he died in May 1930.

Alternative 'left' policies were by now coming from Birmingham, where the Scot Allan Young was Sir Oswald Mosley's economic adviser. Would Wheatley have supported them? Tom Johnston, who succeeded Thomas in March 1930, was certainly sympathetic to many of Mosley's Keynesian ideas, but, echoing Scottish Labour's rejection of Lloyd George's 'Yellow Book' proposals, swung Forward against the old enemies – bankers and tariff reformers.

Among moralistic socialists co-existing uneasily with classical economics, this had logic, expounded by the Chancellor Philip Snowden's articulate Scots lieutenant, Willie Graham. In exporting areas, tariffs meant retaliation and further unemployment. Until the crash of October 1929 MacDonald's policy of tariff reduction and disarmament was backed by most Scots Labour MPs, but after it they could only defend welfare benefits. Secretary Adamson, and Graham, resolute as Snowden against MacDonald's stumbling approaches to protectionism, were both found, in Labour's last cabinet division on 23 August

1931, in the minority of nine voting against expenditure cuts. *Forward* went into the November election urging 'Shot and Shell against Bread Taxes', but it turned out to be 1906 in reverse. In Scotland only seven Labour MPs survived.

The National Government

MacDonald's appeal, with some help from John Buchan, helped swing Scotland behind the National Government. In Wales Labour was the main party with fourteen out of thirty-four MPs; in Scotland it collapsed when co-ordinated Liberal and Unionist voting turned a 2:1 majority in votes into a 6:1 majority in seats. Not that this huge majority helped the coalition parties much. In September 1932, when the government negotiated the Ottawa agreements and broke with free trade, its Liberal supporters split. Secretary Archie Sinclair and four of his MPs chose opposition. His successor, Sir Godfrey Collins, commanded the National Liberal remainder. Wrangles continued in the Scottish Liberal Federation until 1935, when the 'Nationals' were expelled – to become indistinguishable from the Unionists. The latter found the landslide actually made their MPs even less representative of Scottish business than they had been in the 1920s.

This disadvantaged Scotland rather than benefited Labour, which made no by-election gains and only took twenty seats in 1935. It was plagued by a bitter feud with its old component, the ILP. Maxton's party claimed four of the seven surviving MPs, but disaffiliated in 1932. Many of its Scottish members wanted to remain, and later that year set up the Scottish Socialist Party (SSP). Dollan was its effective leader and it made off with most of the ILP's 127 Scottish branches.

ILP membership fell by 75 per cent. Infiltration rapidly destroyed its organisation in all but a few seats, and the CPGB took over as the representative of the far left – but with difficulty. Moscow made it change its line in 1928, turn on the Labour Party and support breakaway trade unions. This led to its increasing isolation, save in the 'Little Moscows' of the Vale of Leven, Clydebank and Fife, where Willie Gallacher broke

from the NUM with his United Mineworkers of Scotland, despatched Adamson in 1935 and stayed till 1950. By then, under
the threat of Fascism, the Communist line had changed once
again, to the Popular Front.

In the 1920s Scots Labour MPs were powerful in the
Westminster party; after 1931 they vanished. Policy renewal
came from 'next door', after Labour under Herbert Morrison (of
Scots ancestry) won the London County Council in 1934, setting
up a socialist laboratory just across the Thames. The SSP was
stymied by legal battles over the property of the ex-ILP branches
it affiliated. It died in 1940, to the relief of Transport House,
which didn't like the left-wing company it kept. The Peace
Pledge Union and the Left Book Club thrived, but not among
Labour's economically parched grass roots, where the Co-ops
declined. Visiting Fife in 1936, Jennie Lee, now married to
Aneurin Bevan, found herself mourning 'all the vigour, the bel-
ligerency, the robust certainties' of only a few years before.

SMALL-N NATIONALISM, 1935–50

NPS to SNP

The year 1935 confirmed the Unionists in power. Labour had
been checked; Liberals were disintegrating, Communists were a
tiny minority, the Nationalists no bigger – though they went on
to provide a unifying theme. 'The Condition of Scotland' had got
relatively worse, raising problems for government and chances
for the opposition. This issue didn't upset the dominance of the
two parties, but their manipulation of it gave a distinctive tone
to Scottish politics.

Political nationalism was garrulous – we know more of it
than of the parties for which 90 per cent of Scots actually voted
– but mattered more than its low membership and few votes.
The National Party of Scotland (NPS), founded on 23 June
1928, largely by intellectuals of the Scottish Renaissance and
former ILPers, gained 5,000 members by 1929 – level with the
Scottish ILP. But its leaders floundered in a hostile environment,

internally divided over strategy. Voters had settled into a new two-party structure, and didn't want to budge. Events in Europe made nationalism look dangerous. Was the NPS to compete with Labour, or try to fill the vacuum created by Liberal implosion?

The NPS, largely run by the ex-ILPers John MacCormick and Roland Muirhead, started on radical lines, unsuccessfully. In 1929 it averaged under 5 per cent in two contests, in 1931 got 10 per cent in five, but in subsequent by-elections improved little. MacCormick now switched tack, trying to attract dissident Unionists (stirred up by Lord Beaverbrook and his new *Scottish Daily Express*) and former Liberals who launched, in September 1932, the Scottish Self-Government Party. A disastrous by-election result in East Fife in February 1933 (Eric Linklater polled only 3.6 per cent among a menagerie of fringe candidates) moved MacCormick to purge the NPS of its fundamentalists in May 1933, and in November back the Scottish Party leader Sir Alexander MacEwen at a Kilmarnock by-election. MacEwen polled 16.9 per cent, and in April 1934 the two parties amalgamated, largely on Scottish Party terms, as the Scottish National Party. Membership, however, fell steeply, to only 2,000 in 1939. There were some promising by-election results, but the 1935 vote didn't improve on 1931.

The right

Scottish grievances persisted, however, even among the government parties, hence the Scottish National Development Council of 1930. In 1932 MacDonald, advised by Buchan (frustrated as a Tory MP), reverted to his earliest convictions and hinted at a measure of home rule. Scottish Unionists repudiated this in manifestos and a petition – branded the 'Ragman's Roll' – in 1932–3, but yielded on administrative devolution and economic measures. This 'climate' aided the creation of the Scottish Special Area Commissioner, the Scottish Economic Committee and the Gilmour Committee on Scottish Administration, together with the energy of Elliot, Secretary of State from 1936 to 1938.

Elliot wanted to legitimate the Unionists as a party of moderate, statist reform, incorporate the Liberals and attract the working class. Despite 1931, there were problems in both areas. He succeeded remarkably – aided by factors from rearmament, the arts and cinema to diffident George VI's energetic Scottish consort Elizabeth Bowes-Lyon, who charmed Smuts and de Valera among Commonwealth premiers.

But might matters have gone differently? Many Unionists bitterly distrusted the Liberals. As a future Secretary of State, James Stuart, wrote, 'they form a race apart, sitting on the fence and incapable of deciding whether to jump down on one side or the other'. A century's enmity could not easily be overcome. So did right-populism, like that of Ulster where much of the Protestant working class had turned Unionist, have a chance?

Unionists had an interest in militant Protestantism. Until the 1920s officials of the Orange Lodges had sat on the Scottish Council, but this link was dropped before 1930. Because Liberals had to be courted? Because Orangemen were less deferential than they ought to have been? Witness the actions of some of them in supporting the General Strike. Certainly, Protestant militancy went beyond Unionism, then and subsequently. One of the first things that Lanarkshire migrants to Corby in 1932 set up was an Orange Lodge; by 1960 there were six, but Corby Council hadn't a single non-Labour member. In the 1950s Catholics voted disproportionately for Labour, but the Protestant vote split roughly on the British average. Orangeism seemed more cultural than political.

Showing such a reservoir existed, populist right-wing movements rose in the 1930s – the Scottish Protestant League in Glasgow and Protestant Action in Edinburgh. The first had four councillors in Glasgow by 1934; and the second became in 1936 the second-largest party in Edinburgh, with 31 per cent of the vote, returning a maximum of nine councillors. The rise in the poll it caused – of 50 per cent in Edinburgh in 1936 – was compared by some to the SNP's municipal impact in the 1960s. It had some vaguely Fascist overtones – it directed propaganda equally against Unionist landlords and Catholic control of the Labour Party, its Edinburgh leader, ex-serviceman John Cormack, claimed a bodyguard and an armoured car – but did it have real connection with economic grievances? It did better in prosperous Edinburgh than in Glasgow at the worst hour of the depression, and waned in the west as it grew in the east. Even in Edinburgh, it broke up in the late 1930s. Apart from it, the radical right was absent. Mosley had important Scottish confidants – Charles Raven Thompson, Dr Robert Forgan and John Scanlon, all of whom had a left-wing background – and some Conservative MPs voiced pro-Hitler sentiments, but the only time Mosleyite candidates stood, in 1937 municipal elections, they were humiliated.

The Popular Front

Elliot's economic achievements figure in Chapter 2. In summer 1937 he met by chance the young Communist Hamish Henderson in Paris and gave him lunch, discussing MacDiarmid animatedly at the International Exhibition: 'Next year we'll knock this into a cocked hat in Glasgow!' But in May 1938 Neville Chamberlain moved him from Scotland to the Ministry of Health. In October he reluctantly supported Chamberlain over the Munich agreements with Hitler, thus sealing his fate in 1940. Churchill dropped him, and he never held office again.

The loss to Scotland of the only first-rank British statesman who identified himself with Scottish issues was a severe one, and it was particularly acute for the Unionists, who were just beginning to lose ground to Labour: in Westminster terms poor but making up ground in local government. They captured Glasgow in 1933, Motherwell and Clydebank in 1934, Dundee in 1936 and Falkirk in 1937, and claimed the industrial counties: a new and powerful interest, and one that Elliot actually encouraged by increased housing and educational programmes, which redounded to the credit of the local authorities.

This was also matched by a revival of home-rule agitation on the left. Tom Johnston became in 1935 Labour's Scottish affairs spokesman. Like Buchan a Commonwealth man, shifting to the centre and towards administrative rather than legislative devolution, he continued to encourage agitation for home rule, through groups like the London Scots Self-Government Committee. Run by a couple of energetic journalists, it made the unsurprising discovery that it was easier to influence Scottish affairs in London than in Edinburgh, and organised an imaginative range of meetings and pamphlets which at least gave the impression that Labour, up to and including Clement Attlee himself, favoured Scots self-government.

Various things helped this, not least the 'Popular Front' line adopted by the Communists in 1935. Casting around for common causes with socialists and liberals, and worried at its own tiny Scottish membership (2,815 in December 1938) it adopted nationalism. Where it went, the stage army of the Popular Front followed; Ritchie Calder and J. B. S. Haldane, Krishna Menon and Jawaharlal Nehru addressed meetings organised by self-government groups, while on May Day 1938 the Communists paraded in tartan, carrying banners of Bruce and Wallace, Burns, Calgacus and (rather oddly: he was a high Tory) R. L. Stevenson.

Such activities increased as the international situation worsened. Scots companies fought in Spain in the ranks of the International Brigade, sustaining heavy casualties, and in December 1938 a strong challenge to the Chamberlain government came when the Duchess of Atholl contested her Perthshire seat as an independent backed by the Popular Front. She lost, but only narrowly. Despite the imminence of war, cross-party nationalism continued to bubble away, encouraged by MacCormick, who also tried to stifle neutralist and pacifist activity within the SNP. There was to be a great convention to launch an all-party campaign for home rule in September 1939. There was war instead: 'imperialist war' to the Communists, and the fundamentalist nationalists who joined them in opposing it.

Labour policy-making proceeded, meanwhile, on two levels. We already know, from Chapter 2, the more significant. Hugh Dalton's inquiry of 1937, his move to the Board of Trade in

1942 and the preparation of the Direction of Industry Act of 1945, on which a generation of Labour prescriptions were based: a success secured in the corridors of power. Labour would show a much more nationalist front in wartime Scotland.

World War II

The war boosted Labour's political recovery and helped to reinforce the apparent distinctiveness of Scottish planning and economic policies. There was widely articulated cross-party support, a surprising amount of success for the SNP, and in February 1941 the desire for change was focused on Johnston, whom Churchill appointed Secretary of State.

In contrast to World War I, industrial relations were tranquil; Johnston considered the loss of only 0.07 per cent of work days on Clydeside through strikes as laying the ghost of 'the Red Clyde'. But Ministry of Information surveys showed great dissatisfaction with the way the war was being run. This verged on disloyalty, borne out by vociferous criticism by MPs both of left and right and mounting third-party success. In July 1943 Sir John Reith recorded a conversation with Johnston:

> He is very bothered by Bevin and other English ministers who do things affecting Scotland without consulting him. He thinks there is a great danger of Scottish nationalism coming up, and a sort of Sinn Féin movement as he called it. The Lord Justice Clerk [Lord Cooper] had said in a letter that if he left off being a judge and went back to politics, he would be a Nationalist.

In terms of its past performance and its political history the SNP did well. William Power got 37 per cent at the Argyll by-election in April 1940, and although its home rule and independence wings split bitterly in June 1942, John MacCormick going off to form Scottish Convention, it got 41 per cent at Kirkcaldy in February 1944 and won Motherwell in April 1945. It took on in Scotland many of the radicalising functions of Common Wealth, although CW, whose Scottish organiser was David Cleghorn Thomson, claimed an early success when Tom Wintringham nearly won North Midlothian in February 1943. He backed home rule, as did Sir John Boyd Orr, returned in April 1945 as an independent for the Scottish Universities. Such pressure was astutely managed by Johnston to get increased autonomy for the Scottish Office.

Johnston's *Memories* invest this process with rather more symmetry than it actually had. He demanded from Churchill a Council of State, composed of all living ex-Secretaries, to vet all proposed Scottish legislation. If the Council approved it, the cabinet was to press parliament to legislate with minimum delay. It would be advised by a body representative of Scottish business, trade union and local authority opinion, and Scottish MPs were to meet regularly in Edinburgh. It took six months for the Council to meet, and then its remit was confined to post-war problems, while the Scottish Council on Industry, the larger body, was independently convened by Johnston on 2 February 1942. There were a couple of meetings of MPs in Edinburgh, which were not successful. That the Council of State shifted to concentrate on wartime administration was largely the result of a forcible intervention by Elliot in December 1941, arguing that post-war reconstruction could not be divorced from attracting wartime industry. Thereafter the Council met regularly until May 1943.

The parallel Scottish Council on Industry was not the fully fledged development commission for which James Bowie and the Scottish Economic Committee had pressed, but it countervailed the *laissez-faire* attitudes of the central office of the Board of Trade, strengthened its local representatives and gave comprehensive backing to efforts to attract industry and plan the economy. Around it Johnston set up thirty-two specialist committees tackling subjects from hill sheep farming to teaching citizenship in schools. Substantial practical gains were registered: Scotland received a full and varied quota of war industries; a committee under Lord Cooper cut through the knot of environmental and vested interests that stopped the Caledonian Power Bill before the war, enabling Johnston to set up the publicly owned North of Scotland Hydro-Electric Board in 1943.

The public sector in medicine was extended; the Scottish Office gained planning powers, set up planning groups for the major Scottish regions well in advance of legislation and liaised subtly with de Valera's Eire, neutral but critical to the UK's food and labour supply.

Was all this a move towards formal devolution which Johnston's successors betrayed? Not really. Johnston disliked London government, but preferred efficient administration to 'partisan political strife'. His Scottish success coincided with the capture of the 'commanding heights' of Whitehall by moderate collectivists – which Paul Addison has seen as crucial to Labour's 1945 victory – building on Labour's Scottish local authority captures. The system that resulted – a form of 'government by consultation' – incorporated local Labour and guaranteed the key policies that sustained it: low-rent council housing and denominational schools. It was confirmed by Labour's sweeping victory in the 1945 election, dispelling (for the time being) the nationalist apparition, and cutting the Unionists from forty-two seats to thirty.

Johnston left politics in 1945, subsequently becoming head of the Scottish Tourist Board, the Scottish Forestry Commission and, in 1948, the Hydro Board. In 1946 the Scottish labour movement lost two other major figures. One represented a body that, because of his activities, had steadily grown in influence; the other's party died with him.

The STUC

William Elger, by descent Austrian, became General Secretary of the STUC in 1922. A small and rather decrepit body, dating back to 1897, it differed from the British TUC in including trades councils as well as unions. If it were to survive it would have to establish its independent status. Elger's first survey of trade unionism revealed in 1942 that only about one-third of the Scottish workforce (c. 500,000) was unionised, and of this number only 290,659 were affiliated to the STUC: there was 'no Trade Union Movement as distinct from Unions'. The relatively non-militant east was better unionised than the 'wild red West'; and traditional Scottish unions were decaying in old industrial sectors, like the eleven different unions in textiles, against four English ones. In growing sectors like public employment English unions had a monopoly. Elger concentrated on building up a Scottish 'movement' by winning over sceptical English unions to affiliation, even at the cost of amalgamations between them and Scottish unions. By 1939 he could look back on a 33.8 per cent increase in affiliated membership while the labour force rose by only 10 per cent (the British TUC's affiliates rose by only 5 per cent), and a position in which the STUC had become a respectable part of the government's consultation framework.

This was not unanimous. In the trades councils, Communists were firmly entrenched and occasionally exercised control. Initiatives to secure backing for the National Unemployed Workmen's Movement were sustained but unsuccessful, and attempts to dissuade the STUC from co-operating with 'class enemies' like Lithgow and Bilsland by joining the Scottish Economic Committee in 1936. An executive member, C. W. Gallie of the National Union of Railwaymen, put the STUC's choice succinctly: 'Were they to sit quietly by until they ushered in Socialism and found themselves the possessors of a bunch of derelict industries?' This became a text for STUC policy. Firmly in a minority on the SEC, on the creation of the Scottish Council in 1942 the STUC was strengthened, and its consultative role was enhanced by the post-war Labour government.

The post-war left

The other death was that of Jimmie Maxton. In the Commons his lank, unkempt figure, his wit and his humanity symbolised the 'decency' and moral passion of the left, the spirit of the 'Red Clyde' glowering out of its mists in Lavery's famous portrait. His ILP had for a time that other thorny moralist, George Orwell, as a member. But as a party it was dead. In 1938 its MPs had negotiated to rejoin Labour, but Maxton's pacifism would not accept Labour's conversion to rearmament. When he died, its two remaining members took the Labour whip. Campbell Stephen died in 1948, and the Unionists won his seat. John McGovern, its most undisciplined MP, moved rightwards and ended as an exhibit on Moral Rearmament platforms, testifying to the evils of Communism.

Paradoxically, 1945 seemed to end Labour's golden age. Its personalities were dead or had retreated to the fringes. The local party structure, with its newspapers, choirs, theatre groups and cycling clubs, had largely collapsed. In the 1950s Glasgow had maybe as few as 500 activists: not unwelcome to local councillors who wanted a quiet life, and whose financial probity was not always above criticism – a sequence of corruption trials in Glasgow in the late 1930s and early 1940s made Johnston threaten to rule the place with commissioners. Organisers cast in the mould of Sir Patrick Dollan, Arthur Woodburn and William Marshall concentrated on organisation and discipline at the expense of participation and ideas. The time of the 'wee hard men' had come.

Electoral success compensated Labour – but not the Liberals. Archie Sinclair was an effective air minister in the Churchill coalition, but took little interest in Scottish affairs, rarely attended the Council of State and lost Caithness in 1945. Dingle Foot (brother of Michael) lost the party's other Scottish seat at Dundee. 'The old fire of Liberalism, which had burned so ardently during the great days of the Midlothian campaign, was now almost extinct', noted Alison Readman – even after an Edinburgh meeting feting the party's most notable MP, William Beveridge. An energetic campaign in 1950 got next to nowhere. Liberals gained two seats – though one was Jo Grimond's in Orkney and Shetland – and lost thirty deposits. Need the collapse have been so great? Possibly not, as after the war liberalism of a sort had a remarkable revival.

The Covenant movement

From the pre-war SNP, John MacCormick had courted the Liberals. In 1937 he negotiated a pact with Lady Glen-Coats allowing his party a free run in twelve constituencies of its own choice, and after leaving the SNP he stood as a Liberal in Inverness in 1945. His 'Scottish Convention', backed by big names outside political nationalism such as Sir John Boyd Orr, Naomi Mitchison and Professor John MacMurray, and expertly served in its economic intelligence by James Porteous, formerly of the Scottish Economic Committee, carried on steady pro-home-rule propaganda: its goal to revive the aborted convention of 1939. In 1947 it took place, with 600 delegates, broadly representative of the churches, local government, the Co-operatives and liberal opinion in general. The following year its second meeting approved a Covenant demanding home rule within a federal system, and at the third meeting, in October 1949, attended by 1,200 delegates, this was ceremonially signed. Subsequently it gained two million names. But the general elections of 1950 and 1951 supervened without any home-rule intervention. This was disastrous: by the time MacCormick had produced a continuing organisation, the impetus had passed. The fact that many Labour opponents gave aid to the Covenant movement prejudiced Labour against it from the start. In December 1947 MacCormick had stood against Labour at Paisley as a 'National' candidate. Paisley had a traditionally high Liberal vote, but by accepting Unionist support he alienated it. Though he ran Labour close, his opponents didn't forget.

Joe Westwood succeeded Johnston. He had been a good deputy to him but fell ill and couldn't catch up, and Attlee sacked him – laconically: 'You weren't up to the job' – in October 1947. Arthur Woodburn succeeded him. As Secretary of Labour's Scottish Council he had given guarded endorsement to home rule during the war. He now rejected it, but used the Convention – 'a kind of smouldering pile that might suddenly break through the party loyalties and become a formidable national movement' – to persuade the cabinet to create a short-lived Scottish Economic Conference and to widen the scope of the Scottish Grand Committee. For over forty years it only handled the committee stages of non-controversial Scottish Bills; now it could debate them at second reading – if the House as a whole approved – and debate the Scottish estimates. This still failed to check Scottish Convention, or Unionists protesting against the centralisation of the Labour government's nationalisation policies. 'I should never adopt the view,' Churchill told Edinburgh electors in the 1950 campaign, 'that Scotland should be forced into the serfdom of socialism as a result of a vote in the House of Commons'. After the election Attlee replaced Woodburn with Hector McNeil, a Beaverbrook journalist who had done well as Bevin's junior at the Foreign Office. He had little time to prove himself; on 26 October 1951 Labour went out of office.

The year 1950 was not to be the last time that a Unionist leader played around with the emotions of nationalism, but Unionists' recovery was slow, aided by Labour as it organised in rural areas and split the anti-Tory vote. The Unionists recovered to peak with a whisker over half the seats and votes in 1955, but they were drifting from urban, industrial Scotland. They lacked Labour's connection to municipal politics, in which the right wing was still represented by local 'Progressive' or 'Moderate' parties. But war and post-war growth in agriculture had created a powerful interest which required central representation. Rational reasons, but also constricting ones.

A PART OF THE WHOLE? 1950–64

The 1950s were tranquil. The romantic episode of the snatching of the Stone of Destiny from Westminster Abbey in 1950 – in which MacCormick was involved – proved to be the swansong of the Covenant movement. On coming to power in 1951 the Conservatives set up the Balfour Commission into Scottish affairs, but removed home rule from its remit; the result modestly expanded the powers of the Scottish Office, regulating electricity in 1954 and roads in 1956. The evening of the heavy industries gave a stability absent for nearly half a century, partly through beating Labour at its own game. Secretary Stuart humoured Churchill, got on well with Labour MPs, exceeded their housing programme by over a third and secured substantial transport

investment: the Forth Road Bridge and Glasgow railway electrification. The fundamental economic and social problems of the
country slumbered.

The icy years of 'austerity' lost Labour Glasgow and other big
local authorities (a gradual process: only a third of councillors
were elected annually). In the early 1950s it won them back, for
fifteen years, but its spokesmen were less effective. McNeil virtually left politics for business; his successor, Tom Fraser, though
an able administrator, was unaggressive. Scottish political torpor
may have been deceptive, but coincided with the development of
'behaviourist' political sociology, derived from America. This
assumed a growing degree of British 'political homogeneity' –
with voters increasingly conditioned by 'common' factors like
social class, and 'consumerist' choices between parties replacing
sectional and regional issues. Scotland seemed part of the whole.

In the later 1950s the economic situation worsened, and
the Labour movement got more aggressive, partly because of
an earthquake in the Communist Party. Still subject to 'Cold
War' proscriptions, the CPGB retained many wartime recruits
and in 1956 had 10,000 members in Scotland, a quarter of the
UK total. Although electorally unsuccessful – Gallacher had
lost West Fife in 1950 – its leading figures were hard-working,
well-briefed on the Scottish economy and more corruption-
resistant than their Labour comrades. But in 1955 and 1956
Khrushchev's denunciation of Stalin and the Russian invasion
of Hungary forced many activists to leave the party. One
result was the 'New Left' which grew up around the universities, contributing to developments as diverse as the folk-song
revival and the Campaign for Nuclear Disarmament; another
was Labour's acquisition of several hundred competent and
radical activists. (In 1965, for example, the President, Secretary
and Vice-President of Edinburgh City Labour Party were all
ex-Communists.) The result energised the left, but could those
who had obeyed the Kremlin for decades also provide imagination and originality?

This was also true for trade unions. The STUC grew faster
than the TUC. Its affiliated membership from 1939 to 1959

increased by 128 per cent against 93 per cent. Elger's policy of co-operation with the Scottish Council and the Scottish Office was continued by his successor George Middleton, and the STUC, as 'honest broker' to incoming companies, ensured that non-union shops met union rates of pay and conditions. It and many trades councils were strongly anti-Communist until the mid-50s but ex-Communists steadily pushed it leftwards, and developed links with unions in eastern Europe. This shift was accelerated by economic downturn after 1958, but Middleton (who looked like an ogre but was the STUC's Metternich) turned matters round through charming Harold Macmillan, helping direct industries north *and* creating a regional planning consensus. The influence of the left also meant the return of home rule, traditionally backed by the Communists, to the STUC's programme in the 1960s, but the importance of this should not be exaggerated: union pressure had always been directed at equalising Scottish and English wage rates. Regional wage bargaining, a central feature of German devolution, was never acceptable. Whatever their declarations to the contrary, unions were unionist.

Between 1958 and 1959 Scottish unemployment doubled. 'You've never had it so good' didn't go down well that October, and Labour won four Unionist seats. Although Macmillan and his Scottish Secretary John Maclay exerted themselves to establish new industry, introduced the concept of economic planning, using Alec Cairncross, one of the 1930s pioneers, and reorganised the Scottish administrative machine to cope, they were frustrated by other parts of their own government's programme, such as Beeching's drastic railway cuts and the run-down of the coal industry. Although it got widespread support in Scotland, the Toothill Report (1961) was not infallible, but scarcely had Maclay announced in March 1962 the creation of the Scottish Development Department (taking over planning and housing from the Department of Health, and roads, electricity and local government from the Home Department) he vanished in Macmillan's July purge. His inexperienced successor, Michael Noble, not only faced incessant attacks from Labour benches, after March 1963 well co-ordinated by William Ross, but increasing indiscipline in his own ranks.

As rural Unionism was now more an interest group than a political force, it was vulnerable to a rise in the political temperature. In the early 1960s the Liberal revival was at hand. The party hit a low during the 1950s, although a popular candidate, like the broadcaster and former rugby internationalist John M. Bannerman, could produce an occasional good result. But under Jo Grimond, charismatic if a bit Olympian, after 1957 it showed its teeth. As a result, indiscipline and individual protests on the Unionist backbenches grew, until Scottish debates tended to become a martyrdom for ministers. Labour, too, was pressed – in April 1961 Bannerman ran them very close at Paisley – but a clutch of by-election setbacks promised Unionist humiliation in the approaching general election. In this respect at least the 'evolution' of Sir Alec Douglas-Home as premier in October 1963, after Macmillan's enforced retirement, served Unionism well. Under an antique exterior, Home had the unsentimentality of his class, and spoke to the agricultural interest. Unfathomable to the political correspondents who followed his election campaign in Kinross and West Perth, it helped secure him a triumph.

The Unionists did not do too badly in 1964. Labour gained three seats from them (a lower swing than in the north of England) and the Liberals gained three, coming second in another eight. The SNP, a lowly presence in Scottish elections during the 1950s, but second to Labour in the West Lothian by-election of February 1962, performed poorly, giving little forecast of the trouble it would cause by 1967. But a closer look would show an accession of membership, money and organisational ability, under the imaginative leadership of William Wolfe and Ian MacDonald, while on the Liberal side there was a growing divergence between its Scottish support and British aims. Its successes showed that a strong radicalism still subsisted beneath the two-party system, with home rule an important component. Yet Grimond and his successors still looked south, and to the notion (apparently demonstrated at Orpington in March 1962) of capturing the English suburbs. Their failure to concentrate on a Scottish programme repeated Sinclair's mistake in the 1930s and would imperil them, just as Labour would be hoist by the expectations of planning and social welfare it had created.

DRAMATIS PERSONAE

Twentieth-century Scottish politicians didn't have a good press: observers have often contrasted the social irrelevance of the Unionist gentry and lawyers and the inarticulacy of Labour with the frontbenchers of the pre-World War I period. But the latter's 'fortnight once a year' attentions were only possible when the role of government was limited. When Scotland got more politically unstable, frontbenchers left. (In 1910 over half of Scottish MPs lived in England; by 1979 less than 10 per cent.) The Unionist response had logic: switching from business to agriculture paid. Labour's fall in prestige was not due to the party becoming more proletarian, though it suffered from the southward shift of trade union authority. In 1922 its MPs were dominated by miners' agents; in 1964 by local councillors. More than a third of its MPs were 'middle class' in 1922, two-thirds in 1964. A further decline derived from two factors. After 1945 the party was centrally controlled by a small but very well-organised Oxford-educated elite, which (with a five times better chance of office) never made up less than a third of most cabinets. Secondly, the growth of Scottish government absorbed Scottish MPs, creating conventions which barred them from 'British' portfolios in areas devolved to the Scottish Office, such as education or housing.

The press assaulted Scots MPs for silence in parliament. This was unfair. While they spoke less on non-Scottish subjects, they worked hard in the Scottish committees (new ones were added in 1957 and 1962) and on questions to ministers. Questions to the Secretary quadrupled between 1924 and 1962, reflecting his increased powers *and* population distribution. In 1924 (when there were thirty-four Labour MPs) nearly two-thirds of questions concerned the Highlands. Business MPs, overwhelmingly Liberal in 1911, had drifted by the 1920s to the Unionists, whose land and agriculture support held up to the 1960s. Labour MPs represented the organisers of manual workers (18 per cent) rather than workers themselves. Fifteen years after the creation of the Scottish Parliament at Holyrood, its second-biggest single category (16 per cent) was 'political professionals' who had never studied or practised anything else. Was there a difference? Between 1955 and 1964 Labour made Scottish Question Time, with every inquiry wired up to supplementaries, a distinctive and deadly tactic.

The members of local authorities were similar to MPs, their status even lower. In the mid-1970s the 'Progressives' dwindled, while independents ran most county and district councils. After 1929 county power shifted from gentry and ministers to farmers and retailers, outweighed by growing numbers of permanent officials – medical officers, surveyors, directors of education. In the burghs capital shifted from manufacturing to trade; and, after 1945, as house-building and redevelopment increased, to construction. Labour councillors tended to be lower-middle rather than working class: small businessmen, union officials and housewives. Both sides were cramped by the fact that the 'state sector middle class' – teachers, civil servants, council employees – was banned from local office until 1974. The exclusion of a group which provided about 20 per cent of Labour MPs in the 1960s unquestionably harmed Labour in particular – as did the fact that many councillors were employees of council contractors, who thus reinforced their interest.

Twenty per cent of Edinburgh councillors in 1960 were women. Their local government role grew, but their parliamentary role stagnated. At no time were there more than five women MPs (6 per cent) and after 1983 there were only two – although in terms of numbers elected (13.5 per cent of UK women MPs) and years served (11.7 compared with 11.1 UK average) Scotland's record was actually a little better than its macho image, and the trade unions' persistent neglect of women's issues, would suggest. But Scandinavian women were, by the 1960s, over 20 per cent of MPs: this influenced the role of women in the SNP, where they were three out of thirteen MPs between 1967 and 1979.

By 1964 'St Andrew's House' had become 'Dublin Castle', with 7,000 civil servants under its sway, terminus of most inquiries from MPs and councillors, a dynamic in environmental, educational and economic planning growing after 1957, culminating in the Toothill Report. John Mackintosh and others accused it of subservience to Whitehall, yet against Whitehall's secrecy and lack of professional specialism, the Scottish Office's problem-oriented structure made it potentially more flexible. Still, while not an Oxbridge fief – only about 20 per cent of its senior staff, compared with over 50 per cent in Whitehall – did it have the planning and economic skills that new commitments demanded? Scottish administration has still (in 2015) to be anatomised, but tended to draw directly from the Scottish universities, reflecting their deficiencies in the social sciences and the inflections of the Edinburgh professions. Only in the 1970s did it get an adequate economic intelligence department under Gavin McCrone.

Two biographies provide a worrying insight into the development of this secretive institution. John Highton became Permanent Under-Secretary under Elliot in 1936. Working class in background (his brother was Chairman of Glasgow Trades Council) he organised unemployment investigations and adult education in his spare time. He could have given administrative shape to Elliot's innovations, but tragically died after a short time in office. George Pottinger, a dynamic figure of the 1960s, candidate for Permanent Under-Secretary, cultivated an impressive lifestyle. At his trial in 1975 it emerged that for years he had earned £30,000 from the corrupt Yorkshire architect John Poulson. Of this, his colleagues and superiors were unaware. Highton was the sort of administrator the Scottish Office needed. Pottinger was led to his downfall by aspiring to Edinburgh upper-class values. He was not to be the last.

As Scots MPs – especially from Labour – were fairly homogeneous, why did it take until the 1960s for a 'Scottish interest' to emerge? Lack of leadership seems critical. For Max Weber 'imperative co-ordination' – the acceptance of common goals and discipline – depended on a 'charismatic leader'. Parnell in 1880s Ireland linked peasantry, local leaders, Church, exile politicians and MPs: machinery that survived his fall in 1890. Tom Ellis and David Lloyd George might have done the same for Wales in the 1890s, but were weakened by their co-option into UK politics. Neither had a Scottish parallel: the Clydesiders didn't attempt to lead Scottish Labour in the 1920s; there were few to lead in the 1930s. Johnston came close to the Weberian pattern in 1941–5, but chose not to develop a political movement.

What inhibited leadership? The constraints of Scottish working-class consciousness? A relatively open entry into the southern elite, which drew the politically and administratively able away – particularly between the wars? For those who stayed, law, local government, education and the Kirk offered secure and influential niches, but MPs who tried to build up a party following in Scotland as well as at Westminster ran mortal risks. Elliot and Johnston lived beyond sixty-five, but William Graham, Hector McNeil and John Mackintosh died in their forties; Wheatley, Maxton, Keir Hardie, Noel Skelton, Elger, MacCormick and John Smith at around sixty. Stress-based illnesses damaged or ended enough careers to suggest that the lifestyle damaged party politics – particularly on the left – more than the other power bases of Scottish society.

For the traditional institutions had their own elites, too. The reunited Church now eschewed party politics, but it still pronounced on political issues. Although two UF ministers – Campbell Stephen and James Barr – were prominent Labour MPs, they dissented from Church unity, and no ministers followed them into parliament. The lawyers showed their solidarity in 1931, when the Lord Advocate, Craigie Aitchison, the Solicitor-General and most of the Advocates Depute left Labour to join the National Government. Yet Labour still loved a lawyer; in 1936 another advocate, Robert Gibson, was chairman of its Scottish executive. Finally, after 1918, educational politics intensified, with the incorporation of the

Catholic schools, the shifting of the SED to Edinburgh, the Education Authority experiment, central salary negotiations and the growing unionisation of the teaching profession. Yet the result was impenetrability, not dynamism.

Did party majorities matter more than leaders? Probably not. Tom Johnston, leading a minority party from 1941 to 1945, was a success when the Liberal Secretaries of World War I, with huge majorities, flopped. In 1974–9, Labour's eleven-seat majority couldn't counter Bruce Millan's anaesthetic effect on the devolution debate. The Secretary of State was critical. Until 1964, when his Welsh counterpart was created, he uniquely controlled a wide range of government functions and patronage. But as party manager, administrative reformer or national leader? The first role – the line of least resistance? – was taken by the weakest. The second, Elliot as Under-Secretary in the 1920s, meant co-operating with local authorities and creating an administrative cadre. This precedent was followed *de facto* by Collins, Johnston, Woodburn, McNeil and Maclay, and as a matter of principle by Willie Ross: the consensus favoured collectivist reform. But Johnston and Ross also encouraged a *Scottish* will-towards-change: problems came when, with expectations raised, the machine didn't deliver the goods.

Finally, Labour needed an ideological substitute for elite solidarity. Practically all Unionist Secretaries were drawn from, or had married into, the Scottish landed and commercial establishment. They knew how to serve its needs. In the case of the best of them, Elliot, there was an intellectual input from pre-1914 'civic consciousness'. Hence the liveliness of his collaboration with its professional representatives, such as Boyd Orr or Grierson. Until 1941 Labour lacked a socialist concept of Scottish government (Adamson was dim right-wing trade unionism personified) or an explicit power base. Johnston, Dollan and Elger created one, but their pragmatism ruled out policy evolution, not only about home rule, but about any challenge to the powerbrokers in councils and unions. This sterility meant that, when its plans turned sour after 1966, Labour lay open to the challenge of the SNP.

5

Mass Media: High Culture, 1922–64

OUT OF THE SOUTERRAIN

Visitors to Holyrood often find Enric Miralles's entrance hall dark and crypt-like, but he said he wanted to trace Scotland's story to its earliest stone buildings, the 'souterrains', trenches roofed with stone slabs. And indeed spirits rise later as light and space are juggled, and glass waves break between parliament's towers like the surges of a northern voe. An image from my first edition recurs – the great stained-glass windows, *Ethnology*; *Philology*; *History* of Eliel Saarinen's National Museum in Helsinki, 1901–11: Finnish liberals giving their nationalism an intellectual-symbolist basis by concentrating on the descent, language customs and society of their people. In 1911 three million, mainly peasants; by 2010 5.5 million and a per capita GDP 7 per cent higher than Scotland.

Both images implied a process of selection; an exercise in intellectual hegemony. Scotland added something different in aim, though not in actual outcome: the 'great tradition' of British intellectuals invoking 'culture as the great hope in our present difficulties' – close enough to Edinburgh High School's *'Musis Res Publica Floret'*: the intention of Carlyle, Mill, Ruskin, Geddes and so on being to combat tendencies towards materialistic, capitalist and class-divided politics by positing cultural excellence as a 'common pursuit'.

Scotland in 1914 fitted neither tradition, although expatriate Scots largely created the second. No longer a peasant society, its popular culture still stood apart from that of England. The position of the intellectuals within it stemmed from the coincidence of the industrial impact with their ambivalence towards cultural nationalism, not just – as in politics – to Westminster. Post-1914 the nation exerted its pull, but was countered by this 'world culture'. The result would be an intellectual dialectic, a 'Scottish Renaissance' of enormous quality and interest, although its links to politics and culture stayed complex and unsatisfactory.

POPULAR CULTURE AND THE LEGACY OF WAR

Working-class culture, before 1914, was deeply divided: between rural and urban, between respectable and rough, between Catholic and Protestant, between men and women. Landward the literary culture was limited: Littlejohn found in *Westrigg* in the late 1940s that its staples were still the Bible and Burns. Long working hours meant that the same was probably the case elsewhere, though folk song survived in the 'bothies' of the north-east and among tinkers and fisher-folk. But the oral tradition had problems in the machine shop and the mine: the male industrial worker had the choice between respectability and roughness, meaning drink. The first meant 'improvement', through the churches, adult education or the labour movement. But it always struggled against difficult living and working conditions.

Roughness underlined the sheer starkness of working-class life. Football, the 'bevvy', the sluggish Sunday – these were emotional escapes rather than a form of socialisation. There was no elaborate pub society, such as Brian Harrison has described in England. In Scotland the architectural magnificence of pubs was strictly proportionate to the drinkers' income. Instead, devoutness and drink were frequent doppelgangers, among Catholic and Free Churchman alike. Spirit drinking – as in Scandinavia – and 'wee haufs' helped overcome foul weather and draughts (for a majority of Scots males probably worked in the open), and tiny crowded houses. If the result was a certain social inadequacy, it would have been much worse but for the women.

They created a home life and a sort of community politics, even if only through policing by gossip. They stayed away from drink and crime, saved, taught (taking over primary schoolteaching by 1914), organised their families, read and wrote. 'Annie S. Swan', a much-mocked Kailyarder, published 162 novels, had a male alter-ego 'David Lyall' with another forty and a further career as Liberal, home ruler and suffragist. Women were a coiled spring.

War broke up many of these divisions. Although it breached religious sanctions, it also gained some goals of the temperance movement: liquor control and stringent licensing cut heavy drinking. There was one pub to every 424 Scots in 1900; by 1955 there would be one to 806; while drunkenness convictions declined tenfold to 2.6 to every 1,000. Both as cause and consequence of this more cash was spent on other recreations.

Women's wartime gains included access to new leisure: initially the cinema which impacted after 1910 (two pioneers survive, in Bo'ness and Campbeltown). And along with Liberal-Kirk rule there departed much of the power of the churchgoing middle class to control the weekend. Catholics were flexible about the Sabbath, and so was the petrol engine. In 1910 only twenty-one Sunday trains had run on the Caledonian Railway, but buses ran on Sunday and motorists drove whenever they liked. Bus tours – for sport, sightseeing or drinking – car trips to country tearooms, mountaineering and hiking gave urban Scots access to recreations previously confined to the well-off or determinedly secular.

OUTLETS

Sport

If sport of various sorts dominated Scottish leisure time, partly because there was a large land area relative to population, Scotland had been, next to Switzerland, 'the playground of Europe' for the Victorians. A sportive ethos had been created, even if it was initially socially restrictive. It is worth looking at the detail, as it turned up with publicity, and theory. There were three main areas: leisure-class activities, mainly field sports; spectator sports; and participant sports. The first in theory involved participants, royalty at their centre – did any other ruling class go in for such desolation to keep up social boundaries? About 60 per cent of rural Scotland (rock, water, heather) was grouse moor or deer forest: important to the Highland economy, a hindrance to its development and an essential part of Scottish upper-class life. Yachting was more middle class, useful to Clyde ship- and boat-building, even experimental. If the middle classes fished a lot, they seem to have done little shooting, and hunted rarely if at all. To judge by *Scottish Biographies* (1938), participation in sport seems to have been, in Scotland much more than in England, a badge of respectability. Thirty-seven per cent of a random sample of entries played golf, 17.5 per cent fished. Only 2 per cent and 1 per cent admitted to an interest in music or art. But then, only 1 per cent said they followed football.

For most Scotsmen, sport meant football. Watching and discussing it took up much of the weekend; it filled a third of the popular press. Save in the Borders, rugby union was middle class; cricket less so (miners liked to play *in white*) but mainly east coast. Shinty stayed in the Highlands – unlike hurling in Ireland, there was no nationalist attempt at 'Scottish' sports. Football defined class, gender, religion and nationality, and ritualised and contained all of these. Its golden age was 1920–39, years of potential social upheaval. Was it a paradigm of Scotland's situation: skilled men underpaid by local oligarchies, clearing off to richer fields abroad, like the old mercenaries? Inter-war internationals with England, twelve out of twenty won by the Scots, were often the only times the best players represented their countrymen. For George Blake in *The Shipbuilders* (1935), the crowd at 'ra gemme' – drink, swearing and all – stood for the values of the skilled workers: decadence meant the new greyhound tracks, perverted to easy money. Only with TV did gates start to fall – by over 30 per cent between 1955 and 1965. So football tended to become an affirmation of working-class solidarity, a central conversation – with specialist satellites, such as bowls, pigeon-racing, competitive gardening – all badges of artisan worth.

Churches encouraged football, notably in the Boys' Brigade (1873) to ward off threats from drink, employment problems and radicalism. But the same people stiffened social boundaries by imposing rugby on senior secondary schools. They may have seen the enemy as commercialism – football pools took on in working-class homes from the 1920s – and their goal may have been the 'democratic game' of the Borders, but the headmasters forgot that rugby needs grass if it is not to be murderous, while football simply needs a ball. Aristocrats didn't have such scruples, and was rewarded. The fifth Earl of Rosebery was popular in Scotland despite his racehorses, his son because of them, although off-course gambling was not made legal until 1969.

Other participatory sports expanded, admitted women, but remained class-bound, because of expense. Tennis, like curling in winter, spread from the upper to the middle class. With the help of municipal courses, golf filtered further down. The golf club remained a major centre of middle-class socialising – and women's self-organisation. Only in the 1960s did sailing and winter sports cease to be the preserve of the well-off, but rowing and amateur athletics, out of the same stable as the Boys' Brigade and YMCA, involved all classes. Aptly enough, Scotland's greatest runner of the inter-war years, Eric Liddell, forfeited an Olympic gold medal in 1924 by refusing to run on a Sunday. Swimming, in heated baths, a by-product of the public health movement, was the most democratic participatory sport, in which Motherwell, in particular, did well.

Indoor entertainment

Enthusiasm for sport was a blow struck against a malign climate. Indoor entertainment, and the cinema in particular, had technology as well as unemployment on its side; it offered warm and reasonably harmless refuge from drink and overcrowding. Theatres and music halls either withered or blossomed into this new life. Glasgow's fourteen fell to nine in 1940, though some of her sentimental singers and alarmingly ethnic comedians put up a strong fight. The winter pantomimes of such as Tommy Lorne and Will Fyffe virtually merged into their summer seasons at holiday resorts. But by 1929, when talkies arrived, Glasgow had 127 cinemas. Large burghs had three or four apiece by the 1940s, and even the smallest burghs had a 'fleapit' which might once have been a church (in Melrose) or a brewhouse (in Kelso). Even the wilds were reached by the travelling projectors of the Highlands and Islands Film Service. To the Scots the movies were magic. In 1950 Glasgow people went on average fifty-one times a year, and Scots as a whole thirty-six times, while the English paid only twenty-eight visits.

Reports on Scottish youth dwelt on the evils of 'corruption by Hollywood'. Certainly, Scottish cinemagoers were more likely to be corrupted from across the Atlantic than from England. They disliked British films save where these dealt with Scottish themes, and the western wasn't far from the old ballads. There was also a real commitment to film culture, with a leftish film society showing continental films – Eisenstein, Fritz Lang – in Glasgow in 1929, and an 'art' cinema, the Cosmo, opening in 1939.

As important, and like the cinema a 'mixed' activity, was 'The Dancing'. It gripped Scotland in the 1920s and only died with the ballroom style in the 1960s. Young men in their 'paraffin' – three-piece suits and slicked-down hair – and girls would flock, up to six nights a week, to huge dance halls. Glasgow had thirty; in some you could dance for six hours for sixpence. Liquor was banned, anything sexy frowned on; the stress was on skill and style – a classy evening break from 'getting by'. Some dance halls saw clashes between gangs, graphically described in MacArthur and Long's *No Mean City* (1934), whose 'Razor King' would only dance with men. Most halls were fiercely respectable, and Glasgow dancers were by World War II reckoned the best in Britain, if – as Neal Ascherson remembered – challenged by Polish soldiers: 'They had wonderful manners, and they danced like Fred Astaire.'

Literacy and its uses

At the time of the 1872 Education Act 14 per cent more Scots children than English children were at school. This leaven affected popular culture for two generations. The Scots were at home with the 'freedom' of the word, Carlyle as much as Calvin. They endowed literacy, organised it. Public esteem was reflected in splendid libraries, while popular spread came through such mass-market publishers as Collins, Nelsons and Blackies, booksellers and newsagents, and a thriving demotic literature. Libraries had featured since 'improvement' and expanded in the 1900s through donations and state action. Andrew Carnegie presented whole buildings with their books to the larger burghs, while J. & P. Coats gave every parish school shelves of classic works (religion excluded). Finally the 1918 Education Act made school libraries part of the county system, and enlarged them. Dunbartonshire had a private endowment at Helensburgh, two Carnegie libraries at Dumbarton and Clydebank, and a municipal one at Kirkintilloch, and after 1918 added ninety branches in schools and a mobile branch. They were a good investment; inspiring the bairns, consoling the unemployed, who could leaf through papers (with the racing pages pasted over) in the warmth. Utilisation figures didn't always mean literary awareness, but Scots were devoted readers; by 1960 Edinburgh held the UK record for books borrowed per head per annum: thirteen.

The Scots devoured 'the papers'; despite a lower living standard that reduced advertising revenue, they bought as many as anywhere in Britain and probably, in the central belt, even more: Glasgow was until 1957 the only city outside London with three evening papers. The Sunday paper story was remarkable. There were none in 1913, but by 1949 the *Sunday Post* claimed one of the most saturated markets in the world. Lack of advertising ought to have checked magazines, but the products of Thomson and Leng, the 'Dundee Press', went worldwide. Papers were national in tone, but not radical. Labour's *Daily Herald* never broke through but the *Daily Mail* set up a Scottish edition. In the 1920s Fleet Street rapidly took over mass-circulation papers, although Outrams of Glasgow and Findlays of Edinburgh, as well as Thomson and Leng survived. Only Outram's *Glasgow Herald* and Findlay's *Scotsman* were 'quality', with authoritative correspondents and reviewers and full political coverage; the others got by on local issues and sport. Beaverbrook's Glasgow incursion of 1928 caused a circulation war: 'human interest', crime and sport powered his episodically nationalist *Scottish Daily Express*. Scotsmen – George Malcolm Thomson, John Gordon, John Junor – were seniors in his black glass courts.

In 1900 T. W. H. Crosland accused the Scots literati in *The Unspeakable Scot* of 'journalising' all literature. William Donaldson has indeed shown how central the profession was to Scots literature from the 1840s on, with the weekly press a conduit of radical politics and popular enlightenment. By 1900, however, there was some loss of publishing nerve. Although Scots produced a disproportionate number of British books, they tended to specialise in religion and reprints (which often ended up as Sunday School prizes). Contemporary Scots authors had to approach the rather staid concerns of Oliver and Boyd and Blackwoods, but some exploited a shift south in the 1880s which helped create the modern 'literary industry' of agents, publicity and commercialism. And one genre of Scottish literature harvested it.

They key figure was Sir William Robertson Nicoll, his instrument Hodder and Stoughton. He bridged the perfervid mid-Victorians and London literary industry with the *British Weekly* (1886) and the *Bookman* (1891), drawing on the techniques of Scottish industry and the products of education. He brought women in, with the significantly titled *Woman at Home* (also in 1891). Thirty years later, in 'Hugh Selwyn Mauberly', Ezra Pound would pin him down as 'Dr Dundas'. Aptly, for Nicoll ran a new gravy train of patronage – literary, this time – to the south. His 'Kailyard' writers gained a market for the 'Scottish story': would-be authors were well aware of the payoffs.

The Kailyard went English-speaking worldwide: a literature whose content was established by market analysis. It was aimed at Scots, the emigrant community and an uncertain middle-class readership which worried about increasing social alienation and class-polarisation and wanted 'community'. Politically it was, like 'Annie S. Swan', Nicoll's henchperson, gently reformist.

MacDiarmid (brought up in Langholm library) thought the anti-Kailyard novels of George Douglas Brown and James Macdougall Hay, *The House with the Green Shutters* (1900) and *Gillespie* (1913), were 'the same thing disguised as its opposite', but fairly soon even this genre had been swallowed by it, in the novels of Jane Duncan and A. J. Cronin, readable and didactic. The Kailyard strain expanded into a disproportionate Scots presence in general-readership light fiction, from adventure stories through historical novels to animal tales and hospital romances. Behind Alastair MacLean, Nigel Tranter, Mary Stewart, Dorothy Dunnett, Gavin Maxwell, James Herriot and Lucilla Andrews might have been the shadowy lineaments of Stevenson, Scott, Dr John Brown and Mrs Oliphant, but what mattered was the literary machinery that Nicoll and his friends had set up. As time went on, it drew on the more proletarian Dundee Press: the same values with older and less respectable copy. In *The Uses of Literacy* (1957) Richard Hoggart noticed how Dundee's women's magazines specialised in serials where true love came with lots of blood: James Cameron, the greatest graduate of Thomson and Leng, remembered strict rules for drawings: slit throats yes, bare knees never.

Scottish leisure thus changed to cope with *some* increased income, changing relationships between the sexes and increased (if not always intended) free time. Accessible literature and spectacle mattered in a country of small houses. The alternative was organised social activity, provided municipally or commercially. Such commerce was partly Scots-run, as in football, or the revival of local Common Riding-style fests to ward off the slump of 1929–30, but its innovation was also increasingly dominated by large-scale English-run concerns.

Scotland was weak in family activities: gardening, for instance, increased, but not to the same extent as in England with her lower-density housing developments. Coarse fishing never became, as in the south, the most important participatory sport. Those who lived in the country, or could afford it, caught trout; the rivers and canals in the industrial areas were too polluted for carp or pike to survive. Hobbies requiring house room, like model engineering, woodworking, motor car maintenance and 'do-it-yourself' projects, were virtually ruled out. School inspectors criticised Scots girls as cooks and dressmakers, citing the same reasons. Domestic science classes in the schools were a response, but such factors probably explained a general skills decline in the working class. The state provided only inadequate technical education. Voluntary working-class education – through the Workers' Educational Association in its early years and the Marxist National Council of Labour Colleges – favoured political militancy and workshop organisation rather than acquiring new techniques or 'the full rich life'.

UPLIFT AND IMPROVEMENT

Although the expansion and diversification of popular entertainment certainly mitigated the tensions of the depression, it was not planned to do so. However, explicit attempts were made, by voluntary bodies and the state, to direct recreational activities in specific directions. These reflected the waning of traditional institutions of social co-operation, new technological possibilities and new client groups. The main diminution was of religious fervour. Although this had yet to register in terms of Church membership, and the churches still took a leading role in many of the developments to be surveyed, the primacy of 'controversial divinity' had vanished. Instead, the churches developed their social organisations, and some bodies traditionally connected with them provided paradigms for more secular developments.

The Freemason style expanded. Masonry had always been important in Scotland, with about 25 per cent of lodges in Britain and about 10 per cent of adult males as members. One of the few areas of interclass mixing, it increased through ex-servicemen's organisations, notably the British Legion. Such bodies could have become – as in France or Germany – intensely political. The

Legion, headed up by Earl Haig in 1921, provided social activities, quasi-masonic ritual and religious involvement which made it a conservative if mildly nationalist presence. Analogous groups like Rotary – an American import which brought together the 'leaders' of local trade and industry, and established itself very strongly from 1912 on – provided such 'non-political' (and by implication, conservative) bodies with a 'general staff'.

The Legion and Rotary accommodated women – though in separate and subordinate organisations. A similar logic led to the creation in 1918 of the Scottish Women's Rural Institutes. The Board of Agriculture had set them up to increase participation in the war effort, and they expanded until most parishes had branches. Like the Legion, their values resembled those of the legion, but they added a major Kailyard revival, the Community Drama movement, whose annual festival swelled from thirty-five competitors in 1926 to over 1,000 in 1936. Artistically such 'kitchen comedies' were rough and ready. They exploited playwrights, like the radical miner Joe Corrie, who had something serious to say, but before TV they reinforced the life of the Scottish parish.

There were no national youth organisations like the Czech Sokol or the Irish Fianna, although the socialist nationalist John Kinloch tried with Clan Scotland to create something like the Welsh Urdd, and the Scottish Youth Hostel movement, formed after the German model in 1931, had much of nationalism in its early days. But the real growth was in the Boys' Brigade and the Scouts (1908). Both expanded in the inter-war years, and added parallel girls' organisations. The 'BBs' were more urban and proletarian – a white belt and pillbox hat instead of the Scouts' pricey bushveldt gear; they had football, the Scouts had the royals, important in their rehabilitation after the *annus horribilis* of 1936. (A Jimmie Maxton motion to abolish them in 1937 got only ILP support.) As for the Socialist Sunday Schools (in Glasgow, naturally) where humanist hymns by such as Edward Carpenter were sung: they declined along with the ILP, and the Co-op's Woodcraft Folk couldn't compete with bugles and woggles. God had all the best tunes.

The failure of political culture was also evident in the weakness of 'serious journalism' – despite important Scots political reporters such as James Margach, Robert Carvel and Alastair Hetherington. There were no Unionist or Liberal magazines (no need, given the views of the press bosses) and the lefty papers, once so promising, steadily declined, although *Forward* and *Plebs* of the National Council of Labour Colleges limped on until the 1960s. It took individualists – John Wheatley, James Leatham, Guy Aldred – to run such papers, which usually died with them – though the Nationalists' *Scots Independent* has lasted since 1926.

'Institutional' papers thrived, but at the cost of parochialism. The Kirk had the monthly *Life and Work*, the Catholics the weekly *Glasgow Observer*, law the *Scots Law Times*, teachers the *Scottish Educational Journal*. In contrast to these, and to the situation in Wales and Ireland, shots at a national critical review failed, although there was usually a hopeful newcomer around to pick up the guttering torch. Between 1926 and 1934 William Power edited *The Scots Observer*, a well-meaning if ponderous bit of the literary revival; in 1934 the SNDC helped out with *Scotland*, which closed down during the war but performed respectably in the 1950s and 1960s. The left-wing Scottish Reconstruction Committee tried its hand with *New Scot* (1945–50), the Saltire Society with the *Saltire Review* and *New Saltire* (1954–64), but no formula seemed to gain a viable circulation. Dundee's *Scots Magazine* (founded 1739) had a dependable mixture of anecdote, local history and a huge exile sale. It, and for a time Outram's classier *Scottish Field*, proved much more successful.

Such cultural investment depended on patronage, and depression and the southward migration of capital dried this up. Edinburgh University, for instance, couldn't match the scale of the pre-war gifts of the Usher and MacEwan families. Support came from the University Grants Committee from 1918, and ensured that the situation didn't deteriorate further. State action also improved research facilities. Following the 1918 Education Act a Scottish Central Library was set up in 1921 to co-ordinate lending, and the National Library got its Act in 1925, taking over the 750,000 volumes of the Advocates Library. In 1936 its building, to the design of Reginald Fairlie, was started on George IV Bridge, Edinburgh. Because of the war, it took twenty years to complete. After 1956 Scottish researchers had – late in the day – the most convenient and efficient copyright library in Britain, housing seven million volumes.

The state's other major action was more ambiguous. Radio began in Scotland in March 1923 under the private British Broadcasting Company. In 1926 it was transformed into a public corporation. By 1936 it reached over 40 per cent of Scots homes. John Reith was Director-General until 1937, apostle of uplift and improvement, yet architect of an extremely centralised organisation. Although the BBC set up a Scottish Region, the promising attempts to marry its aims to those of the literary renaissance by David Cleghorn Thomson and Moray MacLaren ended in frustration. Under the regime of the Rev. Melville Dinwiddie (1933–57) the BBC in Scotland became a by-word for puritanical parochialism. Many staff stayed even longer than Dinwiddie. Uncles and Aunties became institutions, but at the expense of a service that could have coped better with Scotland's social and cultural problems. Its establishment-nominated Council typified the local branch of a centralised bureaucracy. If talented radicals could be silenced by promoting them to positions at the centre, who would complain, least of all at Broadcasting House?

THE SCOTTISH RENAISSANCE

A provincial culture, distinct from that of England for various reasons, rather than superior to it. An acute awareness among Scottish intellectuals of the power of parochialism and the mediocrity of its cultural values; a sense of attraction to and revulsion against the metropolis. These factors appear to be constant throughout our period. But they were made explicit by a sudden literary efflorescence and, despite its subsequent setbacks, this continued to sustain, and ultimately strengthen, the sense of a distinct national intellect.

World War I recruited Scottish literature as propaganda, if the work of the two Anglo-Scottish frontline poets C. H. Sorley and E. A. Mackintosh be excepted, while a Scots-Canadian medical officer, John McCrae, did create one unforgettable symbol, in the lines

In Flanders fields the poppies blow
Between the crosses, row on row . . .

At Craiglockhart Sanatorium in Edinburgh enlightened psychiatrists W. H. Rivers and A. J. Brock stimulated two battle-scarred officers – Siegfried Sassoon and Wilfred Owen – to publish, after popular literature had done its bit, with 'Ian Hay' and 'Spud Tamson'. John Buchan, uncomfortable Unionist, energetic war reporter and propagandist, loaded Richard Hannay with symbolism and sent him off to the Red Clyde, among other places, in *Mr Standfast* (1919): not wholly convincingly. The tragic impact of the war had to wait for over a decade to be commemorated, in Grassic Gibbon's *Sunset Song* (1932).

But before society had readjusted itself, total war and cultural radicalism gained an articulate aggressive voice. Christopher Murray Grieve, 'Hugh MacDiarmid', son of the Langholm postman, went from being a socialist journalist in 1914 to serve in Salonika. Reared in the library of the great engineer Telford, the war was for him 'the breaking of nations', as he battened on the literature, science and recent history of Europe and turned on Scotland a modernist international mind. His first anthology, *Northern Numbers* (1920), respected older literati like Buchan and Neil Munro; his third series sidelined them for a radical nationalist tone.

Behind this lay Ireland's war of independence (1919–21), economic depression and the didactics of John Maclean. Although James Connolly had been *Forward*'s Irish correspondent, the constitutional left had ignored the Rising and his sacrifice, but now his aim seemed to have succeeded. Poets and socialists had together pulled their country away from the English connection. In 1922 W. B. Yeats became a senator and was awarded the Nobel Prize, James Joyce published *Ulysses*, assaulting the preconceived limits of the English language. To MacDiarmid, associated with the radical *New Age* group, a centrifuge seemed to be at work; the hegemony of English, as well as of the empire, was collapsing. The parochialism of Scottish literary life would have to be destroyed. 'Dunbar, not Burns!', 'Not Traditions – Precedents!' were the watchwords of his *Scottish Chapbook* (1922). He laid down to the teachers of Scotland, between 1925 and 1927, the standards of a new culture to cure the nation and, no less, the world.

Thus far he resembled the great 'political' critics of nineteenth-century European literature – Carlyle, Belinsky, Brandes – but he also punched his message home with poetry of rare muscle and skill:

> O Scotland is
> The barren fig
> Up, carles, up
> And round it jig!
> . . .
> A miracle's
> Oor only chance.
> Up, carles, up
> And let us dance!

By 1925 the French critic Denis Saurat was writing of the 'Scottish Renaissance', a term which MacDiarmid promptly appropriated. For his aims were not simply the achievement of a national literature akin to that of Norway or Ireland, but something consonant with Scotland's recent industrial experience – Telford's 'great working academy' – to be realised by controversy and contradiction. He would confront the debased vernacular with the abstracted rationality of the Scots forced abroad by complacency and social failure. His aim was a perpetual unrest, 'a Caledonian antisyzygy' (he borrowed *that* from Professor Gregory Smith's *Scottish Literature* of 1919). There were other nationalist patrons, like William Power or Ruari Erskine of Mar, who nurtured any and every shoot of Scots literature. MacDiarmid flayed as well as encouraged.

Confessedly anti-English, he was also virulently anti-Scots, where the enemy was routine. This is cut into his tombstone:

I'll ha'e nae hauf-way hoose, but aye be whaur
Extremes meet – it's the only way I ken
To dodge the curst conceit o' bein' richt
That damns the vast majority o' men.

MacDiarmid could have ended isolated: there were many sad cases among the Victorian literati – but his self-confident initiative coincided with debate among talented publicists, home rulers and scholars not just about the Scottish economy but about the survival of nationality in face of the political centralisation induced by the war.

The foundation of Scottish PEN (1926) and the National Party of Scotland (1928) were possibly the key literary-political events, but the decade 1924–34 also saw MacDiarmid's 'A Drunk Man Looks at the Thistle' and his first and second 'Hymns to Lenin', the first novels of Neil Gunn, George Blake, Eric Linklater, Fionn MacColla and Naomi Mitchison, the critical writing of Edwin Muir and the early plays of James Bridie. And then, between 1932 and 1934, hammered straight onto a typewriter in a few weeks out of a short life, Lewis Grassic Gibbon's Mearns trilogy, later to be known as *A Scots Quair*.

What unified these, besides a degree of literary success which, if modest by British standards, hadn't been seen in Scotland since Walter Scott's *Waverley* and a general identification of literature with nationality? MacDiarmid wrote in 'The *Kulturkampf*: to William Power' (1935):

No man can state the truth of Scotland,
But he can establish some sort of relation
Between his truth and the absolute . . .

Artists cannot be taken out of their own times and places
To be shown around – just as the beauty of a tree
Cannot be made visible by uprooting the tree;
Here, they were shown together with their country.

Finding a voice in Scotland, as well as for Scotland, was crucial. Besides the war and the wounds it had dealt, besides resentment at the absence of home rule and the failings of political parties, there was rebellion against parental authority, fascination with sex (could be talked about, even enjoyed), a sheer desire to *write* the nation – much as women had used novel-writing to break their social isolation a century before.

'The Uncanny Scot' – MacDiarmid's achievement depended on a singular sort of mentality that cast back to Thomas Reid's 'common sense' of the eighteenth century: the ability to conceive of a situation as a *gestalt*. Maybe now diagnosable as high-functioning Asperger's, this was blended with rare social grace – 'He'll charm old ladies onto the mantelpiece. And leave them there', as Norman MacCaig put it. An escape from the aristocratic reaction of Yeats and Eliot presupposed Telford's technocracy – along with political militancy. MacDiarmid had seen the recovery of Lallans as both democratic and nationalistic; after the collapse of the General Strike in 1926 he moved to a position both more intransigent and more 'scientistic', lauding supermen just as Carlyle, his model in so many respects, lauded Cromwell and Frederick the Great.

After 1930 MacDiarmid rarely wrote in Lallans, but his relevance would shortly be dramatised by the achievement of Grassic Gibbon's trilogy. Like MacDiarmid, but eight years younger, Gibbon was an autodidact, struggling journalist and clerk in the services, all the time – aided by H. G. Wells – aiming at some great scientific world-view. He then fused his ideas, under intense pressure, onto the experience of Scotland. The result – *Sunset Song*, *Cloud Howe* and *Grey Granite* – like MacDiarmid's 'Drunk Man' combines the sweep of historical change – the transition from rural to urban, the General Strike, the collapse of the 1931 Labour government – with the grip of individuals' struggles with one another, with society or with the land itself, for their own identity.

Gibbon put revolution before nationalism, though his use of the Scots tongue proved its vitality. Yet the *Quair* ends ambiguous, even elegiac. Chris Guthrie, its central figure, returns to farm her father's Aberdeenshire croft, and seems to die. Her son, Ewan, leads a hunger march to London. The old rural life ends, the industrial struggle begins? Yet for Gibbon the rural life seems real, the industrial episodes two-dimensional. And MacDiarmid? The absorption in nature, in character, in the frontier spirit with which he invested his 'muckle toun' of Langholm, conflicts with his 'scientific materialism', his dogmatic, even inhumane, politics.

In 1936 Edwin Muir courted – and got – MacDiarmid's wrath by arguing, in *Scott and Scotland*, that the vernacular had no future. His premises actually resembled MacDiarmid's: English was a foreign language, in which the Scots were falsely articulate. Muir's only remedy was to condone assimilation. Given what MacDiarmid and Gibbon had done, this looked tactless, but Muir hit a weak point. The renaissance still failed to penetrate to the real matter of Scotland. The society that Gunn or MacColla or MacDiarmid or Gibbon celebrated was marginal to the urban life that the mass of the people now lived. Even the Kailyard had managed to make the transition which writers of much greater talent had failed to do. The Scottish Renaissance's failure to supply 'the great bourgeois novel' – anything comparable with the triumphs of Mann, Musil, Proust and Joyce – was not its own fault.

Doris Lessing pointed out that because Britain did not go through, or even seriously attempt, a centralised state formation in the nineteenth century, provincial gentry attitudes remained too strong for too long. Further, in Scotland, the skilled craft tradition, passing from the crofter to the weaver and the engineer, was part of an essentially 'planned' transition to industry and kept alive behaviour that was never wholly of industrial mass society. In *Grey Granite* (1934), Chris Guthrie rounds on an unemployed man: 'My class? It was digging its living in sweat while yours lay down with a whine in the dirt', she is speaking for more than the Mearns peasants – for a series of now-vanishing skills which even in the engine shops had more in common with those of the miller, blacksmith and ploughman than with those of the assembly-line operative. Although MacDiarmid asked in his 'Second Hymn to Lenin'

Are my poems spoken in the factories and fields
In the streets o' the town?
Gin they're no, then I'm failin' to dae
What I ocht to hae' dune

his ambition for his own poetry was rarely realised, and in fact was only intermittently held. The ordinary people still read the Dundee Press and went to Burns Suppers, while MacDiarmid's later poetry grew more cerebral and elitist: 'a sound like talking to God' was not something everyone could hear.

By 1936 the renaissance was over, and MacDiarmid an embittered exile in Shetland. Those whom it had stimulated continued to write – the best novels of Gunn, and the Gaelic poetry of Sorley MacLean and George Campbell Hay, were still to come. But they were no longer part of a movement. Scottish political nationalism, as if in reaction to the word's increasingly unpleasant European connotations, was moderate, centrist and not very effective. Despite the founding of the Saltire Society in 1935 and some patronage from Walter Elliot as Secretary of State, the revival took time to move out of literature into other fields. It had been as paradoxical a development as MacDiarmid had wished for. It was about Scotland, but needed the support of Anglo-Scots such as Buchan or Linklater who aided its writers when they might have been ignored in the north, and the advocacy of Ivor Brown, the Leavises and T. S. Eliot. It was about politics, but these were infinitely varied. MacDiarmid wrote great socialist poetry – 'The Ballad of the General Strike' (1926), yet he prefaced *Albyn, or the Future of the Scots* with texts from Barres and Maurras, pillars of the French right. Grassic Gibbon may have based the plot of *Sunset Song* on Gustav Frenssen's *Jörn Uhl* (1901, translated 1905), a German classic of the 'blood and soil' school favoured by the Third Reich – which also responded to the peasant societies of Eric Linklater and Neil Gunn, both blameless democrats. Linklater, Compton Mackenzie and above all James Bridie took on an ironic, convivial Tory style, rather in the manner of *Noctes Ambrosianae*, far removed from the Marxism of MacDiarmid and Gibbon. Elliot belonged here, but also christened the *Democratic Intellect* of the philosopher George Davie (1961), MacDiarmid's protégé, which heralded the nationalist revival of the 1960s.

Oddest of all, the renaissance showed men – particularly Gunn and Gibbon – writing sensitively about women, while their pub society still kept them in the kitchen. The best women writers, Rebecca West and Naomi Mitchison, still went south. But, just as the one fully aware person in 'A Drunk Man' is the poet's wife, the 'talky men' were kept in order by the quiet civil servant Helen Cruikshank, poet and secretary of Scottish PEN. It was shrewd of a later woman writer, Muriel Spark, to capture the spirit of 1930s Edinburgh in the Machiavellian Miss Jean Brodie, dabbling in authoritarian European politics, but getting her 'set' to think for themselves.

With the renaissance came another characteristic activity of nineteenth century nationalism – the compilation of a linguistic dictionary. Here was also 'transferred nationality': the apotheosis of standard English, the *Oxford English Dictionary* was the creation of one 'lad o' pairts', Sir James Murray, carried on by another, Sir William Craigie. In the 1920s Craigie returned to Scottish themes, and set about a *Dictionary of the Older Scottish Tongue*. MacDiarmid hailed this as reinforcing the literary revival: a conviction confirmed when Craigie circulated the imperial outposts of tartan nationalism, Burns Clubs and Caledonian Societies – and got two replies to 500 letters, both refusing to help. The dictionary compilers divided into two. Craigie's first volume came out between 1931 and 2002; the (post-1707) *Scottish National Dictionary* appeared between 1931 and 1975.

Yet a renaissance on a Florentine scale, which transforms an entire culture, requires patronage provided by economic growth, or political institutions that encourage the artists involved. Scotland's Medicis, if they had not moved south, were preoccupied with not going bankrupt. The money was not around to encourage the art forms that needed it. The literary renaissance came cheap; funds of an altogether different order were needed for theatre, music and architecture.

ARCHITECTURE AND ART

Architecture and design, John Ruskin's 'greater arts of life', were crucial. In the 1890s Charles Rennie Mackintosh laid down the principles of a modern Scottish architecture, combining the vernacular – 'as indigenous to our country as our wild flowers, our family names, our customs, or our political constitution' – and the functional. This was confounded by the economic decline in building in Edwardian Scotland, and by 1914 many of the best Scottish architects had gone south or, like Mackintosh himself, given up. There would be no recovery after the war: 1920s building was effectively restricted to council houses and schools, most of which went to mundane builders in local authorities. There was, however, a reaction. In 1932 the nationalist Robert Hurd restated Mackintosh's case, armed with the achievements of small nations like Finland and Czechoslovakia. Out of this emerged the Saltire Society, and the movement for better town planning.

Under Walter Elliot, the state re-emerged as a major patron, with Thomas Tait's St Andrew's House (1935–9) and the £11m project of the Empire Exhibition, which Tait supervised and which also involved the young Basil Spence and Jack Coia. The effects of this long innurition were to be tragically apparent when funds were released for large-scale planning and building in the 1960s, and a few good modern buildings were literally overshadowed by disasters like the 'year zero' Bruce Plan in Glasgow, the wrecking of Edinburgh's Princes Street and George Square and the multi-storey housing programme. In design the situation was, if anything, worse. The Scottish Economic Committee's inquiry into light industry in 1937 found a tradition of expensive hand-crafted work in textiles, furniture and glass, but, below that, design standards were awful. The manufacturers who tried to remedy this were few, though the textile men Alastair Morton, patron of Picasso and Braque, and

Bernat Klein deserve honourable mention. Conscious action over design education, of the sort that enabled Scandinavian countries to compensate for high prices through high-standard mass-produced goods, was almost totally lacking.

If Scottish architecture was disadvantaged by the absence of great patrons, Scottish art was constrained by already having adapted itself to a middle-class clientele. In contrast to mid-nineteenth-century painters like MacWhirter and Faed, engraved versions of whose sentimental studies of Scottish country life and scenes from Burns could be found on artisan walls beside samplers and family photographs, the 'Glasgow Boys' of the 1880s and their successors, the 'Scottish Colourists' – E. A. Peploe, F. C. B. Cadell and Leslie Hunter – produced moderately priced oils, watercolours and etchings for a middle-class public, represented by private buyers and the developing municipal collections, run by gifted connoisseurs like Sir James Caw and T. J. Honeyman, and the great Burrell bequest. These deserved their high reputation, but the indigenous art they patronised was domestic in scale and lacked aggression. Scottish art may have avoided the worst rackets of the international 'art market', but public art like murals was non-existent and the innovators – Alan Davie, Colquhoun and MacBryde, Eduardo Paolozzi – got out. If Tretchikov's green ladies took over in living rooms from 'Burns's Meeting with Highland Mary', where was the improvement in that? Even photography, potentially the most radical art form and one that nineteenth-century Scotland had helped create, rarely escaped from the seductions of a photogenic landscape. Fine work was done in Scotland by the Londoner Jim Jarche, the American Paul Strand, the Glasgow-Italian Oscar Marzaroli, but where was the new version of Hill and Adamson's calotype Valhalla?

THEATRE AND MUSIC

As with art and architecture, so with theatre and music? In the latter cases the inter-war crisis complicated a Calvinist legacy which scarcely encouraged such art forms. That the Victorians managed to sustain some dramatic activity and a modest musical revival was remarkable, given the effect of a puritan Kirk, removing the religious music-making which sustained the achievements in England of Parry, Stanford, Elgar, Vaughan Williams and Holst. But just as touring repertory companies survived by sticking to tried formulas and the classics – the radicalism of Alfred Wareing's Glasgow Repertory Company (1909–14), which premiered Chekhov in Britain, was late and short-lived – Scots music also played it safe. The Scottish Orchestra was founded in 1891, but only got a Scots conductor in 1959 – although its direction included at various times Walter Susskind and Sir John Barbirolli. Its programmes included little music by Scots composers. MacDiarmid never hesitated to criticise this, though music was scarcely his strong suit, and to advocate the songs of his friend and collaborator Francis George Scott, Erik Chisholm and the sort of national musical revival associated with Bartok and Kodaly in Hungary. This involved the systematic recovery of the folk-song tradition, and its use in musical education as well as composition. The problem was that this activity had already been pre-empted by a variation on the Kailyard. Following on the rise of pipe-band music in the nineteenth century, Mrs Kennedy-Fraser and Hugh Roberton had made Gaelic song into an undemanding if attractive middlebrow taste.

Another model of national cultural sponsorship was provided by the Irish Free State, which in 1924 made the Abbey Theatre in Dublin the first subsidised theatre in the English-speaking world. The Scottish National Players (1922–34) were directly influenced by the Irish example: though hamstrung by lack of funds, they gave the young Tyrone Guthrie his first chance as a director and produced in 1928 the first plays of Osborne Henry Mavor 'James Bridie'. Both men rapidly advanced to a British reputation, as did many of the actors from another Scottish independent venture, the left-wing Glasgow Unity Theatre (1938–47). During World War II, however, there were two important developments. Bridie and others set up the Glasgow Citizens Theatre, and Bridie was nominated by the Scottish

Council of State, on the recommendation of Elliot, his closest friend, to the Council for the Encouragement of Music and the Arts (CEMA), the forerunner of the Arts Council and of a programme of systematic state funding.

The result of this was something that no one could have foreseen: the Edinburgh Festival. It was not secured by any Scottish initiative but by the owner and manager of Glyndebourne, John Christie and Rudolf Bing, who saw that the ravages of the war had meant that Munich or Salzburg had no chance of mounting their festivals for years. They lighted almost by chance on Edinburgh and on a sympathetic Lord Provost, Sir John Falconer; and Corporation, Arts Council and a public appeal got £60,000 together. In 1947 Edinburgh found itself hosting Bruno Walter, Szigeti, Alec Guinness, Margot Fonteyn, Barbirolli and the brief, wonderful Kathleen Ferrier. Artistic success was never in doubt. Would the host accept the transplant? The romantic tartanry of the Military Tattoo on the Castle Esplanade attracted the folk, while the rediscovery and presentation by Robert Kemp and Tyrone Guthrie of Sir David Lindsay's renaissance morality, *The Thrie Estaites*, in the spectacular setting of the Church's Assembly Hall, showed that Scottish theatre now had the skill and talent to rise to this challenge.

The Festival took time to permeate Scottish life. Even in the 1960s, to defend it in the political forum was regarded as callous elitism. But gradually it helped dissolve middle-class philistinism, and led to a great expansion in musical activity, culminating in the launch of Scottish Opera in 1960, directed by the Scottish National Orchestra's first Scots-born conductor, Sir Alexander Gibson. If there was still little Scottish music in its repertoire, this was the result of the atonality of modern Scottish composers, such as Thea Musgrave and Iain Hamilton. The post-war period, however, saw, through the work of men like Norman Buchan and Hamish Henderson, and the treasury of Jeannie Robertson's ballads, the reviving of the folk-song tradition. Apart from the fact that it outcropped in the same radical milieu, how to explain why Edinburgh, and Royal High in particular, became the nursery of some of the best jazz talent

in Britain, including Sandy Brown, Al Fairweather and Stan
Greig? But, in the late 1940s, it was.

BOHEMIA OR UTOPIA? LITERATURE, CINEMA, TELEVISION

Royal High was also, through its English master, Hector
MacIver, one of the centres of a literary bohemia in which
the spirit of the renaissance still fermented away. 'The view
from Regent Road', MacIver's pupil Karl Miller, founder of
the *London Review of Books* wrote, 'towards the planes and
declivities of the sleeping Lothians, took in a landscape which
was far from benighted, a hinterland where contributing poets
and pamphleteers lay in their suburbs and country cottages'.

MacDiarmid had written to Roland Muirhead in 1928 that it
would be twenty years before his aims would be understood. He
was pretty accurate. In the 1950s came international recognition, academic honours, republication of his poems in accessible
editions. Scotland also saw rich poetic outflows and 'flyting': the
ironic, contemplative voice of Norman MacCaig, the austere
Orcadian threnodies of George Mackay Brown, the robust bar-
room Lallans of Robert Garioch and Sydney Goodsir Smith.
Edwin Morgan, the Glasgow Marinetti, actually applauded the
planning earthquake that hit the place, Derick Thomson and
Iain Crichton Smith carried on Sorley MacLean's revival of the
Gaelic lyric. Scottish poetry was almost a surrogate politics, with
parties and manifestos – a romantic world, but more interesting
and maybe more realistic than the self-conscious flat-footedness
of England's 'Movement'.

Yet MacDiarmid's self-questioning 'Are my poems spoken
...?' proved as much an epitome of the Scottish predicament in
the 1960s as Yeats's 'We had fed the heart with fantasies, The
heart's grown brutal with the fare' proved relevant to Ireland.
The renaissance had remained intellectual. It had wilfully dis-
tanced itself from the main developments in popular entertainment. In the 1950s there would be another media revolution,
but its consequences would prolong this isolation.

The prosecution case would run thus: MacDiarmid aimed at national regeneration, but his methods were nineteenth-century, or even antique: forms of pamphlet literature like the 'flyting'. He totally ignored the impact of film and radio. Would matters have been different if Compton Mackenzie's attempt to make him edit a critical magazine – *Vox* – on broadcasting in 1929 had succeeded? Could his influence have been swung beside that of the other great Scots innovator of the period, John Grierson?

Like MacDiarmid, Grierson had had his outlook changed by the Russian revolution. He had a vision of a new society in which film – exemplified for him by the work of Eisenstein, Pudovkin and Vertov – became the great public educator, the link between intellectual and people. Much of this was held in common with Reith, and indeed was drawn from that stock of Hegelian ideas of social improvement which floated about the Scottish universities before 1914. But Grierson viewed the media itself as a revolutionary force. 'The imaginative treatment of reality' – his definition of documentary – implied destroying the traditional boundary between culture and society.

Grierson's achievements in the 1920s and 1930s were protean. He travelled to Russia and publicised the work of Russian directors, even impressing the high Tory Rudyard Kipling. Walter Elliot got him to set up the Empire Marketing Board Films Department in 1927, for which he shot *Drifters*, the first classic of British documentary, in 1929. It was about the only film he made by himself: his main aim was to teach, and there were few British directors he didn't influence. Before he left for Canada in 1939 to create the Film Board of Canada, probably that country's most distinguished cultural contribution this century, he had helped reorientate British films towards the realistic treatment of social issues.

His influence was not lost on Scotland. Walter Elliot got his help in setting up Films of Scotland in 1938, and a growing number of films that dealt realistically with the problems and exhilarations of modern Scotland. In that year Michael Powell's *The Edge of the World* was the first of a distinguished line of films – John Baxter's *The Shipbuilders* (1945) from George Blake's novel, Alexander MacKendrick's *Whisky Galore* (1945), Powell's *I Know Where I'm Going* (1945), MacKendrick's *The Maggie* (1953) and Philip Leacock's *The Brave Don't Cry* (1952). Shots at grasping the 'condition of Scotland question', these compared with earlier poems and novels. *The Maggie* – the duel between ruffianly puffer captain and American millionaire – was a comic, dystopic parable of American industry and Scotland. But film, like any electronics-based industry, swung to London or Hollywood. Grierson was a Hegelian; he believed changing consciousness *was* victory. But economics favoured a real Scottish film industry even less than the renaissance.

Like MacDiarmid, Grierson was fundamentally from the artisan class, and required the support of a national body. After his Canadian triumphs he returned to Scotland, and to frustration. The cinema was proving mortal. TV started in 1952, grossing 41,000 sets; by 1962 there were 1,119,000 – more than telephones. The number of cinemas halved, and visits dropped to ten per person per annum. In 1953 'the box' was boosted by the Coronation; in 1955 the BBC was challenged by ITV. In Scotland Reithianism clung on, and the Canadian Roy Thomson, now owner of the *Scotsman*, had to battle to get support for Scottish Television. He didn't help by calling it 'a licence to print money'. No cultural ornament, STV let Grierson present documentaries, but not make them; its drama and current affairs work was poor. With only two million households to beam advertising at, STV was disadvantaged compared with Granada in Manchester, which chose the ablest Scots documentary-makers for its *World in Action*, just as the BBC, in a sharp counter-attack, used many good Scots producers and actors – Jeremy Isaacs, James MacTaggart, Alasdair Milne – in the south. Yet STV did establish a Scottish identity of a sort. Sports coverage and local news were inexpensive and gave career chances for those eyeing a Scottish reputation: fertile ground for politics to grow in.

Cultural life in 1960s Scotland was unprecedentedly lively, and MacDiarmid was able to say, in retrospect, that one of the main aims of my *Contemporary Scottish Studies* has now been realised – the recognition that anything that purports to be a contribution to Scottish literature must be judged by the standards applied to literature in all other civilised countries.

But did the renaissance's successors now have to cope with two Kailyards, one traditional and one electronic?

6

Economics and the Service Society, 1964–99

NOT QUITE THE LAST DREADNOUGHT

On 9 August 1960 Britain's last battleship HMS *Vanguard* returned to the Clyde, where Browns had built her in 1941–6. She took George VI and his queen to South Africa in 1947, did little for nine years, lay 'mothballed' for five. A total of £11.5 million worth of armour, engines and guns, sold for £500,000, was reduced to scrap at Faslane on the Gareloch, ending in autumn 1962. By then Tory premier Harold Macmillan and his Colonial Secretary Iain MacLeod, by descent Gaels from, respectively, Arran and Lewis, had ended much of the empire.

They and their US allies brought a future to the Gareloch and Holy Loch – into whose forty-five-metre-deep waters nuclear missile-carrying submarines could vanish from radar or satellite surveillance. Four such subs made up the US/UK Polaris deterrent agreed in 1962, replacing conventional bombers by 1968. These gave way to four Trident vessels, double the size, in 1996. Three years after the Cold War was won, in 1992 the Americans left the Holy Loch, but by 2014 the Royal Navy was assembling two 65,000-ton aircraft carriers at Rosyth. The cash for these – £7 billion and counting – came after 1978 from North Sea oilfields. This wasn't easy to estimate, because of varying prices per barrel, around $20 until 2000, rising to $100 from 2006 to 2014, and then falling to $60. As a prudent guide, Norway, with the same population as Scotland, set up an oil pension fund in 1990. It was worth $785 billion at the end of 2013.

From 1914 to 1964, the Conservatives ruled Britain for twenty-nine years. There were two periods of coalition government, 1915–22 and 1940–5. Scots voters assented for most of the time; only in 1929–31 and 1945–55 did Labour take most of the seventy-three Scottish seats. This changed between 1964 and 1999. Conservatives still governed the UK for twenty-five years, but in Scotland their vote was never more than 38 per cent (in 1970). Labour Scots mattered little to them but their own seats fell from twenty-one in January 1987 to zero in January 1998. They survived as a 'British' party through the Scotland Act of 1998–9 and Proportional Representation (which they had opposed), returning around fifteen MSPs to the Holyrood parliament.

Only after 1999 did Walter Scott's 'smooth but deep river' hit the rapids, hence the 'blow-by-blow' account of Chapter 8. If the *themes* throughout had a repetitive sound for the nation, we need to examine in this chapter an economy which had apparent continuity throughout, and its impact on Scottish society. We must then, in Chapter 7, turn to party politics, and its mediation in Scottish cultural life.

PLANNING, 1964-STYLE

Churchill was still alive when in October 1964 Labour ended thirteen years of Tory rule. Did political volatility figure? No: Harold Wilson and Labour won in the consensual belief that 'planning and technology' would reverse economic decline. Yes: despite favourable polls, they only just won. Their prescription differed little from Macmillan's, after bitter internal debates on nationalisation in 1959–60. Wilson was a Beveridge protégé (hence a link to the Clyde munitions drama of 1915); he promised dynamism instead of Macmillan's 'stop-go' cycles and intrigues. His 'technocracy' had even less to do with science than with socialism, but in Scotland this was not immediately apparent: the SCDI through the Toothill Report and the STUC had backed consensus 'planning', though Unionists were blamed for rail and mining closures. In 1963 Sir Alec Douglas-Home, welcome in Perthshire or Morningside, was a provocation in the Highlands and the housing schemes.

Scottish Labour MPs, on the right of the party, found 'planning' magic. Their fifteen-seat lead in Scotland clinched a shaky seven-seat grasp on UK office. In *Signposts for Scotland* (1962) they had ditched home rule but, besides increases in health and welfare programmes, they promised 'bespoke' development agencies, at their head the Highlands and Islands Development Board, funded by block grant, which William Ross, the new Secretary of State, carried in 1965. The Unionists called it 'undiluted Marxism': unwisely, as in the 1966 election most Highland seats fell to Labour or Liberals. Labour also set up, in Scotland besides other British regions, economic planning boards and councils to co-operate with George Brown's new Department of Economic Affairs (DEA) in preparing and executing the *National Plan* of October 1965. Supposedly balancing the Treasury, the DEA aimed at 3.8 per cent annual growth between 1966 and 1970.

Never a detailed strategy, after deflation in July 1966 – to keep sterling a reserve currency – growth wasn't even a pious hope. Elsewhere the regional bodies failed. They started without trained staff; when they got them the policy had gone. But the new Scottish Development Department had a Regional Division, and Ross's *Plan for Scotland* in January 1966 was more detailed than any of the English wish-lists. It echoed Toothill's stress on new industries, but it also linked employment growth to social spending. Housing, hospitals, roads and schools: building these would improve the infrastructure and replace jobs lost in the old staples; such spending power would attract much-needed service industries and consumer-goods factories. So inquiries began into Scotland's major social problems, while local teams advised on physical planning, not just in the central belt areas but in the north-east and Borders, with their endemic depopulation.

Initially there was near-euphoria in higher education and the social sciences – a small but growing interest group after the 'Robbins' expansion. Taking on the tasks the Scottish Economic Committee had pleaded for in the 1930s, professionals replaced gentry, clergy and businessmen on public boards and advisory committees; departments of geography, economics, town planning and social work expanded. So much was social science in Scotland the creation of the mid-1960s that for years it was difficult to stand up, look back and see how little was actually achieved.

The crucial issues weren't intrinsically Scots: they reflected the European 'modernisation' – of peasant agriculture and urban rustbelts – after the Treaty of Rome, 1957, and Macmillan and Wilson's approaches (1961 and 1967) to the EEC. But could planning work without state control of investment institutions and with sterling remaining a reserve currency? And when, as yet, there was no cadre of senior civil servants committed to it? In Germany the success of 'social marketism' depended on tight control of savings banks, usually local government/ co-operative, and the devolution of industrial policy to *Land* governments; in France the highly centralised planning of the Fourth and de Gaulle's Fifth Republic (1958) stemmed from the elite of the *Hautes Écoles* in Paris. British government's only effective instrument was demand management, and as Wilson's Dundee-born friend John Fulton found in successive inquiries, notably the Civil Service Commission (1968), 'Sir Humphrey' of Whitehall had problems with technical expertise.

Scotland was still dependent on old capital-goods industries or new industries needing fiscal boosts and public expenditure: so it reacted sharply to injections of cash into the UK economy, *and* was acutely sensitive to deflation. Wilson's enthusiasm for government-sponsored amalgamation within the private sector, as much as nationalisation, increased external control. Could this bring effective understanding? Policy executants were inexperienced on new and treacherous ground, dealing with the unfamiliar and foreign, and well-heeled and ruthless pressure groups outside the old capital/labour dyarchy. The sociologist-criminologist team of John Mack and Hans-Jürgen Kerner drafted a report entitled *The Crime Industry* for the Home Department in 1975. They saw computers, multinationals and tax havens blurring the line between market forces and illegality. Their report was filed and forgotten, though taken up by the veteran krimi-master Eric Ambler. The overlooked intellectual root of 'tartan noir', its toxins would spread in the next thirty years.

By 1970 public spending per head had risen to 20 per cent over the UK norm, largely due to Labour's investment-assistance programmes, but problems persisted. Industrial attraction succeeded, notably the expansion of the electrics/electronics industry from 7,500 jobs in 1959 to 30,000 in 1969 – three times Toothill's forecasts – yet shipbuilding and engineering decline wiped out many of their 'satellites' like optics, hydraulics, control and navigation mechanisms, with good innovation records after 1945. Could inventions from the marine stabiliser to fibreglass have been generated in 'screwdriver' branch plants?

The Scottish Office held that Scots education attracted US firms, but their record was poor. Employing 87,730 *in toto* in 1973, they hired only 250 graduates between 1965 and 1969. Their global map was, in any case, shifting and had at its centre the information revolution in encryption technology and the semi-conductor or 'microchip' – centred on the US south-west and boosted by the Vietnam war (1962–75). At the 1972 Scottish Council Forum an IBM executive guesstimated electronics turnover worldwide at $16bn. By 2008 it would be over $1 trillion.

England, let alone Scotland, never advanced to ownership and direction in this from (1) experiment and (2) the applied level: the worldwide web, online journalism, computer games. Government made no attempt to create Scottish institutions that would countervail this drift. After 1967 Edward Heath's Conservatives tentatively tried a foray into German-style social-market decentralisation, only to self-destruct on taking office.

Regional planning was skewed to stress activities that the St Andrew's House's staff could do, like roads and housing. The Buchanan Report of 1963 was too close to the Bruce Plan of 1946 and – over-influenced by American land-use/transportation techniques – assumed that the state, by building roads and public housing, first injected resources into the economy, and then, second, regulated it by controlling private housing and motoring by varying mortgage and hire-purchase rates: 'Keynesian' management of a sort. But people still used public transport, walked or biked: an effective form of social saving for industrial investment. In 1966 Glasgow had one car for every eleven people, and Surrey had one for every four, but Scotland built Britain's most ambitious urban roads *and* electric-powered multi-storey housing *and* (feeding this) plentiful energy from three nuclear reactors and two huge thermal stations – not long before the oil crisis of 1973. Sir Colin Buchanan's alluring 'comprehensive development' schemes closed or expelled local industry; the high-rise experiment proved catastrophic. In 'conservative' Edinburgh, environmentalists killed in 1969 an urban motorway scheme they saw as corrupt and destructive. Rightly: tens of millions, which could have financed industry or environmental improvement, in fact made things worse.

Post-1966 deflation braked regional assistance expenditure, while unemployment overtopped 1961. Investigations such as the 1967 Cullingworth Report, *Scotland's Older Housing*, exposed problems that would cost and last – making effective propaganda for its critics. There were overdue initiatives – the Scots Law Commission (1965) and the Social Work (Scotland) Act (1967), the new town of Irvine (1969), the Wheatley Commission on local government (1965) – but the central economic failure imposed a mounting penalty. Even Ross's successes accelerated his undoing: uprooting and rehousing, breaking communities and relationships, unsettling old class loyalties – these tempted people to explore a new politics.

LABOUR AND INDUSTRY

Scotland ran a 'balance of payments' deficit, reflecting the growth of public expenditure, especially on industry: in 1964 £15m, by 1973 £192.3m. In real terms this was a ninefold increase, absorbing about a third of the cash available under the Local Employment Act (1964), Regional Employment Premiums and shipbuilding subsidies. Scotland with 9.3 per cent of the

British labour force got 15 per cent of government industrial and agricultural subsidies and 17 per cent of UK cash for roads.

Edinburgh and Leith did well, but were left out of the 'Scottish development area' when they ought to have led it. Instead the stress was on 'jobs' as end, not means. The Unionists in 1964 subsidised the building of a pulp and paper mill in Fort William; in 1968 Labour built an aluminium smelter at Invergordon, *and* shifted the Post Office (later National Savings) Bank to Glasgow, *and* in 1978 sent the HQ of the Forestry Commission from Basingstoke to Edinburgh (most UK trees *were* Scottish, QED).

After a troubled start, the Highlands and Islands Development Board, whose annual budget had grown to £4m by 1973, provided useful and flexible finance for local industry, tourism and transport, and brought Scotland abreast of local development strategies in other countries with remote and underpopulated regions. Manufacturing wages also improved, from 91 to 96 per cent of the UK average, 1961–71. Yet the male workforce fell by 6 per cent, and a 6 per cent rise in women workers still left an overall decline of 1.75 per cent. Unemployment rose from 3.1 to 5.8 per cent, though still shadowing the UK figure. But annual emigration in the 1960s was 16 per cent up on the 1950s.

A total of £641m was spent between 1966 and 1971 in creating 105,000 jobs; in the same five years 156,000 were lost, mainly from heavy industry and agriculture. Mines and farms, traditionally labour-intensive, made up half this figure, yet, besides these 'structural' changes, technological innovation in services – driver-only buses abolished clippies, self-service stores ended 'real' sweetie-wifies – brought sweeping growth in productivity. Its implications? Union leaders were almost as clueless as sociologists.

The first container terminal in Britain, for instance, opened at Grangemouth in 1968; within a decade general cargo-handling had dwindled away; the main Glasgow docks had been filled in and the dockers sacked. By the 1970s, too, 65 per cent of the coal mined in Scotland's dozen or so remaining collieries was being conveyed by automatically loading and discharging 'liner-trains' to the hoppers of the power stations. Over £150m investment in BP's oil refinery and petrochemical complex at Grangemouth had yielded fewer than 2,000 jobs. Even in industries where employment in the late 1950s had seemingly stabilised, such as steel and shipbuilding, rationalisation and contraction loomed by 1970.

Changes in company control accelerated. Wilson nationalised iron and steel and sponsored industrial amalgamation. His technology minister Tony Benn was seconded by businessmen and trade unionists out to get a monopoly position, or a national wages structure. As swiftly as in 1918–22 control shifted south or abroad. Scots held onto small firms, but by 1977 had lost seven out of the top ten manufacturers. Even before Peugeot took over Chrysler in 1978, Scottish-owned firms employed only 41 per cent of workers, with 40 per cent paid from England, 15 per cent from North America and 1.5 per cent from the EEC.

Government money for job creation (averaging £6,000 per job) *reduced* employment, through new technology and rationalisation, and since trade-union pressure now lessened wage differentials, an important incentive to move north got lost. Scottish financial institutions remained healthy, but Scottish industrial capitalism was now marginal. 'Old-fashioned' tycoons like Lithgow and Bilsland had retained a paternalist sense of obligation, which led to planning groups like the Scottish Council, and Sir William Lithgow's Oceanspan scheme with its 'breakbulk' European megaport and German-style design partnerships with Far East manufacture. It stayed on paper. Such an idea wouldn't even be tabled in London or Los Angeles boardrooms.

Some of the new transplants looked shaky by 1970. The vehicle factories at Linwood (Hillman Imps) and Bathgate (Leyland vans) were operating at half-capacity. One reason was bad industrial relations, partly due to the difficulty of adapting a skilled, rather anarchic, workforce to assembly-line discipline; another was the failure of ancillary trades to come north. If 20 per cent of the parts entering Linwood were Scottish, this was a success, but West Midlands' economies of scale kept the average cost of an English part down to £0.096, against £0.246 for the same part made in Scotland. Even when manufacturing was successfully transplanted, the 'generative' elements of the parent companies – research and development, organisation, corporate planning, marketing – rarely came north. In 1972 Scotland came ninth out of ten British regions in R&D expenditure; government research between 1964 and 1973, was only 5.1 per cent of the UK total.

CONSERVATIVES, SHIPS AND OIL

After six years of Wilsonian ductility, the new Conservative government of Edward Heath seemed to know where it was going. Its centrist Scots ministers accepted the principles of the Wheatley Report of 1969 and in 1973 reorganised Scottish local government, creating nine regions with powers over planning, transport, social work and education, and fifty-three districts, mainly dealing with housing and communities. Joint bodies supervised the police, but health services were placed under separate nominated authorities in 1974. Such changes implied that Heath had retreated from devolution, and although the Scottish Office acquired an Economic Planning Department in 1973, its authority slipped back.

Energy didn't equal effectiveness. Heath had pledged to 'roll back' Labour's interventionism, but soon ran into a crisis in shipbuilding. The rescue of Fairfield's Govan in 1965 had shown that the industry badly required government investment. It got it haphazardly. After the Geddes Report of 1966 Labour reorganised and financed the Clyde yards as two groups: Scott Lithgow at Greenock and Port Glasgow, and Upper Clyde, at Clydebank, Linthouse and Govan. In the latter case both sides exploited the settlement, its economics – foreshadowed by the beautiful *Queen Elizabeth 2* built in 1966 for an 'Atlantic Ferry' almost sunk by jumbo jets within a year – behaved likewise. Heath's more doctrinaire ministers demanded near-total closure, but before Upper Clyde Shipbuilders (UCS) reeled into receivership in June 1971, he had to take over the bankrupt

Rolls-Royce Engineering (the limos continued private) and face the Clyde, in the full glare of publicity.

Brown's staged a 'work-in' on 30 July. Led by two articulate Communist shop stewards, Jimmy Airlie and Jimmy Reid, this grabbed media and masses, raising almost £250,000. Heath manoeuvred to retain and re-invest in two of the UCS yards, while after transatlantic drama Browns was bought by Marathon Engineering of Texas for oil-rig building. No one could claim victory: the 'work-in' went beyond a publicity coup, but wasn't it the 'socialism' of an able elite making its own Alex Ferguson-and-Billy Connolly way from TV news to sport and media millions? No German-style joint decision-making or 'dual-system' training emerged. A sequel in 1975–6, when the *Scottish Daily Express* shifted printing to Manchester, and its workers attempted, using cash from Tony Benn and the cloven hoof of Robert Maxwell, to produce the *Scottish Daily News*, was disastrous. But UCS highlighted one problem of industrial reconstruction. 'Old' nationalised industries, like railways, electricity or coal, drew on long traditions of state or local commitment and 'men on the spot'. Could reorganised manufacturing be achieved without this, by remote control from London?

Opinion – among civil servants and on the left – was beginning to shift away from centralised planning towards ecology and regional autonomy: E. F. Schumacher's *Small is Beautiful* came out in 1972. But there was a powerful counter-current, signalled by Marathon. Oil exploration had moved to the fore, and almost 90 per cent of the equipment for it had to be imported. Could the effects of the Yom Kippur War of October 1973 – the Arabs' use of their economic muscle, the sixfold increase in the price of crude – not have been forecast? A famine had been likely from 1967; early in 1973, by suspending oil import quotas, the USA forecast sweeping price increases. Government could have explored some preliminary options; instead, its reactions were hasty and brought Scotland little benefit. North Sea oil exploration had started off Holland in 1959, and the Gas Board was tapping the East Anglian seas in 1965, before in 1970 the first commercial 'Scottish' oilfield – the Forties – was located. This came on stream in 1977, with the whole project yielding 13m tons annually by 1980. Why the time lapse? Problems with difficult fields? Postnationalist boredom with Scottish affairs? A slackening in the Scottish Office? All may have played a part. Later hyperactivity concealed the fact that politicians could do little to control either the rate of oil extraction or the distribution of oil-related contracts. The sooner the stuff was being pumped, the less the pressure on the trade balance: even if this meant surrendering to US command of the appropriate technology.

Marathon apart, no Scots yards built drilling rigs; few built supply vessels. The big stuff was production platforms (vast steel or concrete structures which had to be assembled near the fields) and pipelines. Heath quickly secured seven construction sites, bruising environmentalists. Only five were used, all but one away from the job-starved Clyde, and they got an unstable workforce. These temporary Yukons, or the garish and inflationary affluence of the north-east, didn't compensate for lost chances to co-ordinate development.

On 8 September 1973 the SNP's imaginative oil campaign clicked with the coal and oil crisis *and* the pro-devolution report of the Kilbrandon Commission – rejected by Ross. The SNP's Margo MacDonald got elected for Govan, and the points were switched. The SNP had eleven MPs by October 1974 and might get a majority if the country ran with 'It's Scotland's Oil'. The presence was big, but *was it positive*? Imports of oil equipment in 1976 caused the balance-of-payments crisis that flung the UK's policies before 'the markets' and the International Monetary Fund. This divided minds between economics and the constitutional issue, until – and after – Margaret Thatcher's election in May 1979.

THATCHERISM

Thatcher believed rational Scots ought to appreciate her classical economics, and was distressed (though not disarmed) when they didn't. Scotland kept her in business: oil, peaking at £6bn in 1985, covered 8 per cent of the trade balance. But the petro-pound, peaking at DM 4 in 1980, meant 'sado-monetarism'. One of the worst recessions ever 'cleared' the factories expensively settled in the 1960s and 1970s: Corpach's pulp no more (1980), Linwood's cars and Invergordon's aluminium no more (1981), Bathgate's trucks no more (1986): the Proclaimers from Fife later added up to make their 'Letter from America' . . .

Thatcher deployed such closures, and laws curbing trade unionism, on the labour force. 'Who runs the country?' was settled by the miners' strike of 1984–5, compared by old Macmillan to the West Front attrition of 1914–18. By 2000 heavy industry was down to three shipyards on the Clyde: a last pit at Longannet; nearly all Motherwell steel plant went in the 1990s.

'Silicon Glen' was supposed to gain 'critical mass' from incomers and generate high value-added Scots concerns, but obeyed the 'footloose multinational' rules: new product meant new factory, somewhere cheaper. Good training slowed the collapse, but Motherwell College had 170 engineering lecturers in 1985, serving Ravenscraig, ten in 2005. It was demolished, its expensive successor, on the Ravenscraig site, did 'soft skills'. Without serious work-based inputs even quality production such as woollen textiles and whisky were in trouble. Manufacturing (including energy production) decreased in 1979–86 to under 20 per cent of GNP, employing only 412,000 of the two million workforce; investment fell 40 per cent, from £561m to £339m. Oil production hit a peak in 1986, but this coincided with a slump in the price per barrel to $20. This hit Scotland directly but also destabilised the Comecon nations, living by oil exports: something well known to Mikhail Gorbachev, who on 11 March 1986 visited Edinburgh Castle as Secretary Younger's guest, and exited as would-be social democrat ruler of the USSR. In 1989 Russia's old men tottered from power, succeeded by what Misha Glenny aptly called the McMafia (symbolised by another Clyde visitor: Roman Abramovich's yacht *Eclipse*, which turned up in July 2015: at 12,000 tons fifteen times the size of the PS *Waverley*) and a brief suspension of the Cold War.

Thatcher boosted Scottish house ownership from 38 per cent in 1982 to 63 per cent to match the pattern of working-class England, a level rarely encountered in industrial Europe. She wasn't particularly keen on it, wise old Willie Whitelaw appreciating the stability the council house brought to the Tory counties. In the longer term, however, it set up new polarities and sped up the dynamism of metropolitan and Scots finance, which would after 2000 accelerate Britain's leap into the financial chasm.

Tory Secretaries Rifkind (dodging knives thrown by Thatcherites) and Lang spoke consolingly of Scots exporting more per capita than Japanese; but others (not all on the right: observe the education of Gordon Brown) thought the shift to services inevitable. In the 1980s these came to 62 per cent of GDP: an overloaded grab-bag, from writing computer software to flipping hamburgers. (In 1989–91 Ronald McDonald, not Adam Smith, was 'the West' that East Europe wanted.) But while Baden-Wuerttemberg manufacturing ran at over 40 per cent of GNP in 1987, and 'microcapitalism' backed by powerful regional authorities revitalised textiles and clothing in central Italy, oil in fact accelerated – by offshoring much engineering – manufacturing's fall to 12 per cent of GDP by 2008. Scotland-*Minus-the-Shelf* was increasingly in deficit with the rest of the UK, whose own solvency slumped with the barrel price. Attempts to check this by raising interest rates caused boom-busts in 1987–8, 1992–4 and 2002–4.

MARKETS AND MEN

The year 1981, when the first edition of *No Gods* was published, *looked* much like 2015, something visible in TV clips: cars slightly archaic, girls slender, buses and street furniture pretty much what they were. Bikes had largely vanished from their native land, now motor-fixated. The desktop computer entered, with the floppy disks on which it depended. The pioneer 5¼-inch floppy, which persisted along with green screens for the first fifteen years, relied much on work at the IBM factory

and labs at Glenrothes. For a time in the 1990s, it looked as if
Scotland might take after its Californian prototype, but government put hardware – computers, screens, printers – ahead of
software. In 1988 Scottish Enterprise had only one specialist
in *that*. Some of the new plants survived; the rest vanished as
fast as mechanical engineering. If Ravenscraig Steelworks lasted
forty years, its TV-building neighbour Chungwa died at eight.
The vast Hyundai Dunfermline (1999) was demolished, uncom-
pleted, in 2011.

The microchip plant (1999) was a factor, like the railways
once and the motorways later, that could matter either way. An
alert, skilled community could run with it, settlement was at a
disadvantage. Thatcher's consumer privatisations – telephones,
utilities, transport – meant training and research schemes were
abandoned. This coincided with oil and made her hated. By
1999 her party as a UK force and indeed the Scottish business
class was politically in free fall, and would have disappeared,
but for the grace of devolution, where PR for regional seats at
least retaned a diffused Tory vote at about fifteen MSPs.

The implement that stabilised this was the SDA, closely
co-ordinated to the financial sector. This only just got off the
ground. In 1981 there was a determined effort by Standard
Chartered to take over the Royal Bank. This was beaten off by
the old business oligarchy, which had prudently in the 1970
recruited from nationalist-inclined, free-market decentralists,
such as Professor (later Sir) Donald MacKay. But in the 'Lawson
boom' in 1984–5 the bulk (by value) of independent Scottish
manufacturing was taken over by English or European firms.
This climaxed in 1986, when after an exercise in fraud Guinness
took over Distillers. The Angel of Vengeance was Thatcher
herself, jailing the most prominent conspirators. Such takeovers
did everything their left-economist critics (at that time including
Gordon Brown) expected: benefited investment bankers more
than innovators, shareholders or workers.

A more positive change, perhaps, happened in land transport, a controlled business from the 1930s to bus privatisation
in 1986. This gave two Scots empires a head start and for a

time world dominance, projecting the reach and aggression of Scottish investment banking. Moir Lockhart, the boss of the transport business at Aberdeen Council, built it into First Group, with assets in 2014 worth £4bn. Brian Soutar, from the pacifist Church of the Nazarene via McKinsey, took his firm Stagecoach even further, pretty ruthlessly. Aberdeen and Perth had benefited from the oil boom of the 1970s and being finance centres – and they changed the face of British land transport. Nothing changed in the air. Scotland's only challenge to BA as national carrier, Adam Thomson's British Caledonian Airways, had gone by 1987. No subsequent airline got past being local, and lived. Spaniards ran the airports; the Dutch state ran the trains.

Boom-busts were of a new and complex sort: a literal hurricane plus a stock-market crash in October 1987 segued into compensatory boom fed by Chancellor Lawson 'going European' and 'tagging' the Deutschmark. By mid-1988 this caused a trade deficit, aggravated by the shrinkage of *English* manufacturing, forcing a 'correction' and a longdrawn-out recession, hitting Scotland less than the English south. Unemployment reduced from 15.6 per cent in 1985 to 8.1 per cent in 1990 (UK: 11.8 to 5.8 per cent). In recession it stuck on the UK level at 9.0 per cent.

Despite oil, Scotland's wages fell – from 99 per cent of UK level in 1980 to 93.5 per cent in 1990. South Wales, under its 'wet' Secretary Peter Walker, was using a new geopolitics to lure investment: Cardiff became handier for Heathrow Airport (and after 1993 the new Channel Tunnel) than much of Essex, as oligarch loot poured into 'the United Kingdom of London'.

In 1995 Scottish manufacture was still around 20 per cent of GDP. A remarkable second burst of inward investment in computer and allied factories had boomed sufficiently to compensate for the death of the steel industry. How come? There was by now fast-diminishing academic interest in economic history (a discipline founded on 'looking at the books' was doomed when these vanished into cyberspace) but think of this: the second generation of consumer electronics firms had a huge gap to fill in former communist states denied western information technology, and was now getting to them via Hong Kong (preparing to rejoin China) and the new metropole of Dubai. These were the territories of two modest middle-aged Scots businessmen who had 'gone native': Sir William Purves (born Kelso, 1931), CEO of the Hong Kong and Shanghai Bank up to 1998 when the UK colony returned to China, and William Duff (1922–2014), factotum of Sheikh Rashid al Maktoum, Emir of Dubai; Purves granted finance to Mao's heirs, Duff helped make a quiet port into the Gulf's Manhattan, and the airport gateway to what had been the Asian Soviets.

This second wave of computer investment would not tarry long. It was part of the bridging technology which facilitated the adoption of cheap manufacture in China – not least when transported by the giant 'box-carriers' of the Maersk fleet: built in Denmark, fulfilling for the Danes Sir William Lithgow's Eurospan dream. In Germany the *Mittelstand* joined in, and protected itself through a dense cultural network, with several defences against speculation and exploitation: publicly run banks, short-term loans from local governments, state aid with training, low-cost transport. Scots firms found the accountants (often from Scots-founded firms) a one-stop shop in their difficulties. They got closed down, briskly.

EDUCATION

Modernisation's goals were only partly economic, however, and the limited progress made was partly masked by the social and cultural changes initiated or encouraged by the government, which altered traditional institutions and social life on a scale unparalleled since the Victorians: even, in some cases, since the Reformation.

Education was important in social-democratic theory, promoting equality and economic diversification. Encouraged by inspectors and some teachers, reform was under way before 1964. Adoption of O-grades meant an increase in candidates from 17,175 in 1961 to 83,805 in 1967. Fifteen per cent more were staying on to sixteen, although the leaving age was not raised until 1973. Following Labour policy, Ross and the local authorities reorganised secondary schools as comprehensives. In comparison to England the transition was fairly painless: 98 per cent of pupils were in them by 1974, against under 50 per cent in England. Overall, the size of schools increased: in 1947, 171,193 secondary pupils attended 1,037 schools; in 1974 over 400,000 attended 439.

Primary and secondary curricula were reformed, following a working party report of 1955 and the Brunton Report of 1963, which stressed vocationally centred studies for nonacademic pupils. There were problems within this construct and its social surrounds: how vocational could schools be, when family and industrial structure was in upheaval? The 'youth estate' was dwindling with a growth in migration and a decline in the birth rate. The solidity of 'a job at the pit' or 'in the mills' underpinning communities gave way to not-always reassuring professional clamours. In the 1960s intelligence testing was exposed as so much hocus-pocus. Were there other spectres, the profession asked as it debated its reorganisation after 1966 under a General Teaching Council for Scotland?

To provide teachers *and* the troops of the technological revolution, higher education expanded. Following the Robbins Report of 1963 the great technical colleges of Glasgow and Edinburgh received charters as Strathclyde in 1964 and Heriot-Watt in 1966, as did Queen's College, Dundee, in 1967. A new university at Stirling (1968) helped student numbers double to 33,000 between 1960 and 1969. Three education colleges opened, at Falkirk, Hamilton and Ayr, in 1964–5 and, largely through the Industrial Training Act (a Conservative measure of 1964) technical colleges expanded to 80,000 full-time, day-release or block-release students in 1970. In that year Jennie Lee's Open University unexpectedly won over Education Minister Margaret Thatcher, and opened under the remarkable Edinburgh medic Walter Perry, soon reaching over 10,000 Scottish homes by post, TV and radio.

Yet was expansion enough or in time? Could schools really check Scottish social inadequacies? The Advisory Committee

Report of 1947 placed them in the front line against 'a barely literate populace, debased by vulgarisms and corrupted by Hollywood'. Not the language for the 1960s, yet stressing parents' involvement, while TV, working mothers and marital instability changed the structure of Scots families. Innovation seemed to aid the middle class more. It steered clear of religious schools and, until 1987, 'the belt'. If education meant 'the child in the community' why *two* communities? If it was a partnership, why retain this savagery? Catholic schools had some success with more conventional methods but were subverted by the double-edged challenge of 'vocation': the collapse of a celibate elite – disgraced by scandal by the 1990s – and of industrial training as manufacturing shrank from a third to a tenth of the workforce between 1979 and 2014. The further education college in Germany provided only a third of its famed *Dualsysteme*: workplace and 'shop-floor' with its *Werksakademie* did the rest. This was applicable to eco-hi-tech house-building as much as mechanical engineering, so Scotland lagged in both.

The teaching profession, stabilised at over 50,000-strong after 1973, had grown by 60 per cent in twenty years. Counting universities (c. 12,000 staff) and further education (11,600 lecturers) it outnumbered all but three groups of manufacturing workers, yet despite strong unionisation teachers were remote from the working class and internally divided. Graduates (mainly male) declined from 46 to 39 per cent, increasing tension with largely female non-graduates. A profession 66 per cent female remained as subject to male control as engineering before 1914.

There was, moreover, little unity between it and the anglicised staff of the universities, and tensions grew in the 1970s devolution debate as 'British' universities seemed likely to remain aloof from 'Scottish' education. The first largish generation of Scots postgraduates confronted a conservative but tenured university establishment, recruited in the 'Robbins years' of the mid-60s. Scottish studies, in its broadest sense, was the fruit of the economics and politics of the 1970s, but it tended to the literary or theoretical, rather than the business practicality of a Cairncross or a Bowie – unsurprisingly, as the industrial underpinning of higher education either got diffused internationally to branch campuses, or shrank.

By 2000 higher education had become a major service sector, with foreign student numbers up to nearly 30,000 and bringing in £337m annually in fees and direct expenses, with additional income of £441m. Small wonder that Principals mutated into CEOs, controlling multinational campuses, with rewards to suit, but remoteness from their staff. Against this, Holyrood diverged from New Labour's increasingly marketised English norm, scrapping fees and restoring grants, focusing the radicalism which had earlier gone into the Open University and community and gender studies.

But, sustaining this, were the bairns all right? MSPs found charm and enthusiasm in the primaries, but what happened after that? Idealised programmes – 'Higher still' or 'Curriculum for Excellence' – hit teenage hormones, obsessive new technologies, social media, social inequality. A strange Chicago-influenced symposium, *New Wealth for Old Nations* (2002), pushed the game back to the earliest years.

Forty years of the comprehensives had worked: the evidence was there on Holyrood's benches, particularly among women. But by then were the schools no better, broadly speaking, than their catchment areas? Was exam expertise overstretched? At all-ability Kelso from 1956 to 1958 I learned history, geography, art, worked in wood and metal and encountered the 'Renaissance' at Royal High. With 2Bs and 3Cs I wouldn't have got university entry today. And the ghosts of A. S. Neill and R. F. Mackenzie would have been furious. The Curriculum for Excellence, invented under Labour, enacted by the SNP and promising to combine subject competence with a developed social sense, ended 'vacuous and unambitious' in the view of one idealist, Professor Lindsay Paterson. He thought more highly of the Tory Michael Gove: but was this the Tory or the 'Teacher's Pest' from Aberdeen? Neighbourhoods with prospects: good. But could one size fit all? Particularly when faced with the tracklessness of new media – *and* multiple deprivation, family poverty, regional blight?

HOUSING: HIGH RISE AND FALL

Housing started and ended as an economic problem – but with a magical interlude. Between 1960 and 1970 completions rose (quite literally, in multi-storeys) from 28,500 to 43,100, roughly double the rate of demolitions, with smaller or older houses now increasingly occupied by young couples or single people. Yet Barry Cullingworth confirmed in 1967 that a third of Scottish families were living in 'inadequate' accommodation, and much of this was steadily deteriorating into slums.

Rent control and low council rents meant that private landlords could never undertake renewal, and although Cullingworth suggested that private rents could be subsidised by grants to landlords, Labour would never wear this. Owner-occupation in large old tenements involved difficult modernisation problems as well as rising mortgage rates. That left co operatives or associations, or council policies of renewal rather than demolition. By 1970 both were being pursued, but progress was slow. As private tenants (21 per cent in 1977) dwindled, owner-occupiers (26 per cent) and council tenants (53 per cent) grew. In industrial burghs such as Motherwell over 80 per cent of households rented from councils. But St Andrew's House gained more central control over rents, which in 1967–8 moved to more realistic levels – and brought a bonus to the SNP in local elections.

Housing-management got to problematic from there: not just anti-social families and ailing 1930–60 slum-clearance schemes. 'Point-blocks' were compared with the liners the Clydesiders had once built. But even the *'Queen Mary'* lasted only thirty years at sea. Hundreds soon had design problems – leaky windows, lifts too small for stretchers (and coffins), irregular maintenance. Some were 'insolubles': underfloor electric heating was compulsory but costly; if switched off, condensation and mould appeared. Poverty bred inefficiency; families and pensioners could be stranded 100 feet up. By 1980 several ambitious projects, such as Sir Basil Spence's lauded Gorbals Hutchesontown towers (1965) had become uninhabitable. Their demolition in 1993 was by explosive and bulldozer; little escaped landfill.

Labour suffered because low-rent policies narrowed its municipal constituency while the lack of alternatives to council housing tied improvements too closely to government expenditure, under threat from deflationary policies. Wholesale clearance destroyed communities; building-contract awards and house allocations led to corruption cases. Labour losses in 1966–8 cut dead wood out of the councils and improvement came in the early 1970s, after a survey based on the 1971 census showed that Scotland had 77.5 per cent of Britain's 5 per cent of 'worst areas' for social deprivation. Ironically, reforming Labour councillors such as Robin Cook were often neither tenants nor working class.

Under Thatcher 'right-to-buy' measures bit into the public housing stock, and house-building halved to 20,000 a year; by 2014 it was 14,000, 3,000 of which were notionally social housing. 'Arm's-length' housing associations replaced council departments, but couldn't use sale proceeds. Private builders skimped: plywood, breeze block, aluminium foil would never raise thermal standards from low C to the continental B standard. Holidays and cars were the Scots' compensations. What they'd failed to manufacture dominated their lives. MSPs admired the healthy Danes clambering up the five-storey steps of 'Borgen', their parliament, but took the lift. Thirty-nine per cent of Copenhageners walked or biked to work; 6 per cent of Stirling Council employees did the same.

HOUSEKEEPING . . . OR GOD, SEX, DRINK AND CRIME

Economists reckoned the Heath years, 1970–4, to be statistically the nearest the UK ever got to equality. The trade unions, depending on one's political view, 'protected working people' or 'held the country to ransom'; rents were controlled, council house building ran at 40,000 units a year, bus fares were cheap. The STUC had held out better than the Scottish banks, or the UK TUC, retaining, in 2013, 740,000 members out of the 850,000 it had managed in 1977. But these were now predominantly in the public sector, in the civil service, local government and education.

Back then ... the TV still competed with the pub, or the 'Miners' Welfare': poverty was around 10 per cent. It was a declining land, statistically, and as William McIlvanney admitted in *Docherty* (1975), but it was still recognisable in the sprawling council-house 'villages' of South Ayrshire, or the 'Little Moscows' of Fife. It was also religious by habit, and depended on church groups for much social life, scouts and BBs, guides and guilds. Communism was just another tabernacle.

In 1960 almost 70 per cent of Scots over the age of fourteen were Church members, closer to Ireland, which managed 90 per cent, than to the pagan English at 23 per cent. This was the Kirk's peak, and after 1970 Catholics too declined. TV and Sunday's new career, begun under the frequently Christian Thatcher as 'Big Shop Day', would entice many whose faith was nominal. The middle class still 'believed' in a way that would have puzzled, say, John Stuart Mill. The trusted Royal Bank boss Charles Winter was in 1986 the organist of Longniddry Kirk. But students and teachers shifted to secular social or political organisations, adequate or not; so did local elites in law or commerce.

Was this a victory for Carlyle's 'philosophy of clothes' with 'extension' converts falling to the 'laid-back' ethos of the 1960s? The Kirk's politics – earlier leftish under popular theologues like William Barclay and George MacLeod – now trod uneasily between diffuse ecumenicism and American bible-belt; the latter compromised by the Ulster crisis. Catholics were strong enough to rally to the election in 1979 of John Paul II – pugnacious and populist – until revelations of bullying and sexual misconduct undermined Rome from the 1990s on. The Kirk got its first female Moderator, Dr Alison Elliott, in 1995, and by 2010 most new ordinands *were* women – facing emptying pews and church halls. Dr Callum Brown, historian of the Kirk's decline, found his agnosticism compromising with the need to revive his local community: 'Annals of the Parish' still counted.

Households grew 1981–2012 from 1.6 to 2.4 million. The largest group were now 'single' or secular. A new freedom? A 1999 attempt to forbid teaching about same-sex relationships led to a Holyrood–Church–tabloid clash, but gay marriage in 2014 followed civil partnerships in 2004, without fuss.

'But what remains when disbelief has gone?' asked Philip Larkin. Churches, liturgies, fascinating buildings had been a barrier against calculating corporatism: that Sunday 'reckoning' more thoughtful and socially just than the *Sunday Times* or *News of the World*. On drink, puritans could cite the Scots and alcohol: 89 per cent of the UK level in 1955, this rose to 109 per cent by 1970. Why? More affluence? More consumers? Fewer abstainers? A combination of all three? Licensing hours had been extended, women were accepted in most pubs, young people were no strangers to drink. The Clayson Report of 1975 said it 'could now become a civilised accompaniment to life', and after it, opening hours took on a continental pattern in 1978. But Scots alcoholism ran at five times the UK rate; smoking levels were destructively high, even though most pubs now offered food. After Wembley 1977 and crashing out of the World Cup in 1978, Scots football supporters sobered up a bit and became a droll attraction for the continentals. Spend per head on drink fell back to 102 per cent of UK level in 1990, when only 36 per cent of the male population said they smoked, compared with 51 per cent in 1980. It was banned indoors in July 2006, with ambiguous results. If they couldn't have a smoke with their pricey drink, Scots would stay home. As a result, a third of country pubs had given up by 2014.

A wholly healthy Scotland? Anything but. Registered drug addicts rose from 90 in 1980 to 525 in 1990. Both were fictive figures, given the spread of Aids and the 'crime industry' that Mack and Kerner had feared in 1975, moving north as hoods (often from Belfast gangs) bought into Mediterranean rave culture. A 1996 Commons Select Committee put the problem at 1,500 cases and £600m a year for west coast Scotland alone. By 2012 'regular drug use' affected about 3.5 per cent of the over-16 population, about 130,000, and 60,000 were 'drug-dependent'. The death rate was just under 600 a year: about the highest in Europe. But this was just the cherry on a cakeload of 'illth'.

Disasters didn't help: Ibrox, 1971, with sixty-six crushed to death; the Aids epidemic after 1977 with at least 1,860 dead; Piper Alpha (167) and Lockerbie (270) in 1988; Dunblane (18) in 1996: some avoidable, none straightforward. Grim winters without extra payments: a reputation that dragged down the Tories, a North Sea more hazardous to Scots than to Norwegians, and always a steady nibbling at the welfare fringe. After the 1979 election and Thatcher's measures, culminating in the miners' defeat in 1984–5, poverty doubled to around 20 per cent, 30 per cent in Glasgow. Responses could seem paradoxical. *Half* the Scots population was reckoned as overweight, over 20 per cent as clinically obese, the result of unemployment or deskwork, fatty convenience food, sedentary leisure spent before screens, obsessive motoring – to school, to work, to supermarket, to takeaway, to sick or elderly family members – reducing cycling, public transport and walking; not helped by deteriorating welfare and indeed deteriorating weather. One consequence was the rise of Type 2 diabetes to over 235,000 cases (5 per cent of the population) by 2011. In that year the Scots actor Brian Cox (socialist and diabetic) surveyed four 'sweet temptations' for the BBC: sugar, drugs, drink, tobacco – how they evolved, how they took effect on the brain, what they cost in social terms. The effect was unreassuring for the Scots' *better* selves: from Morningside's 'Can I press you to another macaroon?' to Motherwell's 'Cum oan, ah'll gie yiz a ride tae Tesco's!'

Retail had rationalised, and became a battlefield. Scotland was small shop, not market country. In the 1980s the Co-op had a continuing, though fading, presence in many middle-sized towns, and there were several local chains, notably William Low. But with growing car ownership in the late 1980s the English chains moved in – Tesco took over Willie Low's in 1994 – building big sheds on out-of-town fields, old railway property. 'Bogof' offers caused overbuying, 40 per cent of food got junked, uncooked, and Europe's fattest folk over-ate. In the noughties, the big sheds themselves were hit by 'budget food' scandals. Discounters, mainly German, yet compatible with tolerable urban life, took their trade, and that of East European immigrants.

Small shops moved to fast food: Cupar in Fife, a town of 8,000, had twenty-three outlets. Coffee chains chased declining pubs, but competition wasn't what it seemed as many of their back-room operations were offshored for tax purposes. The Fifer Adam Smith, stickler for commercial transparency, suspected 'gatherings ... for play or merriment' that turned into 'conspiracies to raise prices'. These he found totally unacceptable, yet they dominated the 'market' which claimed him as patron.

7

Politics, Culture and the Better Nation, 1964–99

PARTY PIECES, 1964–74

In James Robertson's political novel *And the Land Lay Still* (2012) is a photo of a football crowd, taken in around 1958. The men – out of perhaps 200, there are just two women – know they're on camera, and are each individuated: different ages, social classes, temperaments – as many futures as faces. 'A far horn grew to break that people's sleep' ends the Edwin Morgan poem that gives the book's title: a line from some technocrat on Morgan's spaceship?

Economic improvement needed – but didn't get – a 'wake-up call': a reliable political system, just as the 1950s family environment was restricted by where you could bike or bus to; football games or holidays being the exceptions. Politics happened down the road, at burgh hall or county buildings, on national service or at faraway Westminster. Local government was antique; the income of councillors low, status variable, party control sketchy: especially in the Labour West where insiders mistrusted activists: 'Ye canna join. We're fu' up for the year!'

Corruption, greater than in England because of 50 per cent-plus council housing, was serious enough; failure to apply any political perspective to 'planning' spread it further. Labour, as the traditional Scots majority party, was home to professionals, planners and social scientists, but incomers soon got to know Robert Michels' 'iron law of oligarchy': being suspect as socialist 'theoreticians' or 'capitalist' journalists. Labour's leader in

1964, William Ross MP, and party secretary William Marshall wouldn't let the articulate John Mackintosh, *the* authority on Cabinets, anywhere near one. Middle-class local politics was for Independents or Moderates, from Kirk or Rotary – few Conservatives stood as such. But what would happen when Labour *was* the government? Would press and public view the advance of the SNP with some indulgence?

The SNP was learning, but it wasn't alone. Communists, under an intelligent Scots leader John Gollan, developed initiatives from the pre-war planners, and ideas about community. Janey and Norman Buchan (later on, a Labour MEP and MP respectively) and Hamish Henderson used folk-song and Marxian theory to promote a democratic, cultural internationalism; until the two shocks in 1955–6 of Kruschev's denunciation of Stalin and repression in Hungary caused the Buchans and more to defect to Labour. The first devolution probes, however, came from the Tories under Heath, in 1966 still reckoning a revival in Scotland was possible. They had, after all, run 'their own' devolved government since 1922 – when they thought about it. James Callaghan went to the Home Office in December 1967 and asked for material on Northern Ireland, for which it was constitutionally responsible (Terence O'Neill's modernising agenda, somewhat resembling Scotland's, was in sectarian trouble). He got a few A4 files. Within months the place blew up.

Scotland even in the early 1970s looked superficially like the 1920s: 'traditional industry' troubles reinforced Labour loyalties. Yet beneath this were non-volatile trends: old convictions weakened, the 'national' option grew. From only 9 per cent when first polled in 1945, it had doubled; by 1992 it vied with devolution at around 35 per cent. Much support came from the left. Scots intellectuals, influenced notably by George Davie's *The Democratic Intellect* (1961) and the journalism of travelled men like Neal Ascherson and Tom Nairn, no longer dismissed it as 'Brigadoon'. Being Scots, like being Polish, Catalan or Czech, was now seen as important in a Europe shifting through *les événements* of 1968 from established capitalism or Communism in favour of individual rights, gender equality, community and the natural environment – even if such enlightenment was still muffled by the strictures of the Scottish class system.

MARCHE ÉCOSSAISE!

Harold Wilson had won the March 1966 election convincingly, returning forty-six Scottish MPs, but instantly ran into a seamen's strike, in an industry being destabilised by containers and airlines. Ineptly handled, it disrupted life in the Scottish islands, provoked a run on the pound and a cabinet battle between the 'Keynesian' DEA under the erratic-to-alcoholic George Brown and Treasury-backed Chancellor Callaghan. The latter won, but central planning fell away; unemployment started to increase, bringing right-wing and Liberal gains in the May local elections.

In July Lloyd George's daughter Megan, long a Labour MP, died and in Callaghan's Welsh fiefdom Gwynfor Evans of Plaid Cymru unexpectedly won her Carmarthen seat. Within two years Wilson's 'Scottish problem' became 'coping with the Nats'. Most Labour folk saw this as a protest against the government's non-socialist economic policies. To a minority it reflected the remoteness and inadequacy of Scottish politicians, and there was no dodging the fact (or compelling fantasy) that SNP members had in eight years grown from 2,000 – perhaps fiftyfold!

Scotland was open to a third party. The Covenant had been quite recent. The Unionists were shadowed by Ulster: working-class Protestantism and a cosy agricultural lobby were both under threat. Enough ditched their 'Liberal' wrapping to enable 'rebranding' as Conservatives in 1965. But 'real' Liberals revived under Jo Grimond in the Northern Isles, took three seats in 1964, Roxburgh with David Steel in 1965 and in 1966 West Aberdeenshire. As in south-west England and Wales, they represented individualist radicalism as well as the problems of remote areas, though the English 'centre' also beckoned, when opinion polling (at its peak under a Canadian Scot, Robert McKenzie) briefly put them ahead of the 'big two'.

Though fickle, 'Orpington Man' diverted Grimond, and after 1967 Jeremy Thorpe, from Scottish policies. The division was replicated in Scotland itself. Outside a few burghs like Greenock and Paisley, activists tended to be '*Guardian* herbivores', remote from the working class, even if sympathetic on Scottish issues. Liberalism in the Northern Isles or the Borders was more regional than national, and after a fumbled courtship in 1964 it kept its distance from the SNP.

The SNP inherited many of the liberal home-rule ideas of Scottish Convention, although its constitution decreed an 'early Sinn Féin'-like route to full independence. Its MPs would withdraw from Westminster when they took thirty-seven seats out of seventy-three. Unlike Convention, it saw elections as central – and their results both sustained and betrayed it.

By-elections were a UK specialism: PR systems with lists can live without them. Harold Wilson depended on them, but after 1966 their huge fluctuations unnerved him: Scotland, with a gaggle of elderly Labour MPs, was especially fragile. On 9 March 1967, at Glasgow Pollok, the SNP got 28 per cent, letting in a rare Tory academic, Professor Esmond Wright. In May its local election poll rose from 4.4 to 18.4 per cent, *and* Tom Fraser left his safe Hamilton seat to chair the Hydro Board. A six-month by-election campaign saw Labour organisation fall apart, just when the economy worsened, making devaluation inevitable. On 2 November a young, articulate SNP candidate, Mrs Winifred Ewing, with an ILP and CND background, trashed a 16,000 Labour majority. The following May the SNP local election vote hit 30 per cent.

The cabinet was divided: 'revisionist' right and 'Bevanite' left saw the SNP as a protest – to be faced down or met with 'socialist policies'. To others the SNP, coupled with huge fluctuations in British local elections, demanded a rebalancing of central and local government. Paradoxically, the 'territorial' ministers, Ross and Welsh Secretary George Thomas, were timid, while English institutional reformers, notably the flamboyant Richard Crossman, Minister of Health and later Housing, were bold. Studies of the SNP could be made to back either interpretation.

It plainly mobilised people whom the parties had hitherto failed to reach. Municipal voting rose sharply in 1967 and 1968, and much SNP support came from working-class non-voters. Football-patriots vitalised by SNP propaganda? The new councillors had little experience. Only about 40 per cent of a sample had been SNP members for more than three years, and only 13.5 per cent had belonged to other parties. This, and the naivety of many of them, chalked up 'protest vote'. Yet the SNP did better in new towns, and in landward east Scotland, while new demands for self-government came from beyond the kirk and the STUC, from bodies as diverse as the New Left and the Tories.

The Scottish Unionists had called for devolution in 1967, and in May 1968 Edward Heath set up a committee of churchmen, constitutionalists and ex-ministers, under Sir Alec Douglas-Home, which reported positively in March 1970. Heath's subsequent inaction, and Lord Home's repudiation of devolution just before the 1979 referendum, cast doubt on the party's actual commitment, but it prompted Wilson to set up the Crowther (later Kilbrandon) Commission on the Constitution in December 1968. This helped hold the line in Scotland, while the SNP ran into more conventional left/right debate, with a division between 'social-democrats' around William Wolfe, and a traditional 'independence first' wing around Arthur Donaldson, whom Wolfe defeated for the Chairmanship in 1969. Council resignations and by-election defeats were embarrassing, and the SNP's claims that Scotland was being over-taxed seemed authoritatively combated by Dr Gavin McCrone in *Scotland's Future: The Economics of Nationalism* (1969), in which it was calculated that Scotland still remained indebted to England to the tune of £56m–£93m per annum.

In October 1968 Labour did well in a by-election at Glasgow Gorbals – the large Catholic vote stayed loyal – and in May 1969 the SNP's municipal vote fell to 20 per cent. An Ayrshire by-election brought no gain against Labour's aggressively Unionist candidate, Jim Sillars. Members drifted away; 'heid-banger' fundamentalists worried folk, given developments in Ulster. In June 1970 the SNP did well to take 11.4 per cent and get one MP elected: Donald Stewart in the Western Isles. Heath had a UK majority of thirty but made only three gains in Scotland (one from Labour). His new Secretary of State, Gordon Campbell, still had 38 per cent of the vote, but problems galore, not least in nearby Ulster.

TO THE 1979 REFERENDUM

Britain entered the European Community *and* its own oil age, as cross-party stress and tension ratcheted up a ten-year constitutional crisis, only braked by the referendum and election of 1979. In November 1973 Ross rejected the Kilbrandon Report as the 'Kill-devolution Report', and a second 'blonde bombshell' burst: the articulate leftie Margo MacDonald won Govan. In February 1974, amid Ulster violence, soaring oil prices caused by the Yom Kippur war, a miners' strike and a thirty-hour week, Heath lost sixteen seats and Labour gained three, but the main swing was to third parties. In England the Liberals went up from 13.6 to 24.2 per cent; in Scotland the SNP from 11.4 to 21.9 per cent. Wilson's minority government talked rich socialist rhetoric, but had little chance (or in the Cabinet, inclination) to fulfil it. The SNP lost MacDonald but added six Conservative seats and one Labour to the Western Isles. Wilson, expecting an election any week, had to act on Kilbrandon, to woo Liberals and hold Scotland.

Devolution split Scottish Labour. Its executive said OK on 10 March, but threw out the pro-devolution green paper on 22 June. Wilson and Transport House summoned the big unions and, at a special Scottish conference on 18 August, carried it. Just in time. Labour went into the 10 October election committed to a rather nebulous Scottish Assembly, goading rather than checking the SNP vote; Plaid Cymru lost some ground but the SNP topped 30 per cent and took four more seats, challenging Labour in thirty-five out of its forty-one.

This was the height of the oil crisis. The barrel price would treble between 1973 and 1978, from $4 to $12, and the SNP knew and said – its *Scotland's Oil* (1973) pamphlet sold a million – more about fuel politics than Whitehall (who kept schtum about a second McCrone Report of 1974 admitting that the Scots were potentially as rich as the Swiss). City rumours suggested that a Scottish breakaway might attract international finance, though the arrival of foreign banks really increased external control, while bust-and-boom aided the inroads of English and multinational firms.

Some socialists enthused over devolution in publications like Gordon Brown's *Red Paper* of May 1975. The boys (no woman figured among the twenty-eight writers) got some kudos, but devolutionists had to contest big Labour majorities in the new regions of Strathclyde, Central, Lothian and Fife, who wanted to establish and uphold their power. Distaste for the idea still existed, not only at Labour's Scottish grass roots but among English MPs and the cabinet itself. This affected the drafting of the white paper, and a battle – now between pro-devolution territorial ministers and hostile English departmental ministers – delayed its appearance until late in 1975.

Our Changing Democracy – or Whitehall resisting any real autonomy for the Assembly that cut across the evolution of the Scottish Office – prevented any logical division of its responsibilities. Housing went north, but not mortgages and private housing. Education likewise, but not universities; infrastructure planning included the new SDA, but not economic planning; transport, but not railways; law, but not courts or judges; local government, but not police.

The Secretary of State still retained substantial powers: over agriculture, fisheries, most of law and order, electricity, large areas of economic policy. He stayed in the cabinet, but took on a quasi-viceregal role *vis-à-vis* the 142-seat 'first-past-the-post' Assembly. He would appoint its executive and adjudicate on whether its enactments were within its *vires* or not. Scotland would continue to send seventy-one MPs to Westminster.

This satisfied the Labour establishment, Whitehall and the unions. In Scotland pro- and anti-devolutionists alike argued that its concessions could only be a first stage, though hostility among business groups, local authorities and some unions increased. They got a boost from the EEC referendum of 5 June, when pro-Europeans faced down Labour and the SNP. A January poll of 29 per cent pro-EEC to 45 per cent anti changed to 58.4 per cent to 41.6 on a low turnout of 61.7 per cent. Labour and SNP could not mobilise all their people.

The devolutionist left then made another mistake. Early in 1976 Jim Sillars MP, a home-rule convert, with left dissidents and journalists founded the Scottish Labour Party. 'The Magic Party', socialist and devolutionist, was popular – for a short time. It gained about 900 members (maybe 25 per cent of regular Labour activists?) but also attracted left-wing sects, and had no 'bottom' in the trade unions. Sillars would preside, ineffectively, over a stramash between middle-class ideologues: a disaster which isolated the country's most eloquent left-winger and weakened his cause within Labour.

Nor was it aided by Harold Wilson's sudden resignation in April 1976. Callaghan, his successor, sacked both Ross and Lord Crowther-Hunt, Wilson's constitutional expert. The new Secretary, Bruce Millan, a competent administrator, fatally lacked Ross's public personality. Difficulties mounted. The Scotland and Wales Bill, tabled on 13 December by Michael Foot, was literally incomprehensible: it didn't transfer control but cut-and-pasted clauses from existing legislation. The Conservatives, since February 1975 under Margaret Thatcher, tasted blood and worked on the division between cabinet, unenthusiastic back-benchers and discontented Liberals, denied proportional representation. Trapped in a committee-quagmire by 350 amendments, even Foot's concession of a referendum was in vain. An attempt to force a 'guillotine' on 22 February 1977 failed by twenty-nine votes.

Nothing much happened in Scotland: no placards, let alone riots. The SNP went to 36 per cent in the polls, but the pause before the new bill was tabled, on 4 November, deflated the issue. Folk were cool towards the Queen's Silver Jubilee in June 1977 (a fascinating topic for the *intellos*) but devolution was sapped by unemployment, the result of Labour's tight monetary policy – up from 3.6 per cent in 1974 to 7.5 per cent in 1978. When John Smith, a convivial Labour advocate, argued the new bill through the House, Scots MPs sat silent. 'Antis' slipped in a clause making its ultimate enactment depend on over 40 per cent of the whole Scots electorate voting 'Yes'. During this gap, on 13 July, John Mackintosh, one of its strongest proponents, died, aged only forty-eight. The Assembly might have given him the chance of high office that the Labour Party had continually denied him; his eloquence was certainly needed to save it.

To Labour the Act seemed to have paid off. English by-elections were disastrous but it swatted the SNP challenge, even in Hamilton (1978 was not a year for patriots: Scotland's eleven flopped in the World Cup in Argentina). But trouble was on its way, from the trade-union power that had forced devolution in 1974. Callaghan postponed the general election until after the referendum, then announced a rigid pay policy. The result was catastrophic; in January 1979 union discipline collapsed. Badly organised strikes coupled with the worst winter since 1947 aided the Conservatives while demonstrating working-class disunity. The intricate compromises of the Scotland Bill offered no answers to this, or to Scotland's growing economic problem; both Labour and the SNP again failed to get their vote out. Both had coherent minorities hoping that devolution would fail, and the imaginative ideas for using the new Assembly canvassed by its young, mainly middle-class, supporters were almost drowned out by the well-heeled 'Scotland says No' campaign's constant harping on expense, bureaucracy and disruption, amplified by the *Scottish Daily Express*, whose new owner, Victor (Lord) Matthews, takeover king and cockney Thatcherite, ditched Beaverbrook's home rule in the interests of 'the boss'.

On 1 March 63.63 per cent of the electorate voted. The highest poll was 67 per cent in the Borders, the most hostile mainland region; the lowest was 49.4 per cent in the SNP-held Western Isles, which voted 'Yes'. These almost epitomised the whole. The Labour heartlands – Strathclyde, Central and Fife – ensured a 'Yes' majority, but only Highland joined them. Lothian was only just 'Yes', Tayside only just 'No'. The main

Liberal or Nationalist areas – Borders, Grampian, Orkney and Shetland – were all hostile. The Assembly won, but only by 32.85 to 30.78 per cent, 7.15 points short of the 40 per cent hurdle.

Radicals as well as Tories preached the doom of social democracy. It was realised between January and May 1979. The devolution compromise wasn't just felled by the unions; councillors clung to their town halls and an antique landed class produced two Old Etonians with the charm of dynamite: Tam Dalyell and Lord Home. The SNP ended an uneasy parliamentary presence by rejecting Callaghan's offer of all-party talks and backing the no-confidence motion that on 28 March ejected his government. In the election on 3 May Labour removed the threat to most of its seats, while the SNP's vote fell to 18 per cent and it lost (albeit usually by narrow margins) nine of its eleven seats, eight to the Conservatives. But this success was dwarfed by Labour's shattering defeat south of the border.

'WE IN SCOTLAND'

The 1980s was an extraordinary decade. The Scots did not enter it with hope, and the election of 1992 was anticlimactic. The digital revolution was fact, marketised first by the 'Pacific Rim' states, then by Chinese 'Leninist capitalism'. So too was its one vivid *empowered* personality: Margaret Thatcher. Both European leaders, Mitterrand and Kohl, were constitutionally inhibited by opponents (Chirac in the *Assemblée Nationale*, the *'Sozis'* in the *Länder*); Ronald Reagan was amiable but dim. Well-placed by the oil and her 'elective dictatorship', Thatcher was borne up by many right-wingers of Scots descent – Rupert Murdoch, and under him Andrew Neil of the *Sunday Times*, Dr Madsen Pirie of the Adam Smith Institute, Professor Norman Stone. Yet her Scottish policies unravelled throughout: she fought a losing battle with voters, Kirk, local authorities and the media, and was wounded in April 1990 in a hard-fought TV interview with Kirsty Wark. On 22 November that year, nemesis came from her own backbenches.

Thatcher often came north. Why? Scots Tories craved prime ministerial indifference. Yet Scotland figured in the ideology of this 'absolute bourgeois'. Her relationship with the English establishment was ambiguous: deferential to the crown, neutral in religion, manipulating the honours system. Yet in Scotland, she seemed to believe, her values could come into their own. Charles Moore suggests a brief romance with a tight-fisted Essex-Scots farmer, duly passed onto her sister. The grossly inegalitarian 'poll tax' was born of a Scot, Douglas Mason; and her most drastic (and among the English bourgeois, most unpopular) shot at law reform followed her appointment of a talented, humane Highland Calvinist, Mackay of Clashfern, as Lord Chancellor.

Yet her monetarist experiment from 1979 to 1981 caused, besides inflation, an outflow of funds and a 20 per cent collapse in manufacturing. The Scottish Office under George Younger, aided by the amiable wettish Willie Whitelaw, checked her while Labour lurched leftward and pushed out the centre-left Social Democrats, who gained two Labour MPs and in March 1982 took Glasgow Hillhead (the city's last Tory seat) with Roy Jenkins. Then came the Falklands war, unpopular in Scotland despite historic links: many 'Kelpers' were Scots by descent and even their Argentinian name 'Malvinas' derived from Ossian's girlfriend. Her victory was like Jutland in 1916: its price heavy naval losses. General Galtieri's fall also triggered the collapse of the South American military dictators whom her US supporters favoured as economically safe. Tam Dalyell quit mauling devolution and mauled her instead over the captious sinking of the obsolete cruiser *Belgrano*, with 350 dead.

Rejoice? Scotland did not in the June 1983 election. But in England Labour held only three southern seats outside London: red flecks in a sea of blue. Foot gave way to Neil Kinnock, little loved in Scotland, though his ally Robin Cook switched back to devolution. Thatcher's next battle, in 1984–5, was with the miners under the veteran Communist Mick McGahey, better regarded than Ian MacGregor, the tough Scots boss of the Coal Board – or the shrill leftist Arthur Scargill. Overinvestment in electricity paid off and saved governmental face. Deep-mined coal promptly vanished, save for two mines, Monktonhall and Longannet, which struggled on until 1997 and 2002.

Political Scots also shifted to the civic, which drew on the renaissance bequest, higher education expansion and many of the cultural linkages. The then-unique Poetry Library in Edinburgh's Old Town – the brainchild of Wolfe and Tessa Ransford – opened ground for cross-party action. 'Unthank' in Alasdair Gray's *Lanark* (1981: an *éclat* of native sci-fi, Carlyle-to-Patrick Geddes spectaculars and Gray's own unique graphics) apotheosised the baroque, put-upon, industrial towns of the central belt, though it was in the country districts and suburbs – natural Tory territory – that 'Tory-free' bodies started to combine in tactical alliances. The BBC ran a pro-devolution TV series, *Scotland 2000*, in early 1987 (Thatcher sacked the Director-General Alasdair Milne). At the October election the Tories lost 4 per cent of their vote – but over half of their seats.

The revolt was polite and prudent, but had links with the growing greenish resistance in Germany and Eastern Europe, Poland in particular, through the dynamic Edinburgh multi-talent Richard Demarco. In May 1986 Chernobyl nuclear plant in the Ukraine blew up, scattering caesium over Scottish hills, and in autumn 1988 Govan again surprised: Jim Sillars (now married to Margo MacDonald) captured it for the SNP. In a Christmas atrocity, 270 died when a Pan-Am flight was blown up over the small town of Lockerbie; twenty-six years later the intrigues surrounding this had yet to dissolve.

By then the focus was on the 'Claim of Right', demanding a convention to structure a Scottish Parliament, first advanced in 1985: a representative centrist bunch, really the Covenant Movement without the 'mass' element, the Free Kirk minus God. In 1989 its first session (Labour and Liberal MPs, Churches, trade unions, representatives of civil society) convened in the Assembly Hall on Edinburgh's Mound, but without the SNP's presence: not the last canny manoeuvre by its new young leader Alex Salmond, who reckoned he was best placed to push it from outside. It was managed by a resourceful clergyman, the

Rev. Kenyon Wright, and backed one crucial policy: that the parliament would be elected by proportional representation: a 'modified d'Hondt system' along German lines. This would lessen the chance of a one-party government; its adoption in 1978 might have secured the earlier attempt.

Mediating with Reagan, Thatcher cleverly patronised Gorbachev. He failed to achieve his *perestroika* (restructuring), and fell only ten months after her, in August 1991. The 'shock therapy' of instant marketisation was visited on the former Comecon. Was this 'the end of history'? Not for long. McMafia schlepped wealth from gangster states to London, rarely further north. But the whisky trade did well.

John Major, premier from 1990 to 1997, initially gained from not being Thatcher. He had to cope with a sophisticated IRA campaign against the London finance metropole, and an economics of shadowing the Deutschmark which ended in the 1992 slump, yet remarkably survived the challenge of Kinnock and John Smith. At the April 1992 election their reindustrialising policies didn't play in the south-east, leaving Major with a small majority, to be martyred by increasing Conservative anti-Europeanism. Smith, the first Scot to be Labour leader since Ramsay MacDonald, enjoyed near-consensual support at home, but 'the boys from the north' were divided. The 'settled will' of the Scottish people was seen by the ambitious Anglo-Scots around him as stepping stone to a British hegemony. They got this chance when, on 12 May 1994, he suddenly died. A power-bid was made by two young men willing to take chances on economics and the constitutionalism: Gordon Brown and Tony Blair in their 'Granita compact' took Walter Bagehot's 'efficient cabinet' to bits.

'WORK AS IF YOU LIVED IN THE EARLY DAYS OF A BETTER NATION . . .'

Consider, for a moment (few in London did), how cultural life in Scotland had evolved since the 1960s. Then it livened up, if only for a minority. Although the commercial theatre was now all but extinct, experiment thrived at the Traverse and the Citizens and on the Edinburgh Festival Fringe. It even became less remote from the pubs and housing schemes, as John McGrath's 7:84 Company, the indescribable talents of Billy Connolly and the work of such as James MacTaggart, Eddie Boyd, Roddy Macmillan, and Peter MacDougall for television gave it a greater demotic edge. Sir Alexander Gibson, appointed conductor of the Scottish National Orchestra in 1959, helped set up Scottish Opera in 1963, and by 1980 the country's musical life had caught up with the Edinburgh Festival and borne fruit, with the help of local authorities and government.

Public money talked. Scotland's share of the Arts Council budget had dropped from 8.4 per cent to 6. 3 per cent between 1948 and 1963. Under the Fifer Jennie Lee, Bevan's widow and now Wilson's arts minister, it climbed back to 11.4 per cent by 1970, subsidising painting, literature, Gaelic culture and folk music. MacDiarmid died in 1978: an honoured national institution, courtly and infuriating: 'He'll charm old ladies onto the mantelpiece/And leave them there', as Norman MacCaig put it. Age would claim the other Renaissance folk but poetry and the short story thrived in quality daily and little magazine. The 'high road to England' had less allure. Writers like James Kennaway, Robin Jenkins and William McIlvanney saw the Scots experience not necessarily as positive, but fricative. George Mackay Brown and Iain Crichton Smith captured the distinctive experiences of Norse and Gaelic Scotland; Muriel Spark and (on stage) Cecil Taylor and Ivor Cutler the remarkable dialectic of Scot and Jew.

Incomers mattered: in 1962–3 a couple of literary conferences caused a splore in douce Edinburgh – with wild men like Henry Miller and William Burroughs overdoing it; acute readers remembered that D. H. Lawrence's Lady Chatterley had been Constance Reid from Glasgow. Scottish publishing activity, in history writing, reviewing and reprinting, coped with the reverses of the 1970s and 1980s: perhaps deceptively. Did bogeyman Knox loom too darkly and too many dash from loom or lathe to the psychiatrist's couch? R. D. Laing worked in London like Karl Miller, and also linked psychotic states with the divided state that housed the *Justified Sinner* and *Jekyll and Hyde*. Miller himself, out of Hector MacIver's Royal High School by Leavis's Cambridge, contributed to the analyses rattling out anent the first rise of the SNP and commissioned the Marxist philosopher Tom Nairn's first (hostile) bout with nationalism. His *Break-Up of Britain* (1977) soon became central to an unsentimental debate. 'Lads o' pairts' returned home, imagination sharpened by analysis; work by Scots and about Scotland, in history, politics and economics, was as distinguished as anything since the eighteenth century.

In the 1970s everyone talked politics, though Neal Ascherson, political correspondent of the *Scotsman*, worried about the absence of the sort of literary movement that nationalism ought to create. Most big publishers closed down or moved key offices south – Nelson, Oliver and Boyd, Collins. Scots literary and political reviews had short lives. *Scottish International* from 1966 to 1974; the student-based *New Edinburgh Review* and *Cencrastus*. When many were overcome by post-referendum *accidie*, *Radical Scotland* (1982–91) under Alan Lawson invented the 'Doomsday Scenario' – '*You* may be the government, *We* are the Scottish people' changing the language of Scottish political discourse. Between 1980 and 2000 the quality papers, now edited now by the sons of 'Renaissance' men – Arnold Kemp on the *Herald* and Magnus Linklater on the *Scotsman* – rivalled anything coming from London; and the BBC and STV showed initiative and a European sense.

The sentence 'Work as if you lived in the early days of a better nation' came from the Canadian poet Dennis Lee, borrowed by Alasdair Gray, from whose books, resembling Geddesian *Masques of Learning*, there flooded out the pent-up experience of the country from the Reformation onwards. Happily, Lee's advice was taken. Gray's fellow Glaswegians Tom Leonard and James Kelman were formidable, though uncompromising and pessimistic. Kelman used the Scottish vernacular at its dourest, causing the London oracle Sir Simon Jenkins to emit an essay which became an anthology item: 'a Jilly Cooper of the Gorbals, a Barbara Cartland of the gutter', etc. Such well-bred vapouring would get its chance again in 2014, now christened 'love bombing'.

But a symbol from a Kelman novel, *A Disaffection* (1989), sounded a more general patterning, its Victorian career researched by Leonard and William Donaldson. Patrick Doyle, a put-upon teacher trapped in Glasgow, is drawn to the transcendence of the German poet Hölderlin. He creates a religion around organ pipes which, he tells his pupils, can communicate across the ages: Jung would have called this the 'chthonic'. Others recalled the arresting organ chords Mark Knoepfler gave to Bill Forsyth's literally 'wonderful' *Local Hero* in 1983, in which mad American oilman Happer arrives as *deus ex machina* by helicopter to stop the Ferness folk lynching their local prophet, and recovers his soul through the phenomenon of the Northern Lights (real and quite worrying solar events). This feeling related to the accretion of symbols and techniques that – given close relation to poetry – could stiffen politics with something both questioning and resilient as well as spurring collective action.

Behind such ideas were the education reforms of the 1960s, new courses, seminars and libraries, maturing in the years after the *débâcle*. The development of 'Scottish Studies' counted here, like Gray's graphics, boosted by the exuberance of women as performers, historians and editors as well as creative writers: Liz Lochhead, Janice Galloway, A. L. Kennedy, Jenny Wormald, Carol Craig. But experimental growth also stemmed from the multiple layers of language, society, environment, though that often misled; Scots could often claim success in fundamental ideas, but in the absence of a small-and-medium-size enterprise (SME) culture (Wolfe's communitarian enterprises were premature) their application to manufacturing remained remote.

In Greenock IBM's staff had fiddled about with their first desktops in 1981, putting paper and ink on notice. Football under Scottish managers and media moguls became the religion of the new and unlovely Rome unfolding from tabloids and satellite TV in the British cities. This flow wasn't linear – or even progressive. Maybe it paralleled the schizoid states of Hogg or Stevenson, the Murdoch press proving more resilient than Thatcher's dynamic bundle of Home County prejudices.

'THE SCOTTISH PARLIAMENT . . . IS HEREBY RECONVENED!'

Out of power, Thatcher's shadow fell over her party, through its increasing Europhobia, though in Scotland her poll tax boosted John Major because rebels fell off the electoral roll. Seething Eurosceptic backbenches, and a Major defensive swerve, brought Michael Forsyth back. Now an anti-parliamentary nationalist of a sort, in 1996 he greeted Mel Gibson's *Braveheart* – alias 'Woad Rage' or 'Mad Mac'? – with what looked like enthusiasm. The civic-to-Marxist folk winced, but the Stone of Scone came back. Labour tied itself in knots over the timetabling of devolution, which bored Blair, but the result of the British general election in May 1997 was that not a single Scots Tory MP survived.

The Scottish settlement was unspectacular, compared with the peace process in Northern Ireland, which would follow on its heels. A referendum was held on 11 September. Shortly before, England had been convulsed by the death of Diana, Princess of Wales in Paris; but the result was victory by 74 per cent to 26 per cent, a switch spectacular enough to drag Welsh devolution – only just – to 50.3 per cent a week later. Following a struggle in Blair's cabinet between Donald Dewar and Lord Chancellor Irvine (who had run off with Mrs Dewar: Anthony Trollope's fingers would have itched!) the Scotland Bill was tabled in November and became law a year later. Debates on it, left largely to Scots ministers and English right-wingers, were humdrum. Only six former MPs came to the parliament that opened in the Kirk's Assembly Hall on 12 May 1999, Dewar having won the first Scottish general election on 6 May. A coalition between the Lib Dems (eighteen seats) and Labour (fifty-six seats) took office.

'The Scottish Parliament, adjourned on the twenty-fifth day of March 1707, is hereby reconvened!' pronounced its senior

MSP, Mrs Winifred Ewing. Which would have surprised the bag-wigged legalists who had thought it buried forever.

Yet the infant Holyrood was confronted with a gulf between its largely welfare powers and the rapidly changing shape of the UK economy 'reserved to Westminster'. The 'United Kingdom of London' had been dynamised by air transport from Heathrow, Gatwick, Luton and City airports, the Channel Tunnel (1993), Docklands redevelopment and the investment/recreational 'social overhead capital' seeded by international plutocrats. There was no parallel in 'Scottish' popular politics. The latter was to do with income, property, cars, shopping, beach holidays, law-and-order, the NHS and death. Apart from the last three, none were run from Scotland. Moreover, MacDiarmid's 'wunds wi' warlds to swing' were gathering force, with natural disaster, terrorism, epidemic.

A regionalist culture – partly Scots-generated – initially thrived in post-wall Europe, but it was evicted by the 'national' discipline of readying currencies for the euro (for accounting from 1 January 1999, as currency from 1 January 2002). This reinforced London, under *its* devolved ruler. An unusual radical, agnostic about his Scots roots, Ken Livingstone calculated a public-sector, public-transport-driven metropolis *against* any regional rivals. His 'servitor capitalism', 1980–6 and 2000–8, squashed by Thatcher, was revived to house investment's London end, through the dynamism rushing in from multinationals, the BRIC (Brazil, Russia, India and China) newly industrialised countries (NICs), and a computer-driven international division of labour. Its guardians became the Jekyll-and-Hyde pair that created New Labour, legitimising him to lead a new London Council.

Blair and Brown bought devolution, divided Bagehot's unified cabinet in favour of juggling with oligarchs, Chinese millionaires and the economics of fashion, media, 'financial services' and semi-mercenary warfare. In all of this, the Scots back home were useful, though 'not quite in on the act'. Their *qui vive* was risky but the bad news was already happening as Comecon broke up, nuclear power – Chernobyl 1986 – went wrong and Mischa

Glenny's *McMafia* (2005) mocked civil society. Yugoslavia had been in the 1960s a lefty near-utopia: goulash Communism, cheap wine, girls sunbathing on Adriatic beaches. Visiting half a century later, the shrewd Peter Geoghegan, successor to James Cameron and Neal Ascherson, whose *People's Referendum* exhilarated in the Scots debate of 2014, found *Republika Srpska* (Serbian Bosnia) not civic but toxic.

The Scots had lived from 1968 to 1998 with terrorism only twenty miles from Stranraer, but kept it in bounds. West Scotland became (for a time) a sort of 'special economic zone' – resembling Alasdair Gray's 'Institute' in *Lanark*, remote from the usual disciplines: this eccentric economy-minus-investigation was subject to mysterious shifts unknown to national statistics. It was reckoned in January 2015 by the para-police of the Scottish Business Resilience Centre – a would-be Fraud Squad – that Scottish business was hit by £3bn a year (2 per cent of GDP) in fraud alone.

This led to a tolerance of economic risk, just as London and Tony Blair bargained City and Docklands tranquillity from Sinn Féin in 1998. Halved by the takeovers of the mid-1980s, and with oil bumping along as low as $10 a barrel until 2000, Scottish capital didn't dabble in overseas finance, it plunged. Chancellor Brown's trusties mocked the German 'flexible specialism' in manufacture he had once praised in *Where there is Greed* (1989). There was some logic to this given the rise of the NICs and travelling Scots like William Purves and Jim Duff. Foreign investment fields would balance one another; inflation would yield to cheap consumer goods made abroad. So said Philip Green, Richard Branson, Terry Leahy, Rupert Murdoch, old uncle Tom Hunter and all! Eternal nylon, frocks and slacks, would join millions of yesterday's computers/phones/video hardware on every Scottish dump.

After the shocks of reunion, manufacturing was refinanced in Germany by Schröder and Merkel, through local, state-run incubators, and social saving from public transport, while house prices stagnated; the place was serious and shabby, like Attlee's Britain, while London, ministering to Ferdinand Mount's plutocratic *New Few* (2012) and their satellites, glittered. This was reflected in a few fortunate Scottish places, though far less flagrant than Kensington: New Town flats in Edinburgh (until about 2012 keeping up with London), big ranch-style houses near golf courses, seldom-used yachts bobbing off western piers.

In 2002 my brief book on Scottish transport, *Deep-Fried Hillman Imp*, was bulk-bought by the Chinese Railway Academy. Based on cloning German technology, a new rail age was under way, schemes radiating from Beijing past the Himalayas far as Dakar in West Africa. The Scots looked on. The damage to their innovative technology dated from well before Thatcher, with the 1960s Pressed Steel and NB Loco closures in Linwood and Glasgow. Only in 2015, with HS2 impending, was the UK's disinvestment in rail technology (temporarily) reversed: but the new Hitachi rolling-stock works went to Durham. Would privatised transport change things? It brought growing orders from Stagecoach to Alexander's busworks at Falkirk, but its rival First, certainly worldwide, seemed less perjink than strayed.

In 2011 three-storey trains of Chinese imports thundered eastbound past Laramie, Wyoming on the freight-only Union Pacific (we were at the university, conferring on Walter Scott). There was one bus a day, each way, at 3.50 a.m. from the Greyhound stop. A note told any locals with problems to complain to First Group at Larbert, Scotland, FK5 3NJ.

8

'Point of Departure?', 1999–2015

BLOW-BY-BLOW?

The Union's 300th anniversary fell on 1 May 2007; inside Catalan Enric Miralles' Holyrood, strongly 'national' in style, the new SNP establishment would form a government within days. Early-eighteenth-century turbulence was being matched Europe-wide, and didn't abate much over the next decade. The mood-music was similarly hypnotic. Gordon Brown's 'light-touch economy' halved manufacture to concentrate on nebulous financial services, encouraged by a press itself halved by an opaque 'new media' between 1995 and 2010. Sober company balance sheets gave way to 'high-velocity', algorithm-propelled financial gambling. Neo-liberalism staged a triumph in Edinburgh and Kirkcaldy in January 2005 when Brown feted Alan Greenspan, Federal Reserve chair and acolyte of the 'anti-altruist' Ayn Rand. This preluded the greatest economic crash in peacetime Britain, in which Westminster MPs bobbed about in a plutocratic City which looked less dynamic than – in the Mack-Kerner sense – a 'crime industry'. Sober savers were looted as interest fell to 0.5 per cent and post-Communist oligarchs grabbed London property which soared in value: the price of an Islington flat costing £40,000 in 1984 rose twentyfold by 2014, while family houses in Brown's Fife constituency crawled from £100,000 in 2001 to £129,000 in 2007; by 2015 they were back where they started.

Some observers of the scene used the phrase 'creative destruction' from J. A. Schumpeter, late of Austria, careful to be in

Harvard between 1932 and 1950, when things hit the European rocks. His Swedish contemporary Thorstein Veblen's 'technocracy' influenced the more practical Scots-Canadian J. K. Galbraith. Nuclear power and 'consumer electronics' *were* world-changers, yet were financed in part by the US imbroglio in Vietnam, and by London as convention-breaking eurodollar megalopolis. A 'planned, baby-boom' generation moved in the 1960s through the joy of sex – 'peace and love' satisfying at low cost David Hume's 'passions' – to Aids after 1977. Initially tragic, this proved manageable: there were 7,384 Scottish cases of which 25 per cent were fatal. Booze, reliable old hitman, killed 600 a year in Glasgow alone. Scotland's Medical Officer of Health, Sir Harry Burns, reckoned that the 'illth' that took the average Glasgow Calton male at fifty-four stemmed from despair at the absence of secure, rewarding work. Western work culture – Walt Whitman to Woody Guthrie – was being upended by a Chinese 'Leninist capitalism' steering (and ultimately restructuring) Western 'brainworks' while retaining attitudes to workers' welfare that would appall Robert Owen.

Scots had played little part in California's Silicon Valley, though early on career-myths were rejigged, with smart Hungarians like the father of 'MacIntyre' in *Local Hero* reckoning on Scots names. By 1985 Bill Forsyth's running gag – ringing Houston from a 10p phone-box – was silenced by new technology; just as *The Simpsons*' Springfield, the property of Rupert Murdoch (grandfather from Rosemarkie; the next-door parish to 'Ferness') went on the map. Its Scots, from primitive Groundskeeper Willie to aged and evil C. Montgomery Burns, didn't encourage.

Scotland contributed to bestsellerdom: in the well-crafted and soon-comfortable worlds of J. K. Rowling, Ian Rankin, Irvine Welsh and Sandy McCall Smith. In 2014, captivated by the Glasgow Commonwealth Games, many found dancing teacakes and Scottie dogs great guilty fun. But the Clyde was on defence-contract life-support; Ferguson's, its last civilian shipyard, closed (happily only temporarily) a fortnight after the athletes left.

Table 8.1 Scottish Parliament general elections, from May 1999

1999 (6 May) Turnout 59%

	Con		Lib Dem		Labour		SNP		Other	
	%	MSPs	%	MSPs	%	MSPs	%	MSPs	%	MSPs
Constituency	16	0	14	12	39	53	29	7	8	3
Region	15	18	12	5	34	3	27	28	8	3

2003 (1 May) Turnout 49%

	Con		Lib Dem		Labour		SNP		Other	
	%	MSPs	%	MSPs	%	MSPs	%	MSPs	%	MSPs
Constituency	3	0	15	13	35	46	24	9	n/a	2
Region	12	15	12	4	29	4	21	18	12	13*

*Greens 7; Scottish Socialists 6; Independents 2

2007 (3 May) Turnout 49%

	Con		Lib Dem		Labour		SNP		Other	
	%	MSPs	%	MSPs	%	MSPs	%	MSPs	%	MSPs
Constituency	17	4	16	11	32	37	33	21	n/a	n/a
Region	14	13	11	5	29	9	31	26	n/a	3*

*Greens 2; Independent (Margo MacDonald) 1

2011 (5 May) Turnout 52%

	Con		Lib Dem		Labour		SNP		Other	
	%	MSPs	%	MSPs	%	MSPs	%	MSPs	%	MSPs
Constituency	14	3	8	2	32	15	45	53	n/a	n/a
Region	12	12	5	3	26	22	44	16	n/a	3*

*Greens 2; Independent (Margo MacDonald) 1
Seventy-three constituency seats, fifty-six regional seats based on the old
European Parliament constituencies.

Much of this was published/publicised by Murdoch. He sold
sex on Page 3, transmitted footie to every time zone, helped
extend 'Leninist capitalism', undermined British monarchs *and*
Magna Carta, compromised London cabinets. In 2015 might he

end the UK? Yes! And south of Berwick? No! *Le roi s'amuse!*
The Sun King has fun!

Closer to home the Northern Ireland effect on Scotland's
'Wild West' outlived the 1968–98 Troubles. The conflict trained
specialised troops; the recycling of the ghettos' criminal economy
became linked to Edinburgh, Dublin and London and their
footloose 'cash-nexus'. Its market impact was historically rooted,
long-term and unreassuring. Enlightenment *savants* – the pes-
simist Adam Ferguson and the 'cameralist' Sir James Steuart,
as important in their time as Adam Smith – worried about the
impact of 'luxury and corruption' on 'commercial' society. This
had been juridically sorted by the utilitarian work and value structures of Jeremy Bentham, Robert Owen and later Walter Bagehot
(with Scots echoes and allies in James and John Stuart Mill and
the *Economist*). Ulster would provide a miniature of post-1991
plutocracy, where a London-centred 'age of plunder' looted
Russia and the former Comecon and fanned high-risk Chinese
manufacture. Assessing in his 'Land and Sea' essay in the *Oxford
Handbook* the ecological condition of both, Historiographer
Royal Christopher Smout was grim: after 2001 his Scotland,
with too many deer, polluting cars and lorries, too few fish, 'was
apparently set on the road to environmental disaster'.

In the 1980s North Sea oil had seemed helpful to a circum-
spect commercial community avoiding the corruption of Nigeria
and the Middle East; but Scotland didn't thrive like Norway on
its $780bn pensions fund. The 1997 election threw out the last
Tories, but far from remedying an oil monoculture, Scots-led
New Labour reduced manufacturing. Tony Blair was the son
of Leo, transiting from Red Clyde Stalinism via the army to
the Tory Party. His twin Gordon Brown, ringed by minders,
dreamed of international markets liberated from messy metal-
bashing, winning Murdoch-style multinationals for London.
UK pollution dropped by a nominal 13 per cent. But the toxic
impact of Far East manufacture plus long-distance sea transport
worsened world pollution.

In their 'Granita compact' in May 1994, unprecedently dividing cabinet responsibility, Scotland became one of 'Gordon's

Things' – home policy, prinked with festivals, tourism, whisky, 'tartan noir' – catered for the multinational combines, from Amazon to NewsInt, which dominated publishing and retail, flowing into an emptying Silicon Glen. In Germany technical education and innovation, directed at rescuing the 'Wild East', held skilled manufacturing at over 20 per cent of GDP. In the UK it had by 2005 fallen to scarcely half this. Construction ran at over 6 per cent of GDP, with most projects, a 2013 Chartered Institute of Building report found, 'allocated' by public-private contracts – and quiet verbal deals between firms. Construction work – *'Joabs on ra Tarr!'* – rarely inspired praise, indeed rarely showed skill. Architects wept when the Mackintosh Art School burned in July 2014, but carried on building dull, expensive PPI schools, dreich malls in Edinburgh's 'Caltongate' and civic Aberdeen. Perth Council strove to level its handsome Edwardian City Hall, the stage of much of *No Gods*'s political action.

'Industrialised retail', mail order, 'knowledge industries' and tourism paid low wages: £12,000 a year in a warehouse, £15,000 for the 90,000 in call centres – juggling high rents and motoring costs in a bad-weather Los Angeles, sapped by insecurity. By 2015 the supermarket model itself hit trouble: alarm arose over what went into 'economy mince', then shrinking profits, then milk so cheap it threatened Scottish dairying. In early 2015 German discounters Aldi and Lidl – with fresh food in town centres – maimed Tesco, at 24,000 Scotland's biggest private-sector employer. A fraction of the NHS, but many of the latter's 160,000 staff had to sort out the consequences of 'Bogof' and booze.

Print culture was under siege, replaced by cars, food, drink and TV/social media for 'all of us', drugs and illness for the 20 per cent of have-nots. The parish was hollowed out. The businesses of St Boswells, population 1,200, were thirty in 1955, eight in 2015. Across rural Scotland, Kirk, choir, drama group, schools, pubs dwindled. In an essay on Britain's uneasy 'dual-monarchy' period (1485–1688) Jenny Wormald described how Scots sank or swam in a sea of shifting, semi-economic forces, from weather to politics. Bewilderment and peril revived enough for the historian Tony Judt in his last books to shift from neo-liberalism back to the welfare state. But what of New Labour? Robert Harris and Roman Polanski's *The Ghost* had ex-Bond Pierce Brosnan as a Blair-Brown figure banged up on Cape Cod – 'tartan noir' gone global, with Ewan McGregor – once 'Renton' from *Trainspotting* – as his ghost and fatal nemesis. Shades of James Hogg's 'Justified Sinner'? Hogg's descendant, Canadian Alice Munro, got the Nobel Prize in 2013: she observed frail rationality assailed by globalism *and* parochialism. Was Official Scotland impressed? *'Alice who?'*

The 'break-up of Britain' would shadow the alarming 2015 election, which took its secular cue from a new, ecological, feminising Scottish left, symbolised by products of Alasdair Gray's 'better nation' *mythos*, from First Minister Sturgeon to such publicists as Lesley Riddoch. Yet its market was made by multinational firms in a packed London, William Dunbar's and Andrew Fletcher's 'macrocephalous head' worries about the place forgotten, Ken Livingstone and Boris Johnson's metropolis traded vast sums from natural resources – factored through the tax havens of the residual British empire – lured by a centralised, expensive state-culture paid out of the public pocket. Scotland's regional subsidy had been high in 2000 – £116 to every £100 going to the English regions. But by 2012, £170 went to London, on top of the inflation of its real estate. That summer an Olympic fest, remote from the amateur ethic, was launched with a flourish – by Danny Boyle, director of *Trainspotting* – lauding a National Health ethic which would shortly be imperilled by the American 'free market' in health provision.

HOLYROOD, ENTERPRISE AND THE BANKS

The 1999–2008 career of the new parliament was blighted by its cost. Even before the 9/11 crisis, £120 million was voted, which changed it from Miralles' open 'political precinct' to a fortress. Squaring security with access, *and* feeding Edinburgh's oligarchs, trebled the bill. In 2004 Dewar and Miralles were blamed by the Fraser Inquiry. They were, helpfully, dead. The commercial architects RMJM – founded by the socialists Robert

Matthew and Stirrat Johnson-Marshall – whose young architects excelled in Holyrood's details, fed off big international contracts for a while, until the slump screened as main feature, fusing all the lights.

Only after 2010 did explaining the 'Pinstripe Darien' trouble Scotland's now-anaemic quality press. Had prospective risks been assessed? Problems had been masked by innovations, structural and technologically enabled, in the firm and the public service: both were made part of the drive to 'voice' (for quick profit) and 'exit'. Whitehall moved from mandarins to 'agencies' with flexible appointments, bonuses and tax perks: Scotland may have made the pace with the Highland Board and SDA (1965 and 1975). The old touchstones – profit and loss, career and pension – were dissolved by the age of the consultancy: 'mergers and acquisitions' was now its own business, debt and tax loss could be magicked into economic gain. Ponzi-type financial rackets throve. The electric power-trader Enron (valued at $62bn on 28 November 2001) strode onto the market, stumbled and in 2002 vanished. Where next?

At the modest £ million level of the Scottish Budget, the Tories had decentralised Scottish Enterprise (SE) to 'local business leadership'. Jack McConnell in 2002 recentralised and made Robert Crawford, from the SNP left, its chair. His aim was Intermediary Technology Institutes (ITIs): research-based business generators modelled on the German Fraunhofer Stiftung. These were promised £441 million over 2002–10: to commission bright inventions, marketise them and make millions. But SE staff seemed to get lost between the 'small-is-beautiful' of German *Mittelstand-Industrie* and the Chinese transformation, often managed by graduates in economics and English from Scottish universities. The ITIs clocked up an outlay of over £230 million between 2002 and 2008, but yielded less than £600,000 in patents. Despite ministerial-level salaries, by 2007 they had vanished. Yet when tidal power and counter-inundation schemes emerged from the unique environment of the northern seas, their projectors were told that technology development was considered secondary to 'commercialisation'.

Wendy Alexander touted *New Wealth for Old Nations* in a Chicago-inspired tract of 2005: its free-for-all became economic archaeology within months. It was back to naval shipbuilding, the construction cartel, unfathomable 'regulated markets' in once-predictable utilities, unwritten agreements and political decisions. The pattern was of Scots entrepreneurs 'cashing in' by selling out (Scottish & Newcastle, Wood Mackenzie, Optos, Wolfson, Macallan, Miller) or being pulled down by multinationals rationalising after bingeing on 'mergers and acquisitions'. Dutch Vion closed in 2012 the Grampian meat-processing plant it had acquired in Broxburn in 2005 through the boys from HBoS. Two thousand workers went 'down the road'.

In 2012 GDP per capita in Scotland was £17,500; in Baden-Württemberg £27,200. The car:people ratio was the same, just under 1:2, but bikes, walking and public transport were formidable 'social savers' in Europe's Stuttgarts, with the dividend going to industrial and training investment. In Scotland, 2007–14, Salmond squashed the Lib–Lab coalition's ill-planned Edinburgh Airport rail link, and reluctantly accepted trams. Their European success as low-cost transit was mangled by Transport Initiatives Edinburgh. One km cost £51m, against £14 million in Germany. He continued with McConnell's 'gold-plated' Bathgate–Airdrie Railway, and added the £1.5bn Queensferry Crossing road bridge, Chinese-built, over the Forth. Edinburgh remained four hours from London by 1970s-built trains. Paris was only three from Marseilles.

New Labour used MSPs as *Harry Potter*-like 'house-elves' tending its Westminster big-hitters' seats (a third of the front-bench in 2000 was Scots). The Holyrood coalitions of 1999–2007 did not have the resilience to withstand this (reinforced by twenty-nine Labour and nine Lib Dem peers, at £29,000 per annum per head). Handling ten different 'Scotland Secretaries' from London's new 'Scotland Office' between 1999 and 2015 meant meetings on the shuttle or at Heathrow. Local potentates, folk said, 'knew where the bodies were buried'. Some promising steps came from the Fifer Henry McLeish until 'a muddle, not a fiddle' to do with a sub-let office felled him on the

BBC's *Question Time* in November 2001. His successor Jack McConnell knew west-coast Labour, but Gordon Brown didn't want to know him.

The Chancellor courted one side of Edinburgh. Danny Boyle's breakthrough film *Shallow Grave* (1994) was set in its finance world: high stools, ledgers, sex and sawing people up. Around 2002 this changed. The Scottish banks – HBoS and RBS – had profited in the 1990s by going online, pocketing the savings of this from depositors, doing well from the rail privatisation (1997) that made Britain's trains the most expensive in Europe. The surpluses of this went on funding feral dealers, their 'handheld-technology', lauded by corporate lawyers and 'animal spirits' recalling 1920s Wall Street.

Sandy McCall Smith in *The Sunday Philosophy Club* (2005) got the scene. Dr Isabel Dalhousie witnesses the violent death of a young man in the Usher Hall. Did he fall, or was he pushed? An insider opens up a cash-driven world where dealing in 'Scottish Colourist' paintings masks tax dodging. A non-toxic explanation – accident plus personal grievance – reassures the *Edinbourgeois* concerned. Would this have worked after the 2008 crash? In March 2014 Douglas Fraser, the BBC's shrewd economics man, noted that for the remaining bankers to warn about the risks of independence sounded odd: 'You'll have had your moral hazard?'

Blair had obsessed on world policing after 9/11. Resolute and 'difficult', Brown was backed by voters as well as the City, until in 2007–8 'mark to market' popped the share-bubble. Not before geld had flowed from finance into property – besides fine art, country mansions (up to £7m a go in 2006) and farmland – through seamless 'enterprise'. Tax-avoidance and ballooning credit stretched worldwide through the treasure islands of the UK's tax havens.

Asked at 9 a.m. on 8 October 2008 by Holyrood's Economy and Energy Committee how the Royal Bank's SIVs (Securitised Investment Vehicles) worked, its Group Economist said 'maybe three people in the firm' knew. CEO Fred Goodwin had staked the RBS's huge cash reserves on his target bank ABN Amro but its magic money evaporated and RBS shares went into in free-fall; by tea time it was under Whitehall control.

The formal banking structure was damaged, the 'new banks' (ex-building societies) wiped out. Scotland produced its first billionaire in 2004, the 'serial philanthropist' Sir Tom Hunter, but in 2009 he took a £500m hit and left the *Sunday Times*'s 'Rich List'; the 'corporate bankers' that made him had vanished; though by 2015 Scots billionaires numbered ten. Chancellor Alistair Darling, grumpily beside Brown during the typhoon, retrospectively blamed banking 'Scottishness', comprehending little of life at RBS after a visit in 2003 as part-time Scotland Secretary. Gill Tett of the *Financial Times* wrote *Fool's Gold* and saw 'tribal' dealers high on hand-held computers, testosterone and serial dough, ripping off and getting out. New York's Bernie Madoff was jailed in late 2009 for a $70bn Ponzi scheme. He said he 'had no innocent explanation' but was no worse than the private equity houses he fed.

Some of the new/old banking order got fired, but all stayed free; even Mrs Thatcher had jailed the guilty Guinness men in 1986. After autumn 2008 Brown and Darling and after May 2010 David Cameron's Con–Lib Dem coalition looted welfare by devaluation to balance the City's books, turning the billions that the 'working poor' had – in pension funds and money-market accounts – over to rescue the youths who had driven their 4x4 'bankers' tanks' to country houses.

Getting a railway back to the 30,000 folk of the Central Borders, opened in September 2015, was a struggle against this 'gated community' and its media men. In an intriguing symposium of May 2006, *Scotland's Ten Tomorrows*, the latter completely ignored the banks: though their 'creative chaos' stimulated the rogue insiders who baled out in time, and went on consuming billions in Payment Protection Insurance, fiddling the Libor rate and so on. Post-slump Edinburgh remained a finance centre, but now had only six of the UK's 300 top dealers. Its 'back offices'/call centres were always vulnerable to 'rationalisation'.

Gordon Brown MP, self-described as an 'ex-politician' and rarely seen in Westminster, cost (with detectives and offices) £316,000 a year to run. Lena Wilson, CEO of Scottish Enterprise, pulled in £210,000 plus a further £68,000 for a day a month with a private London consultancy: more than the First Minister. But after the Pinstripe Darien what did her quango actually do? The 400 workers at Tullis Russell's newly modernised paper mill, Markinch, lost £13.5m over seven years. In April 2015 the accountants KPMG closed the works down, sacking most of the men, who part-owned it. The papers carrying the story said elsewhere that the dodgy banking bill still stood at £19bn.

THE NEW NORTH SEA?

In the mergers and acquisitions frenzy of 2005 BP sold its Grangemouth refinery and petrochemical complex to Ineos, a Swiss-based, Chinese-funded private equity lash-up which, in October 2013, closed it down after a strike by Unite, the old Transport and General Workers' Union: a by-blow of Labour constituency intrigue. After some melodrama a rescue plan involving union concessions was carried thanks to intervention by Holyrood and Whitehall. Salmond reaped praise, yet his SNP lost to Labour in a by-election in Dunfermline, equally dependent on one huge project: building at Rosyth the aircraft-carrier HMS *Queen Elizabeth*, 65,000 tons and costing *at least* £7bn. She and her sister HMS *Prince of Wales* were simply hulls and engines: 'stuffing the carcase', that is giving them planes, munitions and crew, would treble the cost. They hadn't survived on strategic grounds but because BAe's lawyers, after killing a Serious Fraud Office investigation in 2006 (over bribing Saudi princes: Tony Blair signed the papers), drafted lethal cancellation costs.

Grangemouth and Rosyth: these two 'difficult cases' made up perhaps 30 per cent of the country's remaining manufacturing – leaving aside the economics of the Clyde-based Trident nuclear deterrent. The UK's North Sea took risks – its helicopter crash rate much higher than Norway's – but it empowered privatised BP, until its worldwide strategy literally exploded. Its

Texas City refinery blew up in March 2005 (cost: $1.6bn) and in April 2010 in the Caribbean the Macondo deep-sea well blew out (cost: $43bn). Heads rolled, Americans took over, and with oil over $100 a barrel, complicated 'fracking' got going on the near-unpeopled prairies.

Scotland's long-term energy resources in 2014 might be even bigger than in the oil-rich 1970s, though prospects were shadowed by linguistic as much as manufacturing decline: language study fell by more than 50 per cent in a decade. Young Scots thought you could succeed by being English-monoglot. So too did Sir George Mathewson: 'The Deutsche Bank board speaks English!' But in the huge Voith electric engineering combine *Fachsprache/* shoptalk was in German.

The first challenge was embodied by another leviathan, the catamaran 'Pieter Schelte', designed on computers at Swan Hunter Newcastle and building for Dutch Allseas-Heerema in South Korea. A one-stop harvester of the North Sea's oil platforms, jackets and pipelines which were now falling out of use, it could winch the decks into one central dock and the eighty-metre 'jacket' into the other, cut them up and crane reusable equipment or scrap onto barges.

Scotland's marine scenario could grow in six related fields, of which – first – came this recycling. Cost: up to $76bn by 2045, but bringing $46bn worth of business to UK ports, in dismantling and reconditioning. Second, the oil was still there. Though thirty billion barrels had been extracted in the period 1978–2011, between fourteen and twenty-four billion remained. In 2013 each was worth $100, but would this last? As viable as 'fracking' at $60 a barrel (the $10 barrel was last seen in 1999) other new technologies such as Carbon Capture and Storage (CCS) could raise cash from industry and power groups – notably Dutch and German – which needed to bury the lethal stuff in oil-bearing strata. Old fields tapped with primitive techniques could have a second life.

Third, low-carbon energy of at least 12,000m tons of coal-equivalent *every year* sloshed around in Scotland's waters. In contrast to Germany's limited coastline (the western

Wattenmeer dry for much of the day, the Baltic tideless) the accessible fraction of this could potentially supply – through wind, wave and tidal power – a quarter of the EU's electricity. This could be coupled with capacitator technology to expand pump-storage in Highland hydro schemes and direct-current (DC) transmissions: innovations under test, mainly in the European Marine Energy Centre (EMEC) in the Orkneys. We are, the Germans said, where James Watt was in 1760 before he thought of the separate condenser . . .

Fourth, energy demand itself could be lessened by building 'passive' houses to reduce heating to near-zero; replacing the finite oil and rubber of commuter cars with cycles and electric public transport, and decentralising generation to combined heat-and-power units. This was still a German or Scandinavian specialism (*their* houses were at least 'B' in European thermal efficiency grading, in the UK few reached 'C') but could become a critical option for new manufacturing.

Fifth, Arctic ice-melt paradoxically aided low-energy marine transport. A new 'North-East Passage' emerged north of Siberia, cutting 7,000km off the sea-route from Japan and China. Icebreaker-shuttles would need break-bulk ports in Orkney and Shetland, shifting freight into smaller vessels which could bypass congested ports to access the European rivers. Sixth – and long-term the most important? – was the need to combat the inundation which would menace half of the world's people by 2050. Sea levels rose to meet the folk and factories moving to coasts and flood-plains easily accessed by giant freighters: the Danish speciality. Its costs became rapidly apparent – and unavoidable – in 2004: the Indian Ocean and in 2009 the Fukushima tsunamis. Hurricanes Katrina and Rita struck New Orleans in 2006 and Storm Sandy hit the US north-east in October 2012. The last cost $65bn, beyond the range of insurance institutions.

In developing the technology and co-ordinated research necessary to combat this, Scotland seemed uniquely well placed. The oil epoch had carried it close to Europe's booming marine manufacture and it had an unparalleled 'library' of historical experience and environmental understanding. The strategy was complex and would take time. North Sea oil's 'new era' of computer-controlled production and sub-sea electrics took from 1977 to the 1990s to evolve from the Forties Field. But no one doubted that a carbon-free package – generators, power storage and cheap transmission – was possible. Scotland had the key role, with inputs initially coming from Germany and Scandinavia. Where was the place for high-carbon, high-risk London?

Suddenly, in mid-2014, overseas crises and faltering Chinese growth met American-fracked 'light oil'. During the politicking of Scotland's independence referendum, Brent crude remained at over $100. Then it started to fall, and by January 2015 had nearly halved to $50. The 'close call' of the 18 September referendum was lucky for one ex-oil economist, Alex Salmond.

SALMOND'S LEAP

Were such prospects reflected in Scottish government *organisation*? Energy (and with it engineering) was partly a 'subject reserved to Whitehall', represented at Holyrood by four minor ministers. Salmond hadn't the power to enforce co-ordination, and Scottish Enterprise's career didn't encourage. Germany had after 1996 used well-developed federal funding to overcome post-unity strains: innovative manufacture was over 20 per cent of GDP. In Scotland it was 12 per cent, and 'offshore' or 'defence' siphoned off its trained manpower: allowing for population, there were five German engineers to every one Scots engineer. 'Renewable Scotland' would, in the short term, have to rely on a co-operative Eurozone.

Salmond, born on Hogmanay 1954, had the staying power of Angela Merkel, born 17 July the same year. She took power in September 2005, he in May 2007, after a period when the SNP was challenged by the independent left and the Greens. After gaining a majority in 2011 (thought impossible under the d'Hondt PR system) 'the Eck' deployed Holyrood's internal lines of power and concentrated them against David Cameron's weak

London coalition, under pressure from the 'English nationalists' of UKIP. By autumn 2012 the two agreed an independence referendum on 18 September 2014.

This suppressed some problems. Not only the Labour-led opposition complained about local authorities – only thirty-two, eccentric in size and organisation, little loved – or about a concentration of power in 'arms-length' quangos under well-paid but unimpressive 'Numptocrats', often recruited from other political parties. Fire and rescue services were amalgamated; in 2012 Police Scotland became under Kenneth MacAskill as Justice Secretary a national *gendarmerie*. It had a prominent ex-Scotland Yard boss in Sir Stephen House, affected worrying black shirts and fierce-looking guns, but lacked a reliable political chain of command. House was set to go in 2015. The *quality* press devoted a quarter of its print to equally frail football, no longer charming TV companies, shrunk to tiny gates and 2 per cent of the income of the mighty English Premier League. Rangers' finances became more interesting than its games.

The historian Michael Fry, unabashed free-marketeer, who knew his 'Scotch Managers', converted himself to home rule and compared Salmond favourably with his Regency hero Viscount Melville, though he lacked the latter's alluring 'London end' of India and the Navy. Salmond was resilient. He didn't frighten; he left the Merkel shunting-engine stuff to his efficient deputy Nicola Sturgeon. Humane and witty, he could turn on the charm: Walter Scott's Bailie Nicol Jarvie, never Rob Roy. Assess the anti-Salmond forces in 2014, and in *Scottish* politics Cameron's 'Coalition' strength (Conservative and Lib Dems) might keep only fifteen Scottish MPs at the 'fixed-term' May 2015 UK election while Scots Labour, internally divided and (in contrast to 1997–2010) overlooked at Westminster, might fare even worse. This was, it turned out, crazily optimistic.

Growing interest in independence from outside the SNP had a lot to do with suppressed Scots fury, not least at Westminster's reluctance to prosecute its City paymasters. London bankers were loathed not as Englishmen but because they were less public than expense-fiddling MPs, yet capable of far more irresponsible acts. A substantial minority of Scots seemed to tend towards independence. But what sort of independence? Salmond wasn't a 'big bang' operator. In practice he would probably have settled *pro-tem* for 'devolution-plus' – what Gladstone offered Charles Stewart Parnell in 1886: less federalist than 'confederalist' – like the pre-1861 USA or the Austria-Hungary of 1867–1918. The latter shadowed Ireland's original Sinn Féin under Arthur Griffith in 1905 – the year that saw Norway end its federal link with Sweden – and the SNP's own constitution, through which a majority (thirty out of the fifty-nine MPs) could withdraw to *Dáil Alba* and legitimise secession. Dominion status had attractions for the Queen: ahead of the centenary of Easter 1916 she could add a successful Dublin visit to the memory of Eamon de Valera's admiration for her mother as Commonwealth diplomat in the 1930s. She and Salmond were both Buchan folk: Balmoral and Strichen had racehorses in common.

But Cameron wasn't a free agent: his rival Boris Johnson touted the near-anarchy of London's plutocrats. This reflected the arcane tax expertise of the City, and the opportunistic Europhobia – if not English nationalism – in Tory think-tanks and blogsites, themselves menaced by UKIP. Paradoxically his autonomy as premier made him dependent on his Lib Dem allies, while Labour could only gain a Westminster majority through its insecure Scots. In early 2014, the 'Better Together' coalition pushing a 'No' vote in September made defensive sense, but grated against a London politics whose life blood was party confrontation. The anti-SNP Holyrood parties had set up the Calman Commission (2007–9), but by diluting Unionism they actually strengthened Salmond. A crushing victory over him seemed both necessary and difficult.

By spring 2014 'Yes' had gone from 30 per cent to just under 40 per cent, enough to keep the issue in play, whatever the result, and to put 'Better Together' under the enduring threat of a 'Neverendum' – and *that* was the Unionists being optimistic. Salmond saw UKIP damaging Cameron–Clegg in the May European elections, though it got one Scots MEP,

David Coburn, elected on the single list with 11 per cent of the poll. His own 'Bannockburn 700' fest on 23 June was checked by a Cameron-orchestrated (and free) 'Armed Forces Day' at Stirling, though in July–August Glasgow's bonhomie captured the Commonwealth Games. But Grangemouth had only just survived; the Clyde stayed on defence-contract life support.

CITIZEN KANE AND JEAN THE COMMONWEAL

Pat Kane, blues singer and *politologue*, was the country's *troubadour-intello*: his *Play Ethic* book (2004) anticipated a media expansion far bigger than that surfed by Carlyle and Walt Whitman through the steam-press in the 1840s. He fronted the first 'Yes' meetings. The Scottish Parliament got part of it right. Its franchise age – starting with the referendum vote – was reduced to sixteen in 2012. Were the kids all right? Essential to make 'online' work, their politics on social media asserted and irritated (like boy bands, CGI explosions and indeed the word 'like' . . .). Did sex-and-violence sagas – Ossian/*Game of Thrones* – permeate teen viewing, before Isis screened the real thing?

But uncertainty played to an SNP speciality. For those dodging college, call centre or supermarket, there were now multiple 'Black Swans': 'unknown unknowns' . . . not least Chris and Colin Weir, SNP loyalists, who won the 2012 Eurolottery and £161m, and pushed £3.6m Salmond's way: levelling things with the City rich of 'Better Together'.

In the chat rooms lurked ghosts from earlier conflicts: could a rattled Argentinian government reopen its Falklands claim, with UK naval response impossible? Would Northern Ireland implode if Sinn Féin became the biggest party, north and south? In real life west-coast Protestants drummed-and-fluted through the chaotic finances of Rangers and *its* Union Jack. Putin turned on Ukraine, disregarding London, his oligarchs' tax haven of choice, while 'liberated' Iraq went critical with fanatics (propelled by Islamism or 'social media'?) posting horrors on Twitter. From early 2013 high-speed broadband

Table 8.2   European Parliament election results, 1979–2014

	1979		1984		1989		1994	
	%	MEPs	%	MEPs	%	MEPs	%	MEPs
Con	34	5	26	2	21	–	15	–
Labour	33	1	41	5	41	7	43	6
Lib Dem	14	–	16	–	4	–	7	–
SNP	19	1	18	1	27	1	33	2
UKIP	–	–	–	–	–	–	–	–

	1999		2004		2009		2014	
	%	MEPs	%	MEPs	%	MEPs	%	MEPs
Con	20	–	2	18	1	17	1	17
Labour	29	3	26	2	21	2	26	2
Lib Dem	10	1	13	1	12	1	7	–
SNP	27	2	20	2	29	2	29	2
UKIP	–	–	–	–	–	–	11	1

All elections were held on fixed dates in early May. The European Elections Act, 1999 replaced eight European seats with one single Scots constituency.

(touted as serving 'industrial growth') brought pleasure – even if showing celebs or footballers behaving badly. Now in 2014 Armageddon, World War I and friends, came in on cue.

Carlyle in his *Sartor Resartus* 'philosophy of clothes' mode would have twigged the clash of signs: black for Holyrood, funerals, court appearances – and gun-toting police. Sport irrupting with overpriced strip; weddings (back in fashion) with compulsory kilts. Clothes talked: 'distressed' meant shabby chic not despair. Cub reporters found everything 'iconic' yet nudged 'kenspeckle' awake, which greeted a possible community. Service societies could swim against the industrial tide in grand style, even if Scotland battled Middle America in the fat stakes and big people in the shrieking day-glo of the public services jazzed up grim winters in a 'Greater Springfield' where cars, up by 16 per cent from 2003 to 2013, lurched and crashed on pitted roads. But 'Reforming Scotland' reverberated online, stretching from the bucolic (with deep roots and sharp people, as Christopher Smout and Kathleen Jamie reminded) to women activists, posting on abounding, argumentative websites *from all over* – Bella Caledonia, National Collective, the Scottish Review – bursting out in the villages. If building, football and Catholicism – great male markers – were close to skid row, Catriona Macdonald's retrospect *Whaur Extremes Meet* (2009) showed the twentieth century as a social market, multiplying choices to a point where Volunteer Hall or Kirk could house the National Collective or Lesley Riddoch's *Blossom*. Taking last things for granted, Margo MacDonald, Holyrood's exuberant conscience, reduced the menace of physical pain. Her 'right to die' campaign dissolved ritual just as old-type churches dwindled, and cardinals got vulnerable. Not just in the books of Unionists such as Allan Massie or Andrew O'Hagan did macho Scotland seem, once deindustrialised, to face the 'flag or freakout' choice.

Billy Connolly and Sean Connery grew old and mortal, Richard Demarco passed beyond eighty, John Bellany seemed to walk into the Eyemouth tide, commemorated by his eldritch paintings and Peter Aitchison's astonishing *Children of the Sea*. The loss of the village's fleet in 1881 was set meticulously between Thomas Chalmers and Joseph Conrad: a dissenting parallel to Le Roy Ladurie's *Montaillou*. Its women unquestionably were powerful, and among their daughters the elixir of education worked: aid and nursing brought martyrs and heroines.

Doubt clouded youth's prospects: boredom, in a society now only vestigially industrial, little to keep you at home. How would the enfranchised bairns react? Only 18 September 2014 would show. James Robertson, a fine novelist troubled like James Bridie by his last acts, wrote *The Professor of Truth* (2012). In the uneasy Meghrahi aftermath of Lockerbie – 'first the flood then the fire!' – he battled to a bleak but far-sighted humanism, through the furnaces of climate, surveillance, intolerance.

Trained for the 'knowledge industries', youngsters wanted

more than warehouses and call centres and outside them tattoos, booze, curries, graffiti, drugs. In Glasgow an over-electrified piece of modernism burned on 23 May 2014, and Scotland's greatest building, the Mackintosh School of Art, went up with it. John Arden, 'Britain's Brecht' out of Edinburgh's Art School, had once divided the world into 'fat and thin men'. But ... when fat meant poor and blue-collar? Arden's last year, 2012, was enlivened by assaulting, with Fintan O'Toole, his adoptive Ireland's criminal rich. A sombre prophet was John Buchan, who ended governing Canada, sometimes *against* a Scots Liberal premier, Mackenzie King, who thought Hitler a good thing. His Last Things in *Sick Heart River* (1940) were like Robertson's, of ice. He ate little and at his end in 1940 was scarcely bigger than the tiny Mohandas Gandhi who would close the empire down in 1948. His pessimism about human fanaticism endured. What separated the Covenanters who shot women and children after Philiphaugh in 1649 from Islamic State?

Some provided slick neo-liberal answers. Niall Ferguson didn't improve on Carnegie, fondling international wealth, using the hype of Buchan's (and Murdoch's) Free Kirk to devalue the Muslim world. Edward Said's subtler *Orientalism* (1978) had misread the Scots Presbyterian tradition of Robertson Smith, Duncan MacDonald, Sir Hamilton Gibb, but his case against 'Civilisations in Conflict' ideology stood. Conservative Zionism provoked its Islamist-militant correlate. Scott and Carlyle had been more subtle.

These weren't surface problems. Economic crises deferred a realistic political discourse. Scottish genetic research devised Dolly the cloned lamb, but just when experiment started to give the young 'technosphere' reality, complex attempts to develop manufacture failed. In the country of Penicillin Fleming and Beta-Blocker Black, there was no analytical history of that taciturn seventy-year-old giant the NHS. And while the homeland of 'tartan noir' listened for 'There's been a murrder!' in places where there had never been one in centuries, the standard work *Policing Scotland* (2005) had no history in it, no mention of

fraud. In 2015 a police-backed 'Resilience Centre' report reckoned insider fraud *alone* might clock up £3bn a year: 2 per cent
of GDP.

Youngsters averaged five hours a day before a screen, mainly
computer-gaming. This and an Anglophone webworld threatened the great translation tradition – from Urquhart (Rabelais)
to Carlyle (Goethe), Scott-Moncrieff (Proust) and Mackie
(Neruda). But as if jagged by such problems, the Referendum
campaign gathered momentum. A small cloud in September
2012, it remained for two years low in pollsters' interest, with
'Yes' stuck at 30 per cent. But when the London coalition began
to prepare for the (unprecedented) fixed general election date
of 7 May 2015, it swelled. There were other issues: first the
London economy, salient in Olympic year with its magnetic
effect on migration and house prices; then commemorating
1914, along with endless touting of 'Great British' this and that,
provoked resistance. In the polls the Lib Dems got sicklier and
Labour's Ed Miliband failed to charm.

Rejigging 'No' in terms closer to the third 'Devo Max'
option Salmond had earlier wanted to offer, could Cameron's
'most successful partnership' marry the suddenly reanimated
Gordon Brown's 'broken system'? London media jerked from
plaintive to aggressive. UKIP at by-elections threatened, then
took, safe English Tory seats. Scots Catholic leadership went
secular: yet the 'reliable' Catholic historian Tom Devine,
courted by Brown and knighted in summer 2014, plumped
for 'Yes'. Labour looked for its once-compact Scots vote, with
anxiety.

By August the race narrowed, with talk of an 80 per cent
turnout (exceeded, as it turned out, at 85 per cent); the 'Yes'
vote steadily edged up. Rattled London celebs echoed bank
and supermarket threats, only to get 'They *would* say that,
wouldn't they?' back. On 7 September a rogue poll predicting
'Yes' at 51 per cent sparked panic in the two-party system: to
the *Daily Telegraph* it dissolved a grand alliance; the *Guardian*
and a clever James Graham play saw Alex and Dave '*Dividing
the Union*' like a CD collection. By 17 September London spied

only one political professional in the UK, and he wasn't in Westminster.

On Friday 19 September he wasn't in Scotland either. Alex Salmond accepted a vote of 55 to 45 per cent against independence and flagged up his departure for November. Only four of thirty-two local authorities returned a 'Yes': Glasgow, Dundee, West Dunbartonshire and North Lanark. Orkney, Shetland and the Borders were two-thirds 'No', suburbs and commuterland over 55 per cent 'No', industrial burghs just over 50 per cent 'No'.

But what did 'No' mean? Better Together accepted a Commission under Lord Smith, the return of Devo Max *and* substantial shifts in Westminster organisation: promised by Cameron, prompted by Brown. Facing election year and with a world crisis eerily resembling 1914, the SNP claimed at least 80,000 members and the smaller 'Yes' parties did well, but Labour was down to 18,000, stuck at 30 per cent in the polls, risking, perhaps, single-figure oblivion . . .

Nicola Sturgeon, a shoo-in as new First Minister, cheered when the Principal of St Andrews, the US-Irish Louise Richardson, challenged the Royal & Ancient Golf Club (£250 per round, per player . . .). When Dr Richardson visited, some members waggled their Club ties at her and smirked, but on 18 September they were beaten by 80 per cent. A few women got in – though not the Principal. She left for Oxford. Rupert Murdoch bought the R&A's world TV rights – *and* Salmond's memoirs.

The Dream shall Never Die appeared on 19 March 2015. It seemed lightweight (at least to non-golfers) but the subtext fascinated: Moira Salmond's weekly parlay with her Turriff ladies presaged the common-sense election team of Nicola Sturgeon and her husband Peter Murrell, the SNP's secretary . . . which cleverly kept the unexpected bonus of 'Yes' voters in the party. On 7 May turnout topped 71 per cent against 66 per cent in England, with swings of 20–30 per cent to the SNP. Labour (South Edinburgh) and the Lib Dems (Orkney and Shetland) joined the Tories (Dumfries) with only a single MP each. After 8 May the Parliament of Great Britain was hollower than under the Stewart Restoration (1660–88), which used a British nobility to create an authoritarian Scottish Council under a Governor in Edinburgh. Not the most reassuring precedent.

Labour was scarcely audible north of the Chilterns, let alone the Cheviots: fear and loathing in North London was muffled by reaction to an oligarchy guilty of war, 'light touch' economics, savings theft. Brown now seemed to provoke more than Blair: earnest discourse didn't fill up his Westminster void. Ed Miliband and Cameron might share a Jewish background, but lacked Disraeli's flair and his grasp of the Scots: their fervour and (via Scott and Carlyle) their imagination.

Was this Boston in 1776, or Dublin in 1916? Or something uniquely pacific and furious, terrible and gay? An explosive Scots curse got the mood. After the pit, steel and factory closures, deindustrialisation, bad diet, bank robbery, fall in oil prices, the country was *scunnered*!

January 2016 saw north-east Scotland and the new Sturgeon ministry flailed by the worst rains since records began. Near Balmoral the tower of Abergeldie tottered on the brink of the swollen River Dee. On the other side of the pond, two Americans of Scottish provenance, not unknown on their native heath, Donald Trump and Rupert Murdoch, stoked up the right-wing vote. Had a Scottish government and intelligentsia rather too keen on 'the gospel of success' found itself entrapped?

It got worse. The Royal Navy's eight Type 45 destroyers, built for a billion each in separate sections at various British Aerospace yards, failed to work properly and had to be withdrawn for rebuilding. Trident, getting long in the tooth, came up for replacement, to find a radicalised Labour as well as the SNP opposing. As we went to press, the spirit of revolt spread to the Conservatives, who declared against the European Union: leaving the possibility of Scotland pro-Europe in an anti-European UK on 24 June 2016.

During the 2015 election, at a televised debate, the women leaders of the Greens, Plaid Cymru and the SNP, arm in arm, launched themselves on a non-plussed Miliband: the three graces rooting for a new politics. And words came back, from Hugh MacDiarmid, sobering up after the General Strike in 1926:

> But Him, whom nocht in Man or Deity
> Or Daith or Dreid or Laneliness can touch
> *Wha's deed owre often and has seen owre much.*

> O I ha'e Silence left.
> 'An weel ye micht', sae Jean'll say –
> 'Efter sic a nicht!'

Further Reading

SECTION I

The original bibliography of *No Gods* tried to be comprehensive, as in 1981 not much historical writing on the twentieth century had been published. However, the fruit of new technology encompasses far different approaches, recoverable online, ranging from documentaries such as the BBC's *History of Scotland* series (2008–9) to the encyclopaedia-style entries in Michael Lynch's *Oxford Companion to Scottish History* (2002) and the concise essays to be found in Jenny Wormald and Tom Devine's *Oxford Handbook of Modern Scottish History* (2012): its Part V deals with contemporary history. Accessing the valuable content of the last two, however, isn't helped by eccentric indexing. Indeed, many important books dealing with the 2007–15 political crisis have no index at all – despite Tony Benn's rueful comment: 'All politicians read books from the index. We're such egomanes!'

Secondary literature has expanded or critiqued this treatment. This first section surveys the main series and online resources, available in libraries, or inter-library loans, or assessed through online critiques: for accessions see the quarterly *Scottish Review of Books* website at www.scottishreviewofbooks.org. Browsing the web can uncover good technical, military or architectural history, but regional coverage on Wikipedia depends on local activity. If there's an imaginative secondary school, museum or local history society, then good – see Coatbridge or Kirkcaldy. But there are dire entries for places that deserve better, such as Motherwell or Airdrie; and overall little guarantee of material surviving, let alone getting regular updates.

As to the old discipline of economic history, the 'dead reckoning' of the balance sheet has vanished with economic principle – as the slump of 2007–9 showed. The promise of 'Modern Studies' to enliven the Scottish secondary curriculum has not been aided by its websites, something sadly confirmed by the author's experience of political education at the Scottish Parliament, contrasted with the German federal state and *Länder*'s statutory provision of political/citizenship education. Dr Alexander Boehm's *Politische Bildung und Regional Identität* (Berlin: Logos, 2006) comparing Wales and Germany is properly critical of UK practice.

Relevant material comes in the last third of Rab Houston and William Knox (eds), *The New Penguin History of Scotland* (London: Penguin, 2001), with period studies by Graeme Morton and R. J. Morris, John Foster and Christopher Harvie. For the first half of the twentieth century there is T. C. Smout, *A Century of the Scottish People, 1830–1950* (London: Collins, 1986). The finest recent Scottish historical achievement has been Colin Matthew's editing of the *Oxford Dictionary of National Biography*, completed in 2004 after his tragically early death. Use your library card to access it online. Deceased notables take about three years to turn up, but – dear editors – do give us some older rascals, like 'Gorgeous George' Pottinger (1917–98), the corrupt mandarin who nearly got to run the Scottish Office.

John Hume and the late Charles MacKean contributed generously to industrial and architectural history and the publications of the Royal Commission on the Ancient and Historical Monuments of Scotland, from which is derived SCRAN (the Scottish Cultural, Resource and Archive Network) storing half a million (and counting) images, from photos and maps to archive interviews and Norman MacCaig reading his Assynt poems. Again, remember your library card. Representation of women remains limited, but is catching up – aided by Elizabeth Ewan, Sue Innes and Siân Reynolds (eds), *Biographical Dictionary of Scottish Women* (Edinburgh: Edinburgh University Press, 2006); and Lynn Abrams, Eleanor

Gordon, Deborah Simonton and Eileen Yeo (eds), *Gender in Scottish History since 1707* (Edinburgh: Edinburgh University Press, 2006).

The *Third Statistical Account* was started in 1942. There was a thorough *Glasgow* volume in 1958, but then it rather limped until the 1990s, though there is often good local detail. In the new century this gap was filled by the *Scottish Ethnological Survey: Scottish Life and Society*, the child of the late Professor Sandy Fenton, which will run to fourteen volumes of 500 pages and more on the gamut of activities – from diet to transport – determining civil society in the 'historical' era. They are 1. *An Introduction to Scottish Ethnology*; 2. *Farming and Rural Life*; 3. *Scotland's Buildings*; 4. *Boats, Fishing and the Sea*; 5. *The Food of the Scots*; 6. *Scotland's Domestic Life*; 7. *Craft and Service: the Working Life of the Scots*; 8. *Transport and Communications*; 9. *The Individual and Community Life*; 10. *Oral Literature and Performance Culture*; 11. *Education*; 12. *Religion*; 13. *The Law*; 14. *Bibliography*.

The Buildings of Scotland (derived from Nikolaus Pevsner's famous Penguins) is similarly, but regionally, structured. Painting is catered for in Duncan Macmillan's remarkable *Scottish Art, 1450–2000* (Edinburgh: Mainstream, 2009). Rosemary Goring's *Scotland the Autobiography* (Edinburgh: Birlinn, 2009) and Louise Yeoman's *Reportage Scotland* (Edinburgh: Luath, 2008), provide good eye-witness accounts. There is also the immense personal contribution of Ian MacDougall, whose twenty-odd books of interviews with working people record the 'sense and worth' of the orra folk.

For reviews consult *History Scotland*, the *Scottish Historical Journal*, *Scottish Affairs* and the *Scottish Review of Books*. For literary history Cairns Craig (ed.), *The History of Scottish Literature*, vol. 7 (Aberdeen: Aberdeen University Press, 1993); Robert Crawford, *Scotland's Books* (London: Penguin, 2005), is comprehensive and succinct though oddly blinkered on the territory common to history and imaginative writing. As for the 'UK bestseller' formula? It's closer to transnational commerce than to empathy or creative imagination: see

Kenneth O. Morgan (ed.), *Oxford History of Britain* (Oxford: Oxford University Press, revised ed. 2010). Neglected surveys like Geraldine Prince (ed.), *A Window on Europe: Lothian European Lectures* (Edinburgh: Canongate, 1993) contrast with the noisy oeuvre of Niall Ferguson. This may explain much about the present political crisis.

As for the present writer's output, and other essays on regionalism, politics and literature relevant to Scotland, Germany and elsewhere, see the *Festschrift*: Eberhard Bort (ed.), *The View from Zollernblick* (Crieff: Grace Note, 2013).

SECTION II

I have concurred here with the alphabetical ordering of earlier *New History* volumes, giving the main sources used and other interpretations. An asterisk represents a take on the subject or period which presents an unorthodox interpretation, stirs things up or is simply well-written advocacy!

Chapter 1

Cameron, Ewen, *Impaled upon a Thistle*, Edinburgh: Edinburgh University Press, 2010
Campbell, R. H., *Scotland since 1707*, Oxford: Blackwell, 1971
Devine, Tom, *The Scottish Nation*, London: Penguin, 2012 [1999]
*Elliot, Walter (ed.), *The New Minstrelsy of the Scottish Border*, Selkirk: Deerpark, 2006
Gallagher, Tom, *Glasgow: the Uneasy Peace*, Manchester: Manchester University Press, 1987
Macdonald, Catriona M. M. and McFarland, E. W., *Scotland and the Great War*, Edinburgh: John Donald, 1999.
MacDougall, Ian (ed.), *Voices from War*, Edinburgh: Mercat Press, 1996.
Marwick, Arthur, *The Deluge*, London: Macmillan, 1966
Middlemas, Keith, *The Clydesiders*, London: Hutchinson, 1965
Royle, Trevor, *The Flowers of the Forest*, Edinburgh: Birlinn, 2007
Strachan, Hew, *The First World War*, London: Simon and Schuster, 2003

Wood, Ian S., *John Wheatley*, Manchester: Manchester University Press, 1990

Chapter 2

Bowie, James, *The Future of Scotland*, Edinburgh: Oliver and Boyd, 1939
Burnett, John A., *The Making of the Modern Scottish Highlands*, Dublin: Four Courts Press, 2011
Cairncross, Alec (ed.), *The Scottish Economy*, Cambridge: Cambridge University Press, 1953
Devine, T., Lee, C. and Peden, G. (eds), *The Transformation of the Scottish Economy*, Edinburgh: Edinburgh University Press, 2005
Dickson, Tony (ed.), *Capital and Class in Scotland*, Edinburgh: John Donald, 1982
McCrone, Gavin, *Scotland's Economic Progress, 1951–1960*, London: Allen and Unwin, 1965
Maver, Irene, *Glasgow*, Edinburgh: Edinburgh University Press, 2000
Mitchell, James, *Governing Scotland: The Invention of Administrative Devolution*, Basingstoke: Palgrave Macmillan, 2003
Payne, Peter, *Colvilles and the Scottish Steel Industry*, Oxford: Oxford University Press, 1979
Ransom, P. J. G., *Iron Road: the Railway in Scotland*, Edinburgh: Birlinn, 2008
Robbins, Nick and Meek, Donald, *The Kingdom of MacBrayne*, Edinburgh: Birlinn, 2006
Saville, Richard, *Bank of Scotland, 1695–1995*, Edinburgh: Edinburgh University Press, 1996

Chapter 3

Abrams, Lynn and Brown, Callum G. (eds), *A History of Everyday Life in Twentieth-Century Scotland*, Edinburgh: Edinburgh University Press, 2010
Craig, Carol, *The Tears that Made the Clyde*, Colintraive: Argyll, 2010
Hutton, G., *Social Environment in Suburban Edinburgh*, York: University of York, 1975
Knox, William, *Industrial Nation: Work, Culture and Society in Scotland, 1800–present*, Edinburgh: Edinburgh University Press, 1999

Levitt, Iain, *Poverty and Welfare in Scotland, 1898–1948*, Edinburgh: Edinburgh University Press, 1988

Littlejohn, James, *Westrigg: a Study of a Cheviot Parish*, London: Routledge, 1981 [1963]

McCrone, David, *Understanding Scotland: the Sociology of a Nation*, London: Routledge, 1992

Orr, John Boyd, *Food, Health and Income*, London: Macmillan, 1936

Paterson, Tom and Cunnison, James, *The Young Wage-Earner, a Study of Glasgow Boys*, London: Nuffield, 1951

*Spark, Muriel, *The Prime of Miss Jean Brodie*, London: Penguin, 1965 [1961]

*Thomson, David, *Nairn in Darkness and Light*, London: Hutchinson, 1987

Wightman, Andy, *The Poor had no Lawyers: Who owns Scotland*, Edinburgh: Birlinn, 2010

Chapter 4

Finlay, Richard, *Independent and Free*, Edinburgh: John Donald, 1994

Fry, Michael, *Patronage and Principle*, Aberdeen: Aberdeen University Press, 1997

Harvie, Christopher, *The Rise of Regional Europe*, London: Routledge, 1991

Hassan, Gerry and Shaw, Eric, *The Strange Death of Labour Scotland*, Edinburgh: Edinburgh University Press, 2012

Hutchison, Iain, *Scottish Politics in the Twentieth Century*, Basingstoke: Palgrave, 2001

*Linklater, Eric, *Magnus Merriman*, London: Penguin, 1987 [1933]

Marr, Andrew, *The Battle for Scotland*, London: Penguin, 1992

Mitchell, James, *Strategies for Self-Government*, Edinburgh: Polygon, 1996

Mitchison, Naomi, *Among You Taking Notes: Wartime Diaries*, London: Phoenix, 1985

Nairn, Tom, *After Britain, New Labour and the Return of Scotland*, London: Granta, 2000

*Roy, Kenneth, *The Invisible Spirit: Post-War Scotland, 1945–75*, Prestwick: ICS, 2013

Torrance, David, *The Scottish Secretaries*, Edinburgh: Birlinn, 2006

Chapter 5

Anderson, Carol and Christianson, Aileen, *Scottish Women's Fiction*, East Linton: Tuckwell, 2000
Bold, Alan, *MacDiarmid: Christopher Grieve*, London: Paladin, 1990
Calder, Angus, *Revolving Culture: Notes from the Scottish Republic*, London: I. B. Tauris, 1994
Connery, Sean and Grigor, Murray, *Being a Scot*, London: Weidenfeld, 2008
*Galbraith, J. K., *The Non-Potable Scotch*, London: Penguin, 1964
Gifford, Douglas, *Neil Gunn and Lewis Grassic Gibbon*, Edinburgh: Oliver and Boyd, 1984
Gifford, Douglas and MacMillan, Dorothy (eds), *A History of Scottish Women's Writing*, Edinburgh: Edinburgh University Press, 1997
Miller, Karl (ed.), *Memoirs of a Modern Scotland*, London: Faber, 1968
Moffat, Alistair, *The Scots: a Genetic Journey*, Edinburgh: Birlinn, 2011
Purser, John, *Scotland's Music*, Edinburgh: Mainstream, 1992
Withers, Charles, *Gaelic Scotland: the Transformation of a Culture Region*, London: Routledge, 1985

Chapter 6

Aitken, Keith, *The Bairns o' Adam: the Story of the STUC*, Edinburgh: Polygon, 1997
Ascherson, Neal, *Stone Voices*, London: Granta, 1993
Blythman, Joanna, *Shopped: the Shocking Power of British Supermarkets*, London: Fourth Estate, 2004
Foster, John and Woolfson, Charles, *The Politics of the UCS Work-in*, London: Lawrence and Wishart, 1986
Harvie, Christopher, *Fool's Gold: the Story of North Sea Oil*, London: Penguin, 1994
Hassan, Gerry and Warhurst, Chris (eds), *Anatomy of the New Scotland*, Edinburgh: Mainstream, 2002
Hechter, Michael, *Internal Colonialism: the Celtic Fringe in British Development*, London: Routledge, 1975
Knox, John and Wilson, Eben, *Scotland '78*, Alva: Wilson and Knox, 1978
*Mackenzie, Robert F., *A Search for Scotland*, London: Collins, 1989 [1982]
Nairn, Tom, *The Break-up of Britain*, London: New Left Books, 1981

Storrar, William, *Scottish Identity: a Christian Vision*, Edinburgh: Saint Andrew Press, 1990

Chapter 7

Brown, Gordon (ed.), *The Red Paper on Scotland*, Edinburgh: EUSPB, 1975
Craig, Carol, *The Scots Crisis of Confidence*, Colintraive: Argyll, 2008 [2002]
Devine, Tom (ed.), *Scotland and the Union, 1707–2007*, Edinburgh: Edinburgh University Press, 2008
Donnelly, Daniel and Scott, Kenneth (eds), *Policing Scotland*, Cullompton: Willan, 2005
Edwards, Owen Dudley (ed.), *Scotland's Claim of Right*, Edinburgh: Polygon, 1990
Gray, Alasdair, *Lanark: a Life in Four Books*, Edinburgh: Canongate, 1982
Harvie, Christopher and Jones, Peter, *The Road to Home Rule*, Edinburgh: Polygon, 1999
Hassan, Gerry and Warhurst, Chris (eds), *Anatomy of the New Scotland*, Edinburgh: Mainstream, 2002
Jamieson, Bill (ed.), *Scotland's Ten Tomorrows*, London: Continuum, 2006
Kane, Pat, *The Play Ethic*, London: Macmillan, 1994
Keating, Michael, *Glasgow: the City that Refused to Die*, Aberdeen: Aberdeen University Press, 1988
Morgan, Kenneth O., *Michael Foot: A Life*, London: Harper, 2007

Chapter 8

Blain, Neil and Hutchison, David (eds), *The Media in Scotland*, Edinburgh: Edinburgh University Press, 2008
Brown, Gordon, *My Scotland, Our Britain*, London: Simon and Schuster, 2014
Fraser, Ian, *Shredded*, Edinburgh: Birlinn, 2014
Geoghegan, Peter, *The People's Referendum*, Edinburgh: Luath, 2015
Harvie, Christopher, *Broonland: The Last Days of Gordon Brown*, London: Verso, 2010
*Jamie, Kathleen, *Sightlines*, London: Sort of Books, 2012

Macwhirter, Iain, *Road to Referendum* and *Disunited Kingdom*, Edinburgh: Luath, 2014
Moffat, Alexander and Riach, Alan, *Arts of Resistance*, Edinburgh: Luath, 2008
Riddoch, Lesley, *Blossom*, Edinburgh: Luath, 2012
Salmond, Alex, *The Dream shall Never Die*, London: Collins, 2015
Smout, Christopher, and Stewart, Mairi, *The Firth of Forth*, Edinburgh, Birlinn, 2013

Chronological Table, 1906–2015

Abbreviations: E. = election; PM = prime minister; RC = Royal Commission; S = Secretary for Scotland (after 1926 Secretary of State)

1906 E. Jan. Liberal landslide: Campbell-Bannerman PM, Sinclair S.
1908 Asquith PM; Education (Scotland) Act.
1909 'People's Budget'; crisis with Lords; Scottish miners affiliate to Labour Party.
1910 E. Feb./Oct. Asquith kept in power by Scots and Irish, Parliament Act.
1911 Scottish Exhibition, Glasgow; Agriculture (Scotland) Act.
1912 RC on Scottish Housing; Wood S.; Suffragette and Labour unrest; Conservatives and Liberal Unionists form Unionist Party; Argyll Motors fails.
1914 Crisis over Irish home rule; outbreak of war (4 Aug.); Rosyth building (to 1916).
1915 Coalition government (May); Labour unrest on Clyde (Sept.); Battle of Loos.
1916 End of Red Clyde by April; Dublin rising (26–7 Apr.); battle of Jutland (31 May); Battle of Somme (Jul.–Nov.); Lloyd George PM (6 Dec.); Munro, Coalition Liberal S.
1917 Housing RC reports; Council of Irishmen; Bolshevik takeover in Russia (Nov.).
1918 Reform Act (Jan.) gave vote to women over thirty, trebling electors; Armistice (11 Nov.), German fleet interned, Scapa; E. Dec.; R 34 flies Atlantic from/to East Fortune.
1919 Forty Hours strike and riot, Glasgow (Jan.); German fleet scuttled (Jun.).
1920 End of boom, unemployment 20 per cent; Labour gains on Glasgow Council; hostilities in Ireland; Communist Party of Great Britain formed.

1921 Railways Act; Sankey RC on Coal urges nationalisation; 'Triple Alliance' of Miners, Transport and Railway workers fails (Nov.).

1922 *E. Nov.* Fall of Lloyd George; Labour gains twenty-two Scottish seats; Law PM.

1923 *E. Dec.* Chamberlain Housing Act; Baldwin PM; Scots railways amalgamated into LMS and LNER.

1924 First Labour minority government; MacDonald PM; Adamson S.; Wheatley Housing Act; Baldwin PM; Gilmour S. *E.Oct.*; National Grid.

1926 General Strike (3–12 May); miners out until November; MacDiarmid's 'A Drunk Man ...'; home rule motion falls; Gilmour becomes Secretary of State.

1927 Trade union powers restricted, Lochaber Aluminium Works built.

1928 National Party founded; women over twenty-one get vote: Scottish Office ends Boards.

1929 *E. May.* Labour government: MacDonald PM, Adamson S; Wall Street crash (October); parish councils and educational authorities abolished; United Free Church and Kirk amalgamate; first talkies shown.

1931 *E. Aug.* Depression worsens; 'National Government' under MacDonald, Labour down to seven MPs; Sinclair (Liberal) S.

1932 Liberals quit over free trade. Collins S. ILP disaffiliates with Labour; the A8 ('the Boulevard') connects Edinburgh to Glasgow; first sighting of Loch Ness Monster.

1933 Roosevelt's New Deal (Mar.); Hitler in power (May); Labour takes Glasgow.

1934 Scottish National Party formed; Scottish Commissioner appointed; Grassic Gibbon completes *A Scots Quair.*

1935 *E. Nov.* Queen Mary completed at Clydebank; armament boosts heavy industries; holidays with pay; Baldwin PM, Elliot S.

1938 Chamberlain PM; Empire Exhibition, Glasgow; Munich treaty; Colville S.

1939 War breaks out (3 Sept.); conscription and rationing, evacuation; *Queen Elizabeth* built.

1940–1 Churchill PM (10 May); Brown S; Norwegians in Shetland; USA and USSR at war. Council of State founded (Oct.); Johnston S.

1942   Singapore lost; Battle of Atlantic; Cooper Committee on Highland power.

1943   Hydro Board set up (schemes built, 1945–62); Prestwick as Atlantic hub; Eighth Army in Italy.

1945   E. *July*. SNP take first seat (April); VE day (8 May); Labour under Attlee PM (late Jul.); Westwood S; atomic bombs bring Japanese surrender (15 Aug.).

1946–8 Power, gas, transport nationalised; Bevan creates NHS; Woodburn S; Edinburgh Festival launched; Kirk revival; snow, freeze, floods.

1950   E. *Feb*. Labour majority falls to five; MacNeil S; Korean war.

1951   E. *Oct*. Churchill PM, Stuart S; Festival of Britain; TV in Scotland; first grid-attached wind-generator, Orkney.

1953   *Princess Victoria* sinks off Larne, 130 drowned (Jan.); Elizabeth II crowned (2 Jun.); Korean war ends; RC on Scottish affairs reports.

1955   E. *May*. Conservatives win 50.1 per cent of vote; Eden PM; STV starts broadcasting; Dounreay nuclear establishment commissioned.

1956   Suez invasion; Russia invades Hungary (*Oct.–Nov.*); UK Communists split; Macmillan PM.

1958   Slump in Scottish heavy industry.

1959   E. *Oct*. Conservatives win but with Scots losses; Glasgow's Blue Trains begin running; decolonisation.

1960–1 Elvis at Prestwick (Mar. 1960); Toothill and Beeching Reports; Industry Act increases public support; NB Loco closes; strip mill at Ravenscraig; motor works at Bathgate and Linwood; Noble S; hydro development stops.

1962   Scottish Development Department set up; Glasgow's last trams run; Polaris programme launched.

1963   Douglas-Home PM; Buchanan Report; closure of one-third of the rail network.

1964   E. *Oct*. Labour wins; Wilson PM; Ross S.

1965   Highland and Islands Development Board set up; motorway and high-rise flat-building programmes; work starts on *QE2* liner, commissioned for 1969.

1966   E.*Mar*. Labour majority increased; 'A Plan for Scotland'.

1967   Steel nationalised; Scottish Transport Group set up; SNP wins Hamilton; oil exploration starts; Cockenzie power station opens.

1968 First Polaris submarines; 'Europe in revolt'; SNP wins in local elections; Crowther, later Kilbrandon RC into Constitution set up; Conservatives back devolution; Wheatley Report on local government.

1970 *E. Jun.* Conservatives win; Heath PM; Campbell S; SNP returns one MP. Longannet power station opens; Open University founded.

1971 Upper Clyde Shipbuilders crisis.

1972 Scottish Economic Planning Department established; Local Government Act sets up eight regions and thirty-two districts.

1973 Miners' strike: three-day week; Yom Kippur war in October trebles barrel price of oil; UK joins EEC.

1974 *E. Feb.,Oct.* Narrow Labour wins; Wilson PM, Ross S; SNP has eleven MPs; Labour wins regional elections; North Sea oilfield development.

1975 Scottish Development Agency set up; referendum confirms EEC accession.

1976 First Devolution Bill; Callaghan PM, Millan S; Hunterston B nuclear power station built.

1977 Devolution Bill fails; Lib–Lab pact: new Bill tabled; SNP gains in district elections.

1978 Devolution Acts passed, subject to referenda.

1979 *E. May.* 1 Mar: 32–30% Yes but 40% needed. Conservatives win general and European elections; SNP have two MPs; Thatcher PM, Younger S. Oil prices plus the strong pound lead to a 20 per cent fall in manufacturing.

1980 Labour recover in local government; steel industry shrinks.

1981 Chrysler, Linwood, Invergordon aluminium close; SDP leaves Labour.

1982 Falklands War (Mar.–Jun.); Pope John Paul II visits (Jun.) – 300,000 at Glasgow Mass; Conservative success in regional elections.

1983 *E. Jun.* Lib–SDP alliance gains in regional elections.

1984 Miners' strike begins (Mar.). Conservatives lose three seats at the European Parliament; Labour gains in district elections include Edinburgh.

1985 Miners' strike ends in defeat for NUM (Mar.); first oil peak; shipyard crisis.

1986 Gartcosh steel mill closes; Rifkind S.; his guest Gorbachev becomes USSR leader; regional elections see heavy Tory defeats; poll tax announced; Edinburgh Commonwealth Games boycotted; *perestroika* begins.

1987   *E. Jun.* Tactical voting reduces number of Tory MPs from twemty-one to ten.

1988   Poll tax introduced; Piper Alpha blows up, 167 killed (Jul.); Jim Sillars, SNP, elected for Govan (Nov.); Pan-Am 747 bombing over Lockerbie, 270 killed (Dec.); Torness nuclear power station opens.

1989   Constitutional Convention meets (Mar.); 'velvet revolution' starts in Eastern Europe (Oct.); Berlin Wall falls (Oct.).

1990   European elections (May), Tories lose last seats; Constitutional Convention adopts PR (Nov.); Thatcher replaced by John Major; Lang S.; Hunterston A power station closes.

1991   Gulf War (Jan.–Apr.), Scots troops involved; electricity boards sold off; Ravenscraig condemned; Gorbachev overthrown (Aug.); Lib Dems by-election success (Nov.).

1992   *E. Apr.* Surprise Major win; fall in Labour regional vote (May); Ravenscraig closed (Jul.); European summit in Edinburgh (Dec.); 25,000 on devolution demo.

1993   Rail privatisation carried (May); Channel Tunnel opens (May).

1994   European elections (May); Tory wipeout in local elections; John Smith dies; Blair–Brown 'Granita' deal alters cabinet government; crisis over Brent Spar demolition; Glasgow rejects water privatisation, with 97 per cent against; Dounreay decommissioning to cost £6bn.

1995   Reshuffle: Forsyth S.

1996   Dunblane shootings (Mar.); *Braveheart*; Stone of Scone returned (Nov.); second oil peak; Trident submarines replace Polaris as deterrent.

1997   *E May.* Scotrail franchised; record Labour win; no Conservatives returned; Blair PM, Dewar S; Diana, Princess of Wales dies (Aug.); Scots (74 per cent) and Welsh (50.3 per cent) endorse devolution.

1998   Legislation for parliament; seventy-three constituency seats; fifty-five list seats; Good Friday agreement, Belfast.

1999   Holyrood elections (May); Lib–Lab government, Dewar FM; Scottish Parliament opens in Assembly Hall (1 Jul.).

2000   Dewar dies (Sept.); McLeish FM.

2001   Outbreak of foot-and-mouth disease (Sept.); '9/11' attack;

Afghan War; economic slump; McConnell FM; Scotland Secretary sidelined; Rosyth–Zeebrugge ferry.

2003 Start of Iraq War (20 Mar.); Scottish elections (May); SNP setback: Greens (seven seats), left (six), independents (four) benefit.

2004 Holyrood building opens; single transferable vote adopted for local government elections (Jun.); Brown's 'light-touch' boom; windfarm expansion on land and sea.

2007 Holyrood and local council elections (3 May); Salmond FM; SNP has forty-seven seats (Jun.); Brown PM; Rosyth gets contract for giant aircraft carriers (Jul.).

2008 Collapse of HBoS and RBS (Oct.); Trump golf course opens (Nov.); Scottish & Newcastle taken over.

2009 Calman Commission (Lab–Lib–Con) reports. Megrahi returns to Libya (Aug.).

2010 *E. May.* Lib Dem–Conservative government; Cameron PM; Papal visit, 65,000 at Mass (Sept.); Tunis revolt starts 'Arab Spring' (Dec.); end of Rosyth–Zeebrugge passenger ferry.

2011 Holyrood elections (May). SNP wins sixty-nine seats.

2013 'Arab Spring' starts Middle East crisis; Cockenzie power station closes.

2014 Independence referendum (18 Sept.); 'Yes' defeated 45–55 per cent; Sturgeon FM.

2015 *E. May.* Conservative government; Cameron PM; SNP wins fifty-six of fifty-nine seats.

WITHDRAWN

Index

UNIVERSITY
OF
GLASGOW
LIBRARY